From Warsaw to Wherever

Published by New Academia Publishing

AN ARCHITECT OF DEMOCRACY: Building a Mosaic of Peace
by James Robert Huntley, Foreword by Brent Scowcroft.
(Memoirs and Occasional Papers, Association for Diplomatic Studies and Training)

PETER STRICKLAND: New London Shipmaster, Boston Merchant, First Consul to Senegal
by Stephen H. Grant
(ADST-DACOR Diplomats and Diplomacy Book)

NATIONALISM, HISTORIOGRAPHY AND THE (RE)CONSTRUCTION OF THE PAST
Edited by Claire Norton

TURKEY'S MODERNIZATION: Refugees from Nazism and Atatürk's Vision
by Arnold Reisman

THE INNER ADVERSARY: The Struggle against Philistinism as the Moral Mission of the Russian Intelligentsia
by Timo Vihavainen

PETS OF THE GREAT DICTATORS & Other Works
by Sabrina P. Ramet

From Warsaw to Wherever

Zygmunt Nagorski

SCARITH An imprint of New Academia Publishing
Washington, DC

Copyright © 2007 by Zygmunt Nagorski

SCARITH/New Academia Publishing, 2007

All rights reserved. No part of this book may be reproduced or transmitted in any form or by any means, electronic or mechanical, including photocopying, recording, or by any information storage and retrieval system.

Printed in the United States of America

Library of Congress Control Number: 2007925260
ISBN 978-0-9787713-9-3 paperback (alk. paper)

 An imprint of New Academia Publishing
P.O. Box 27420 - Washington, DC - 20038-7420

 info@newacademia.com
www.newacademia.com

To Marie – who provided all.

Contents

List of Illustrations	ix
Preface	xi
1. What Is America, Daddy?	1
2. The First Act	5
3. The Walk, the Jail and the Arrival	25
4. Scotland	31
5. Were They My Gurus?	45
6. New York	69
7. Arthur Hays Sulzberger	77
8. Chattanooga	87
9. A Baseball Game	111
10. New York, Once Again	127
11. Benjamin Franklin	133
12. Two Lives of a Salesman	149
13. South America	163
14. Moments of Reflection	175
15. Egypt	187
16. The Lumumba Saga	199
17. South Korea	213
18. France	235
19. The Return	249

20. Vietnam	261
21. Council on Foreign Relations	277
22. The Aspen Institute	289
23. The Last Chapter	297

Illustrations

Figure 1. Zyg and Marysia.	151
Figure 2. The Polish Army in Scotland during the war.	151
Figure 3. Maria, our firstborn, and I in Chattanooga.	152
Figure 4. The snake-charmer, Andrew, in Chattanooga.	152
Figure 5. The Foreign Service in Cairo.	153
Figure 6. Our "extended" Cairo family.	153
Figure 7. The Lumumba Saga and the convertible.	154
Figure 8. Marysia and Zyg in Korea.	155
Figure 9. Marysia (right), the tennis champion.	156
Figure 10. Our daughter, Terry, holding Andrew's firstborn.	156
Figure 11. The Hudson Institute in Vietnam.	157
Figure 12. Our Center For International Leadership.	157

Preface

There is always an urge to leave behind something worthwhile for generations to come. In my case, the worthwhile message is complicated. At first, it depicts an emptiness of days spent as a spoiled young man on a college campus. The emptiness continued when the big war found me in the uniform of an exiled army relocated in Scotland, prepared for a German invasion that never came, where endless hours of bridge filled that emptiness.

The message: do all you can to prevent wars, no matter what your station in life, no matter how inadequate you feel to the task. But should you find yourself – in spite of yourself – a soldier, attempt to fill the emptiness of days, weeks and months spent in the trenches of Vietnam, Iraq or Somalia with a sense of purpose. Your government may not be able to provide that sense of purpose. The only one who would be able to do so is you.

Then, my story jumps across initial parts of going nowhere. The decision to cross the Atlantic was prompted by political developments totally outside of our control. We moved blindly, unprepared and oblivious of what to expect. A series of jobs, some typical for immigrants, some acquired by pure luck, followed.

The message: have the courage to open closed doors; be bold, forgetting your ignorance, there will always be time to learn and to get educated. Above all, never allow yourself the luxury of not trying.

The book that you are about to read does not convey heroism; it does not depict battles of major proportions. It is an attempt to project a journey that was neither planned nor anticipated, a journey of one family's adventure that started as a tragedy yet is about to end as fulfillment. The German invasion of Poland was the tragedy, living the final days in America the fulfillment. The title tells you what to look for. We started in Warsaw. We ended up in Washington. The 'wherever' was in between.

1

What Is America, Daddy?

"Where are we going, Daddy?"
"To America."
"What is America?"
"It is a big country, very big and very beautiful."
"Bigger and more beautiful than Scotland?"
"Yes, much bigger than Scotland."
"But not more beautiful? I know it isn't. My teacher said so."
"Maybe it is even more beautiful. We shall see."
"No, it isn't. Even my friends from second grade told me so. Why do we go there if it is ugly?"
"No one said it's ugly. We are going there to give you a great, modern, lovely school. To have many new friends. To read many new books. To have a lot of fun."
"I can have a lot of fun here. I have a lot of friends. Daddy, where is America?"
"It is across a very big ocean."
"How will we go across the big ocean?"
"On a big boat."
"Daddy, what happens if the boat sinks?"
"It won't. I promise you it won't."
"Daddy, I don't want to go to America. My teacher said it is so big that nobody really knows it well. How will I find my school?"
"I will show it to you. Don't worry. And you know what? They have really delicious ice cream in America, the kind that Scotland used to have before the war."
"Ice cream? Real ice cream? Daddy, when are we going? I can't wait…"

A six-year-old girl asking such questions? Rather normal. But it was up to us, the grown ups, to attempt an answer, an answer trying to describe a huge, distant continent which was to become the little girl's home.

Another pertinent question came to mind and I recall that it was asked and answered by an 18th century philosopher, whom I read sometime ago, J. Hector St. John de Crevecoeur.

What then is the American, this new man?

> He is an American, who, leaving behind him all his ancient prejudices and manners, receives new ones from the new mode of life he has embraced, the new government he obeys, and the new rank he holds… Here individuals of all nations are melted into a new race of men, whose labors and posterity will one day cause great changes in the world. Americans are the western pilgrims, who are carrying with them the great mass of arts, sciences, vigor and industry, which began long since in the East; they will finish the circle… The American is a new man, who acts upon new principles; he must therefore entertain new ideas and form new opinions.

So how did we envision America? We saw America as green and big and open and anxious to share and to give. I also saw America as a country in which you would grow up. I saw you in a classroom full of people your own age but not all of them thinking alike or acting alike. I saw you in a classroom full of different thoughts, ideas, colors and beliefs. I saw you making friends with a black boy, and fighting tooth and nail with a girl from a rich, white neighborhood. I saw you being yourself. Well, I will tell you being yourself is the most difficult thing in the world – it is to stand up for what you really believe in. It means being stubborn about what you think is right; to be obstinate enough to do what you think makes sense in life.

I saw America as a place waiting for people like your mother and me – an America bubbling with excitement when she saw people like us coming over. Why us? Because we were different, because we were arriving full of dreams and hopes that we would be able to transform these dreams into realities. It is surprise that makes life worth living. It is the unexpected that provides challenges. Challenges evoke responses and bring people to the heights of their abilities and creativity.

Like the big war: the one that stood between our dreamland and us.

"What is the big war, Daddy?"

"The big war…"

Scotland was good to us. It welcomed us as members of the defeated but stubborn army, as men (and a few women) who spoke a funny language and barely managed to respond to simple questions in English. "Do you like Scotland?" "Yes," they said, not even adding, "I do." But it didn't matter. The remnants of the Polish armed forces that arrived equipped with rifles, tents and the enthusiasm of a team ready to finish a job, were greeted warmly. Scots opened their homes, their hearts and their war chests to welcome unknown foreigners. And we looked around, built elaborate tents, returned smart salutes from slightly confused British soldiers and settled in for a while. A while turned out to be a rather long duration.

The Scottish intermission arrived after a rapid war drama unfolded in two major acts. The Polish campaign, that lasted twenty-seven bloody days, and the rapid defeat of the French that squeezed our units between hordes of French soldiers throwing up their arms and the fast advancing German army. Before we knew it, a friendly ship, a part of the pre-war Polish merchant fleet, was ready to take us to an unknown destination. We all marched onto an unsteady plank, settled on the upper deck, spreading our blankets and never even gave a thought to the potential presence of German submarines. Two days later, we disembarked on British soil.

It was the first act and it set the tone for the entire drama. All of us, what would eventually be known as the World War II generation, were caught by two feelings: surprise and blind belief in the final victory. The swiftness of the enemy attack and the total absence of the promised, but never delivered, allied help surprised us. But that was not enough to undermine our belief that the war would be short, that the just cause would prevail and the might of allied powers would crush Adolph Hitler and his soldiers. That notion, firmly rooted in our inner beings, made us strong, resolute and beautifully ignorant. As I watched my immediate family see me off at the Warsaw railroad station, proud of my newly pressed uniform, it never occurred to me that the opening scene of the drama was to lead all of us into permanent exile. I was going to fight a just war. It was inconceivable that we would lose it. Should anyone have suggested such an outcome, they would have been declared a traitor. Anyone doubting the solidity of Western commitments to my native land would have been declared a pathetic pessimist. We boarded our train and sang the songs of a joyous army until the first German bombs landed on the railroad tracks.

That was the beginning of my personal saga. I was newly married and newly settled into a job. I was also fresh from a brief seaside vacation with my young bride. There we had walked along the Baltic beaches, not far from the East Prussian border, opposite a naval fort called Westerplatte, which soon was to be the target of heavy German attacks, totally oblivious to the gathering storm. The sky was blue, full of blinking stars at night and I loudly predicted that there would be no war. Germany is not a stupid nation. Hitler knows that he has no chance. He is not going to attack Poland. I stated that in the middle of August 1939, and barely two weeks later, I was dusting off my uniform. It turned out to be the beginning of our journey to America. But we knew nothing of that. We planned nothing of the sort. And we would have defied anyone who would have predicted, or tried to predict, the outcome.

2

The First Act

The preface of the first act of the drama needs to be touched upon. I led the life of a privileged boy, unaware of some of the real problems of the country that I was born into, as well as the oncoming national tragedy. Or perhaps not oblivious, but certainly not fully comprehending the magnitude of the events I was witnessing – events that directly touched my family, events that were brewing outside of my family, and events that were unleashing the destructive energies of a frustrated leader. I existed in a vacuum, and so did my future wife. We were children of innocence and blessed ignorance.

My future wife, who was young, inexperienced, naïve and beautifully firm in her belief in human goodness, was brought up in a family that had suffered a great deal. Caught by the Bolshevik revolution in 1917 – the year she was born – her father was never able to forget. His contempt and distrust of Russia and everything it stood for was inherited by his daughter. He saw destruction, rape, murder and arson perpetrated by the incoming Russian soldiers. He lost all he had. His wife, fragile and totally devoted to her only child, witnessed the debacle. Their house was taken over. From one day to the next, they became refugees, with their tiny baby suffering malnutrition and cold. My wife never fully recovered and carried into her adult life the remnants of her debilitating illnesses. In our old age, when our son served in Moscow as a Newsweek foreign correspondent, she was still unable to shake off her memories. She never visited him, never wanting to cross the frontier dividing Poland and the Soviet Union.

There were days that followed in the newly independent Poland that also left deep scars. The family settled in a suburb of

Warsaw. The girl had to commute to school by foot and by train. The trip was long, weather severe and trains crowded to capacity. Little Marysia returned home at night exhausted and hungry. But there was homework to be tackled and there were chores at home that awaited her. The little girl, determined to be a good student, persisted. A few years later, life delivered a blow to her that she was unable to deal with for years. Her mother, a friend, cherished companion and a vital part of her life, died of tuberculosis.

I never suffered the way she did.

Within my family, which was affluent thanks to father's flourishing international legal practice, an occasional ripple of a crisis brought to my young and not very profound mind a touch of reality. Within the legal profession in pre-war Poland, Jewish lawyers were a majority. They, as all the others, faced perennial Polish anti-Semitism. Father, whose wife's maiden name sounded Jewish and whose views were those of a liberal, was often a target. The more successful one was in those times, the more one could expect personal attacks of a rather ugly nature. It came to a climax at a general meeting of the Warsaw Bar Association when he was elected to its Board. His opponent represented a right, highly nationalistic wing. Father won thanks to Jewish votes. The assembly erupted in indignant shouts. A wall of protectors thwarted an attempt on father's life. I was one of them, swinging my fists left and right. But the threats, the attacks, the sense of insecurity at home persisted. I suddenly realized that we were living in a society full of hate and I was at a loss how to react, how to respond or what to do about it. It was at that time that I discovered my love and passion: writing.

I approached a liberal weekly published by a group of university students and recounted the experience. It was published almost instantly and made me a *bete noire* among the majority of the right wing student body. Once again, I was not fully aware of the consequences. I was not fully conscious of what I was doing or writing about. The mere fact of exposing the ugliness of the legal profession was enough for me to proceed. It was not, however, a missionary zeal. It was simply an urge to write. The public reactions to that act only vaguely registered in my mind.

I was never deprived of the basic necessities of life. I was never uprooted from home. And during my college days, financially secure, spoiled and light-headed, I played more than I studied. Unlike my future wife, my own incentive to climb the ladder was limited. I felt like I was already there. My days were spent around the bridge table, my nights at dancing establishments. I joined a fraternity – called "corporations" in pre-war Poland – whose principle goal was to drink a lot of beer and to have a good time. Our roads to adulthood could not have been more diverse.

Outside of the family, I began to observe another ugly aspect of political life once again, thanks to father's involvement.

The government was run by a group of military officers who took power after the death of Marshall Joseph Pilsudski, the national hero of World War I. It was the Marshall who arranged a coup d'etat in 1926, totally frustrated by the fragmentation of the Polish parliament where over twenty parties competed for power, and a semi-totalitarian regime was established. Father was violently opposed to the methods that were applied. When sixteen prominent opponents of the government were arrested and kept in jail, he volunteered, together with another group of prominent lawyers, to defend them. The trial produced newspaper headlines across Europe and brought him national prominence. For me, the young and green observer, it was a moment of facing another reality: father's willingness to stand firm, irrespective of the effects on his profession, earnings or even personal security. For several weeks, he kept his small suitcase packed with overnight essentials. Rumors were rampant in Warsaw that the lawyers involved in the trial were next on the list of people to be detained.

While all of that was going on, dark clouds were gathering west of the Polish capital. When Czechoslovakia fell, Marysia and I received the news while playing cards in a ski chalet atop of one of the highest Tatra Mountains. We stopped playing for a minute or so and then resumed, unable to comprehend that this was just another step in Germany's march to the East. Did our group think that we were safe? Or were we simply too inexperienced, too naïve to think in larger terms? Father, I learned later, sank into a deep depression.

And on September 1, 1939, the inevitable occurred.

It was a strange, almost surrealistic scene. A platform packed with young men reporting to their respective units, Warsaw still untouched and civilians going about their daily chores. And I was boarding a sleeping car on my journey to war. How did I get it? An authorization requesting my immediate arrival at my unit's location was rather inaccurate as to the class of ticket. The dispatcher looked at it, scratched his head and asked me whether I was an officer. I was not. My rank was cadet officer with stripes of a sergeant. He looked at me with his blurry, blue eyes, smiled and scribbled something on my mobilization paper. Before I knew it, I was assigned to the only sleeping car traveling west. Was I thrilled? Probably not, but I was rather amused and awaited further developments. My three companions – there were four berths in each cubicle – were all civilians. We barely talked. Instead, I put my head on the pillow and slept peacefully until early morning. My alarm clock was of a German make with a whistling sound of a bomb traveling at the speed of sound and hitting the ground in close proximity.

Yet, the journey continued. Directions were changed. Instead of heading west, we turned abruptly east. I was supposed to land in Bydgoszcz, a mid-sized town where I was trained in the school for men assigned to armored division. I was a tank specialist. My tanks were waiting. But where were they? Where was the crew? Men, equipment and logistical support units? Provisions? Medical staff? Our car buzzed with questions, rumors, unconfirmed news about the German air force ready to unleash a major attack on us, and still less confirmed, but awaited with excitement and anticipation, stories about people spotting American and British planes high in the Polish sky. "I swear I saw them last night," claimed a burly farmer watching our reactions. "Did you really?" chimed in a middle-aged woman. "I think that I saw them also but they were flying further east. Maybe to the Soviet Union."

The train stopped abruptly and most of us decided to take a little walk to examine the outside world. Our stationary position, I figured out, would be a perfect target for the German air force.

My inquiries led nowhere, with the motormen either ignorant himself, or uncommunicative. His instructions were clear. Don't go any further and await the arrival of a special cargo. What type of cargo? No one knew. The only immediate visible change was the uncoupling of the sleeping car. All four of us were asked to take our belongings and move two cars up. From the luxury of a bedroom, we were relegated to a livestock car. No one complained. No one looked upon the change as a demotion. Someone started playing a harmonica. The mood changed into that of a typical soldier's barracks with loud laughter erupting. It sounded almost carefree and it proved to be a great escape from the tension of the day.

The cargo arrived. We greeted it with shouts of delight. It consisted of our weapons, tanks, pieces of artillery, howitzers and other heavy equipment. I ran to the tanks. Here they were: huge, cumbersome and slow, but ours. I climbed inside of the lead vehicle. It had two large levers to be used to turn, no steering wheel. At the upper level sat a small piece of artillery. Gunners were to be placed next to it while drivers sat below. "What is the maximum speed?" I inquired. "Eight to ten kilometers an hour?" I gasped. That is just about the speed of an average horse.

"Correct," responded the man who brought the tanks to us, "they are old, but heavy, sturdy and able to withstand direct hits."

"Old? How old?"

"About twenty years. They came from the French arsenal of World War I. Paris sold a bunch of them to Warsaw a few years back. We Poles bought them because they were cheap." And here they were.

We walked quietly back to our cars while the newly arrived cargo was loaded on open flatbed cars hooked to our train. "Aren't they going to be visible to the enemy?" somebody inquired.

"Not at all," came a crisp and cheerful reply. We will camouflage them thoroughly.

The train slowly pulled out of the station.

Historical places are there to be visited, admired and left behind inside various albums of family outings. Only on very rare occasions do they enter into the consciousness of men and women preoccupied with their daily chores. And even on more rare occasions, soldiers wandering around battlefields are aware of the historical significance of either their deeds or their geographic locations. Brest Litovsk, or *Brest nad Bugiem* in its Polish designation, was such a historical place, where the Russians surrendered to the Germans at the end of World War I. It was there that the Polish government in the early thirties interned members of the opposition parties. This was to be the final destination of our tanks, our men and our youthful dreams.

Brest was a medieval fortress. We survived inside the fortress for a full six days, assigned to one of the powerfully built gates. We hugged our metal friends and slept under them, withstanding the heavy, steady German artillery shelling which lasted day and night. Our gate was chipped by shrapnel, our access to other units blocked by the steady rain of heavy shells. I was at times paralyzed by fear. The men whom I was asked to command were less nervous, more courageous and willing to undertake dangerous escapades into other corners of the fortress. At one point, sensing or anticipating German intrusion, I fired my tank's gun a couple of times, not knowing where my bullets landed. Later, I learned that some of our own men were hit from behind. Was I instrumental in delivering what was later called, "friendly fire?"

The first act of the war was rapidly coming to its climax. News of the Russian move into Eastern Poland, linking their forces with their then-allied German divisions, plunged us into the darkest of depressions. We burned our tanks and headed away from the fortress, oblivious to an order shouted at me by a passing officer to turn around and protect units still inside. I continued in the opposite direction. Long, endless columns of men and vehicles joined us. We were in the middle of another exodus of a defeated army, which eventually, without ever imagining it, found its way to a distant Scotland. At that point, however, our goal was much simpler: to survive and see another day.

And survive we did. In my mind, I composed another letter to my bride long before our first anniversary. I did not know where she was. I did not know whether she was still alive. I posted a number of letters, which I wrote as we went along, in various mailboxes scattered around the country. She did the same, but neither of us was ever able to read them because no postman was working. No mailbox was ever emptied. Marching along the trail of escaping humanity, I could not help but to see her and talk to her.

"My dear," I started. "Here we are, you should see us. We are running away from the war. Are we cowards? Maybe. I really don't know. But I would do anything to be able to see you again. Maybe this is why I was hiding under that tank? Maybe this was the reason that I sent one of my men on a dangerous mission instead of going myself? Do you hear me? Do you excuse my behavior? Or are you reading my thoughts in the way any logical person would read them? As a way to provide self-excuses? Tell me, please. I need your response. I need it so badly that only another soldier like myself could understand that need."

Someone interrupted me. It was a young boy, badly wounded, carried on a stretcher. He grabbed my hand, tears running down his cheeks.

"Help me," he asked. "Help me not to die." I stopped, so did the four men carrying him. We looked at each other and almost in unison we assured him that he would not die, that his wounds were not serious, that he would still be able to fight. His face, still wet and lined with pain, suddenly broke into a wide smile. "Thank you, men. Thank you so much. I am sure that you are right. I will still fight. I do want to fight." Then his voice faded, his eyes closed and his head dropped. The bearers picked him up. One checked his pulse and the others just kept walking.

"I am back with you, my dear. Where are you? Are you, by any chance, looking around, the way I do? Seeing nothing but desolated fields and fearing nothing except approaching planes? Or maybe you are hiding somewhere in our house in Warsaw awaiting my return. If you are, stay there. I am on my way and I promise I will make it. I am not going to be killed. I am not going to be captured. I am determined to keep walking…"

I kept walking. The first stop was my grandparents' summer place. Maybe I would find some traces of parents, wife or brother? Yes, they were here. They stopped on their escape route and then they went further south. Nobody knew what happened to them. Our old, faithful, sturdy housekeeper, whose wife and family lived in the house, was optimistic.

"You will find them," he boomed in his masculine voice. Was he treating us the same way that we treated the young, dying boy, providing the narcotic of hope?

My four companions, enlisted men who formed part of our tank crew, listened patiently. They had no place to go, no place to hide and no place to call home. I became an anchor, a leader, someone who had a plan. In fact, I had none. I just wanted to get back to Warsaw, to check on the house, to find the two maids and see how they survived, to look for surviving friends and to do some planning.

A German platoon, composed of about thirty men, arrived at the house where we stayed. The officer was polite but firm.

"We need your place to billet our men. If there will be room to accommodate you, fine. If not, you have to move out." The officer, a man in his late twenties, looked us over: four men of draft age, looking healthy and fit. "Are you soldiers?"

"We used to be," I answered.

"Why are you free? Why are you not in a POW camp?"

I pretended not to understand his German, so I mumbled some kind of an innocuous reply and my men remained mute. The officer gave up and settled in an upstairs room. His unit spread across the house, occupying all available space. Five of us went to the basement, sharing one room with the caretaker and his family. But the officer's questions were dangerous. Throughout Poland, the German High Command had proclaimed that former Polish soldiers had to report to POW camps. Failure to do so called for immediate execution. We simply ignored the order.

That first German platoon moved out after a couple of days to be followed by another and still another. We were lucky that it was the regular army and not a SS unit or the Gestapo. But I decided to stop pushing our luck too far. A way had to be found to begin our journey to Warsaw. Easier said than done. To walk approximately one hundred miles? Our meager financial resources dwindled to almost zero. It was the caretaker who fed us, and it was his wife who cooked for us, buying food in the local store on credit.

"Should we separate?" the four men kept asking. It finally came to that due to the sudden appearance of an old family friend who had a rather ancient but functional car. Destination: Warsaw. Departure: tomorrow. And there was only one spot available in the car. All four urged me to take it. There was little hesitation on my part, but for a long time, years after the events, I continued to think about them. I heard nothing from them. I knew nothing about their fate. I simply hoped that somehow they managed to avoid captivity the way I had. But the feeling that I was a poor leader who abandoned his men lingered with me for the rest of my life.

What an amazing ride it turned out to be. The old car acted almost like a machine gun, with a poor mixture of gas and air causing incessant backfiring. We passed a marching column of German soldiers who reacted with collective laughter. At one point when the car refused to move, a group of Germans pushed it down the hill until the engine caught again. The owner of the car, a prominent landowner in the area, who looked like a typical blue-collar worker, conversed with the soldiers in passable German. All the rest of us were instructed to keep our mouths shut. After all, every single passenger, with the exception of the owner's wife, could be considered a refugee from justice by the German authorities. So we traveled without saying a word, and towards the end of the day, we arrived. I was deposited in front of my parents' house and the rest continued. I stood alone at the gate, hesitating what to do next. Then I rang the bell.

A reluctant head appeared at one of the windows. Then there was a second one, and in a minute, two women ran to the gate, opened it and hugged me with tears running down their faces. They never expected to see me again. They never expected me to be alive. So many have died; so many have been maimed.

Elzbietka was the older of the two. Broncia, young and pretty, worked as an upstairs maid. They were almost like family. Broncia nursed me when I was sick and cooked me dinners when I came home late at night. She made sure that I was warmly dressed in winter, and made equally sure that my younger brother, George, kept his mischief to an acceptable level. Now they were the only two survivors. Where are the rest? Parents? Wife? Brother? They did not know. They only knew that the family had left, that they went away by car, that there was no time to take much of anything, so Father left without his winter coat.

"But they will be back, won't they?" Elzbietka asked, begging for a reassuring answer. I kept walking around the house.

"Where are the dogs?" We had two of them.

"Soldiers had killed them, used them for target practice." Soldiers? Ours? Broncia nodded. They also raped Elzbietka when she went out to buy some groceries.

"Yes, they did," Elzbietka repeated, sensing a look of disbelief.

How do you live in an occupied country? How do you preserve

hope and faith in a bright future? How do you continue to sense the validity of a struggle that may last forever?

A group of us, all of military age, met regularly in a popular coffee house, conspiring, whispering to each other the latest news overheard on the radio from London, almost oblivious to the presence of uniformed German officers at adjoining tables. We also worked. My job was relatively simple. I was determined to repair the house rather badly damaged during the Warsaw siege. I was also determined to look for funds. I discovered them in a hidden safe, which, I later learned, belonged to my uncle. I raided its jewels, sold them promptly to the first dealer I encountered, and went to work. Within weeks, the house looked like new. Even the huge picture window, that used to display exquisite Venetian glass, was replaced by plain but solid glass.

Ok, what to do next?

The answer was simple: escape and rejoin the army. Our grapevine reported that in France, a restructured Polish army was being formed under the French command. How to get there? Doubts crept into many minds. Shall we go East and try to pass through Soviet occupied territory? "Never!" cried my father-in-law, who, at the end of World War I, had experienced life under the Soviets. Go West, try whatever route, even through Germany, but not where the Russians are waiting to send you to Siberia. We listened and continued meeting in coffee houses. We debated until one day, an event occurred which made me decide and made me face what it meant to be living on the edge. Naked reality knocked on my door.

A military staff car pulled up to our house. Three tall, young, very smartly dressed German officers stood examining the building. They rang the bell and I went to open it. They saluted me politely and asked if they could look inside. Surprised by the civility of their approach, I nodded. The three walked in, looked around and whistled a sign of approval. "Great place," the senior man said. "Was this your family home?"

"Yes, it was. And the library…"

"Ah," said the next man, "great library. You even have some German books. Why?"

"My father studied in Germany. He wrote in German. His doctorate thesis was published by the University of Zurich."

"Here it is!" shouted one of the officers. A slim volume, a doctorate thesis, dealing with the legal rights of illegitimate children, was passed from hand to hand. They looked at it, turned a few pages and put it back on the shelf.

"Germany has always been a great place to study and to learn. Don't you agree?" they asked. I smiled without uttering a word. Should I have told them that father was expelled from the University of Berlin for propagating the notion of an independent and free Poland at the beginning of the century?

I looked around. The officers were gone. But I still heard their voices. Where were they?

Our large basement housed the family's help. It also had space for provisions that mother kept for the winter months. Just before the outbreak of the war, she had spent weeks making special preserves. There were raspberry and strawberry jams, marinated cucumbers, herring and other similarly selected items. Next to her domain was that of father's, wines of all kinds, almost all of them French. Bottles were stacked up, with the finest, old vintage wines put in the coolest end of the room.

It was in that room that the three officers stopped and reflected for a moment. They called their driver, barked orders and the husky man, his arms full of mother's preserves, opened the garage door and started loading his loot into the trunk of the staff car. Then he went down to help himself to a dozen or so bottles of wine.

The three Germans were ready to leave. This time they did not salute. "Have you served in the army?" the senior man asked.

"Yes, I have. Some time ago."

"Did you report to the German authorities?"

"Of course, I did. They asked me to go home."

"Are you disabled?"

"Slightly," I continued lying.

The men looked at each other as if unsure of what to do next. The highest ranking, a captain I thought, issued the final order. "We will be back. In the meantime no one should touch anything in the house. And we will check on your story about allowing you to go home."

And they were gone, leaving me with a sudden determination not to wait for their next visit. Two priorities were established in my immediate agenda. One to receive instructions from the Polish underground authorities, which were already beginning to function, and the second, to secure papers that would help me to move across Poland. A friend who worked at the City Hall promised to deliver. He was also ready to move into our house as a temporary tenant. After all, we knew at that time, December 1939, that the war was bound to end soon and a total defeat of Germany was the inevitable outcome.

It was wonderful to be young, to be naive and to be ignorant. But I was not conscious of any of the above.

Marysia wrote me a letter.

My dear Zyg, it is probable that we will be leaving Warsaw tonight. We don't have any idea yet as to where we are going. Maybe to the West, who knows. Everything is so fluid. I am writing this letter today and I am leaving it at home. My other letters sent to the destination of your unit may never have reached you. I have no other address. Don't worry about us even if there will be no news from us for a longer period of time. It looks as though mail delivery does not work too well. Nevertheless, I will continue to send letters.

Date: September 5, 1939.
An addendum:

It is the next morning. Our departure plans had to be changed. All villages and towns that we were planning to go through put out restrictions on people like us. Are we refugees? I refuse to accept this label. Apparently, there is no room for any more people. There are no places to sleep and no food available. As soon as I learn our new itinerary, I will let you know. My dear, we really are trying to take care of ourselves the best we can. We are leaving our home with strong hopes and convictions that we will be coming back soon. But we could not risk remaining in Warsaw any longer. Both your father and brother could have been taken into the army or forced labor. Remember that we are leaving in a very comfortable way, by car. We are all healthy and strong and I have kept faith that God will look after us and after you. And as soon as the danger will be over, we shall return. I have deep convictions that things are bound to turn around and that we will be able to resume our peaceful, good life. Without faith in the future I would be lost. That faith gives me strength to deal with difficult moments.

She was young and deeply in love. She was ready to endure, to go to whatever lengths necessary to rejoin her husband whom she had married barely ten months earlier. Inside the car, which belonged to Father, there were four of them, the entire contingent of my immediate family. It was a luxurious way to travel at that particular time. Along the route leading south, they observed the beginnings of human displacement. They did not know that this was just the beginning, and they looked with horror at the long lines of marchers, pushing their meager belongings in front of them, carrying small children and helping limping grandmothers. It looked as if the entire population of the Polish capital were on the move. And yet Warsaw experienced only a mild version of the German onslaught. No one was able to imagine what was lying ahead.

Escaping, moving and hoping were not enough to shake off German terror. Low flying *Stukas* - German fighter-bombers - scooped low over the heads of escaping Poles. At first they simply observed the human snake of refugees and disappeared on the horizon. But within minutes two others arrived, with their machine guns blazing. The snake broke into pieces, with men, women and children running into ditches, covering their heads, pretending to be dead. Mother threw herself down on the bare earth. Father, always more controlled, followed suit in slower and less dramatic movements. Marysia, the young bride, used the car as a shield. Somehow, a miracle occurred. No one was hit. No one was wounded. German pilots must have been still in the process of training. Their bullets hit the dirt of the road and the planes flew away.

The long snake of refugees continued to move. Marysia and my brother George were designated watchers. It was up to them to warn about incoming planes. It was up to them to spot German dive-bombers whose mission was nothing less than to terrorize civilians in an already conquered land. Much later, as a war correspondent in 1945 and also an allied soldier, our unit captured a contingent of German pilots and kept them confined to a room. They swore openly that Luftwaffe never attacked civilians. It was not easy to control my temper. It was not easy to resist using my machine gun to silence the liars.

The drama of the family saga reached its climax when the moment arrived to cross the Romanian frontier. While the young contingent, Marysia and George, saw this as an adventure - she had never been outside of Poland - father sensed the tragedy. He was leaving behind the fruits of his entire life, his involvement in conspiracy before and after World War I, his early service in the newly constructed government in an independent Poland and his success as a lawyer and public servant. Experienced, savvy and not easily swayed by optimism and dreams, he had a premonition of a long exile, and even of the possibility that returning would never be possible. He was a controlled man, his emotions always hidden behind a stony face. This time he just stood there, looking at the point of no return, waiting beside the vehicle to be cleared by Romanian border guards. The two youngsters giggled, expecting a new adventure. In their minds nothing but a rosy future lay ahead.

Earlier, the group managed to secure passports. When they left Warsaw, no one expected a trip to a foreign country. No one expected to be on the road for more than a few days. Upon leaving the house, Mother appeared with her fur coat wrapped around her shoulders. Father scolded her, it was September, warm, almost summer weather. He told her to put the coat away. She did. It was added to the future German loot.

Somehow, the local officials in a place called Zaleszczyki, the last stop in Polish territory, managed to secure blank passports. Otherwise, even the friendliest Romanians would have had difficulty in admitting anyone. And they were friendly, exceptionally friendly. With Polish currency worthless once the invading German forces overran the country, the family found itself penniless. In one of the first homes encountered on the road toward Bucharest, they were invited to stay. They were fed and housed for a couple of days and a signal was sent to the relatives in the Romanian capital requesting similar hospitality. The four escapees stayed there for the entire month, treated as members of the family.

Marysia, in the meantime, continued searching for me. A flow of Polish soldiers steadily arrived in Romania. She posted notices all over the city describing my unit, my last assignment and my rank. While she was full of hope and total faith that I was still alive and that she would find me, her efforts almost backfired. One day a man, presenting himself as a former soldier, rang the bell of the house where the family stayed. Fortunately no one except the Romanian hostess was home. The man informed her that he was the only witness of my death. That he was in the same unit, and that he read the notice my wife put up and felt he had to let her know that it was useless. Her husband was killed in action.

It was the sensitivity and wisdom of that Romanian woman that decided it was best to keep the information to herself. Even when there were hints in her comments to Marysia and a marked sadness in her expressions when she came home, somewhere in the back of the hostess' mind there must have been doubts about the veracity of the informer's account. It was several months later, when we were reunited in Paris, that my uncle who knew the story, shared it with both of us. The alleged Polish soldier was probably one of the German agents whose job was to undermine the morale of the Polish refugees. They turned out in large numbers with instructions on what to do. They were, in many cases, successful in turning hope into despair.

In our case, despair turned into hope and hope turned into a reality. Meanwhile, in Warsaw, the signs were multiplying, suggesting that hope was indeed a viable commodity.

It was a busy morning inside the City Hall. German officers in full battle uniforms with decorations crowding their chests were getting ready to receive an important visitor. General Frank, who was to be appointed Governor of occupied Poland, was expected to arrive at noon.

In one of the smallest rooms, three Polish employees bent over their papers and kept a silent watch. They knew that one of them, Frank Studzial, had received an important assignment. A couple of days earlier he was approached by a member of the fledgling, barely functional underground group and asked if he could provide legitimate German papers to be used by an important emissary escaping abroad. The man will be instructed to contact the Polish Government in Exile in Paris and deliver a series of important messages.

Frank knew what to do. The perfect moment inside the office had to be chosen when the Germans were preoccupied with other tasks. The very morning before the arrival of the general appeared to offer just that opportunity.

The officers were running all over the place. Their pace was fast, their clicking heels audible all over the building. Frank moved slowly towards the middle drawer where his German supervisor kept official seals. He took one out and, with a swift movement of his wrist, stamped a piece of paper. Then, equally nonchalant, he slowly walked back to his desk. A typewriter clicked while the other two kept watch on the door. Within a couple of minutes the document was safely in Frank's pocket. It spelled the purpose of an official trip by the bearer to Cisna, a tiny village located on the Hungarian frontier. The bearer was a merchant looking for timber. All of the German authorities were requested to assist him in his task. The seal with swastika and "Heil Hitler" prominently displayed added full weight to the document.

Thus I was transformed into a merchant of timber. I looked it up the nearest encyclopedia. Cisna had pine, oak and even cedar. I had to learn about some of the dimensions I was looking for. A young memory offered wonderful opportunities. Within a couple of days I memorized enough data to make my new profession credible.

Another meeting at Cafe Club followed. There were five of us sipping coffee, laughing and on the surface having a great, worry-free time. Next to our table sat an SS officer attempting to seduce a Polish girl. He was absorbed in his task. So were we.

I was cleared almost instantly. My underground companions marveled at the document and its usefulness. "Great," they exclaimed, "just go and make sure that this most valuable piece of paper is preserved. It can be used by others. And when you get to Paris, tell them that we are not idle. Tell them that the country is still in shock. Germans have already started rounding up Jews, ordering each of them to wear a yellow Star of David on their arms. Officers and men who served in the army were ordered to report to POW camps. Those who failed to do so faced the death penalty. Long lines of men formed in front of German manned desks to register for shipments. But we do not intend to be intimidated. Our movement is in the process of being formed. It is too early to give you details. We don't have them as yet. But we need money to buy arms. We need contacts and radios as soon as possible. Maybe they could drop a dozen or so small units somewhere on the Polish soil?"

I listened without doubting for a moment French or English or American willingness at this stage of the war to undertake such a risky operation. Haven't they committed themselves to assisting Poland? "Okay," my instructors continued, "tell them that we do have leaders here. One of them, Zygmunt Gralinski, is ready to give you further instructions. The other, Stefan Korbonski, will have one of the key positions."

"Don't delay your departure," one of the men suggested. "Go and buy as much timber as you can!" the group erupted in a loud laughter. The SS man turned his head, obviously annoyed. Don't interrupt my efforts, his eyes conveyed. I am almost there.

Within three days, two of us, myself and an old friend from college days, were waiting at the Warsaw railroad station for a train to Cracow, our first destination. After that it was to be a long walk: Cracow to Cisna, Cisna to Budapest, Budapest to Barcz, Barcz to Belgrade and then who knows what would be ahead of us. With maps in our heads, the German paper in my pocket, optimism and illusions in abundance and a few hundred of Polish currency hidden in our shoes, we were off. I looked back at my parents' house, warmly embraced the two wonderful women and new tenant of the house as this would be the last time I was close to our real home.

What a great ride. We bought ourselves first class tickets pretending to be affluent merchants. A German captain sat across from us eying us at first, to determine our identity. It took him little time, however, to doze off. The conductor checked our tickets, a burly man with a traditional Polish moustache. He looked at the sleeping German and winked. We winked back. Yes, we knew he was harmless.

The early morning hours, arriving in Cracow, found us sleepy and groggy. But we knew that there was no time to waste. There was also no place to go rest. The long walk had to begin.

It turned out to be a long one indeed, twenty-six days to be precise. But at that point we faced each day as it came, each kilometer as it was traversed. There was neither the intention nor the will to make long term plans. Back roads had to be found and navigated. In spite of the German paper in my pocket, we were determined to avoid direct confrontation. We just marched along. At one point we were plain lucky, a freight train was moving slowly in our direction. We grabbed the chance, jumped on one of the open platforms only to be faced with a group of five young men, former soldiers like us, looking for a way out of occupied Poland. By the time we finally reached the Polish-Hungarian frontier, there were twenty-six of us, almost a platoon.

The frontier area was the most dangerous part of our journey. Local farmers warned us that Germans with specially trained dogs patrolled the border. We were also told that men caught trying to escape were, on occasion, executed on the spot. The lucky ones were shipped back to concentration camps. But once again there was that proverbial luck that hovered over our heads.

Out of the blue, appearing from nowhere, a young peasant boy offered his services as a guide. He knew the region. He was born there. He was ready to take us through. He was armed and we were not. There was a momentary hesitation. Was he real? An agent or German plant? He read our thoughts and smiled. "I know what you are worrying about. Do not worry. The only contribution I can make to our war effort is to see that as many people like you as possible reach our army in France." There was an instant recognition of honesty; there was an intuitive sense of the boy's sincerity. He took us across. He refused to take anything for it. We walked in total silence and when we were already on the Hungarian soil he waved a joyful goodbye. We learned that two months later he was killed while guiding another group of Polish soldiers. At that time, and even now half a century later, I knew and I know, that he was one of the unsung heroes of that big war.

For us, thanks to our guide, the first frontier was easy. "Just watch for Germans with dogs, avoid them and don't go down to the villages no matter how hungry you are. Just keep walking," the guide advised. The snow was deep, sometimes getting close to our shoulders. The menu for all three meals a day, the snow was occasionally boring. We were tired and had to support one of our companions whose strength gave out. But so what? The goal was clear, our optimism high, our young legs strong and our determination unsurpassed. We simply knew that we would make it.

3

The Walk, the Jail and the Arrival

On the Eastern frontier of that tragic, hopeless struggle of the outnumbered and outgunned Poles, another chapter of the battle was unfolding. Soviet troops, allied with Germany, invaded Poland.

"Don't you ever try to go east," pleaded my father-in-law. "You will never make it. The Bolsheviks will kill you or ship you to Siberia. They are worse than the Germans. Believe me. I saw them in action at the end of the previous war." I listened and I obeyed. Years later, a story of the Soviet Polish encounter, between the remnants of the Polish army and advanced units of the Soviet infantry, surfaced in hand written memoirs of one of the survivors confirming the worst possible fears that my father-in-law had voiced. In the meantime, unaware of the other parts of the war-torn country, I focused my concentration on the road ahead.

The second frontier - no Germans, no dogs, just a half-frozen river - proved challenging. The Drava River, separating Hungary from Yugoslavia, was too deep, too cold and too wide to swim across. The only way across was to jump a moving train, which once a day, early in the evening, crossed the bridge. The bridge itself was guarded day and night. But the stupid designers of railroad cars made them so high that our many attempts to jump on ended in small disasters. Anyone who has landed on his face on railroad tracks would be able to sympathize with us.

The other way across was to hire a fisherman and ask him to ferry us to the other bank of the river. Our first attempt landed our group of seven desperados in jail. And this is where the amusement started.

As far as jails go, it was a congenial one.

The room was bare. The guardian, who spoke only Hungarian, was friendly. He pulled out a huge key attached to a heavy chain and instructed us to enter a small room separated from the main one by an iron partition. This turned out to be the only holding pen in the jail. Tired and unsure of what was coming next, we settled on the floor for a much-desired sleep. There was a slight surprise when we woke up. Our guardian, his legs stretched out and his arms looking limp, was fast asleep from too much vodka. The keys to our cell were lying in the middle of the floor. There was little time lost, little hesitation and little eye contact between us. Within minutes, through an engineering feat of belts and a few pencils, the key was in our hands. The group tiptoed around the man after a little note was left on the floor, written in Polish, thanking him for his hospitality, and we were gone. Destination: the local bar.

The second chapter of our Hungarian adventure was about to begin.

Around midnight, at the very time that several mugs of beer made their way to our heads, three armed soldiers arrived summoning the bartender. We stopped drinking and watched the drama unfold. A rather brief conversation ended with an appeal to all those concerned. First in Hungarian, later translated into Polish, the theme was rather simple. Several men apprehended earlier in the day for attempting to cross the frontier illegally, escaped from jail. Unless they are found and returned to prison, the guardian of that prison will lose his job. He is a family man, he is old and he will probably starve. The soldiers just stood there waiting.

We marched back. We were locked up and given an early breakfast before going to court. The judge, slightly bored by another case of former Polish soldiers accused of the same criminal act, gave us a suspended sentence of three months in jail, provided that we would promise not to try again.

We promised.

We tried again the same night, and this time, our fisherman managed to avoid both the border guards and the huge chunks of ice covering the Drava. We landed in Yugoslavia and were promptly arrested as illegal aliens. But the Yugos, probably from experience, did not even try to lock us up. We registered our names and other personal data and were left alone. When we started walking along the nearest paved road in the direction of Zagreb, nobody paid the slightest amount of attention to just another group looking the same, acting the same way and going in the same direction as many others have done since the war began. The Polish exodus of people determined to continue living and continue fighting became a familiar sight.

The rest was easy. A postcard mailed from Hungary reached my parents in Paris. They knew that I was on my way. A series of telegrams were dispatched to still existing Polish diplomatic missions abroad, requesting assistance should I surface. One of the dispatches reached Belgrade. I did surface. A diplomatic passport and a ticket including a sleeping berth on a train going to France were handed over to me. Exhausted, happy and impatient to reach Paris, I fell into a deep sleep. The next stop: Gare St. Lazare.

Within days I was again in uniform. Within days I also became an immigrant, a refugee no matter how I was dressed or how I was labeled. But I knew nothing about that changing status. On one side, I was reunited with my parents and my young wife. On the other, I sensed pride in regaining the common purpose. It never even occurred to me to think in terms of being an immigrant. I was a soldier and this was the continuity. Nothing else. French trenches were to be our next stop. The French army was to be our fighting ally.

Isn't it great to be young? Naive? A dreamer?

France, during the period of *drole de guerre* (phony war), retained the profile and the personality of someone oblivious to the forthcoming dangers. Boulevard St. Michel was full of youngsters having fun. Champs Elysees featured elegant couples strolling around in seemingly carefree moods. There were uniforms about, but soldiers, like all the rest of the population, were not taking the situation too seriously. It was a little nuisance to play the role. It was a little unnatural to carry handguns, but otherwise, life was going along just fine. Maybe the Germans got their satisfaction out of the Polish conquest and would leave France alone?

The Paris metro was crowded. We bought our tickets, stamped them properly and moved in. I was in mufti and we spoke Polish between us. Suddenly, a loud voice behind my back caught my attention. "Speak French," the voice shrieked. "This is France. We do not need any foreigners."

Ready to respond, I had to be constrained by the firm hand of my wife. "Don't," she whispered. "Look at the other faces. They really hate us." My verbal rebuttal would probably have had fairly negative effects. The French lady, whose voice brought us to the reality of wartime moods, kept muttering her objections, looking around for approval.

It was time to immerse ourselves once again in the carefree crowd of wandering Parisians. It was indeed a very strange war in the year of 1940. The dark clouds gathering on the horizon were as invisible for most, as were the similar clouds that I failed to observe a few months earlier on the beaches of the Baltic Sea.

The strange intermission, the strange bloodless and tireless war did not last long. The German war machine, refreshed, confident and seemingly invincible started its powerful engine in full speed. New orders arrived at our headquarters. Once again we faced the prospect of separation. Once again the uncertain future crowded our mental horizons.

Poland fell fighting. France fell retreating. The Maginot Line, a wall of fortifications meant to stop invading foes, was easily bypassed. Neutral lands were overtaken. Before anybody was able to organize a viable defense, the Germans were there. Huge columns of refugees once again moved back and forth. Unlike the Polish scene, the French scene featured both civilians and soldiers. Military organizations collapsed; there was no one to issue orders or stop the steady departure of men in uniform from their units. Within days, it was obvious that German victory was inevitable.

Piolenc was a tiny spec of a village near Mignon. It consisted of a row of houses, hugging the Route Nationale, a bar (where I lived upstairs), and one fairly civilized edifice, which housed our major. He was in charge. In his early forties, with a thinning hairline, stiff posture and a very formal way of approaching his task, the major was still acting as if he were in big headquarters. His problem was linguistic; he didn't speak French. I was summoned to be his interpreter. What fun. The maire of our village would speak for five minutes without stopping. It took only a couple of sentences to get the gist in translation. My chief was not pleased: "Was that all that he said?"

The Walk, the Jail and the Arrival 29

News of the Belgian surrender created a deep sense of general failure. A stream of vehicles with Belgian license plates was greeted with jeers. In the meantime in the bar, local players were preparing for the worst. "When the Boche come, we will simply go about our business and disregard them."

"Oh, yes," I rejoined. "I saw them in Poland. It won't be so easy to ignore them." This time I was totally ignored. After all, I was not French.

I sent a telegram to Marysia in Paris, *'War may be coming instantly to this region. Stay where you are, don't try to join me.'* Her reply from Paris, *'I am on my way.'*

Marysia arrived bright and early. There was no way that she was willing to endure another period of uncertainty. There was no way that she would want to face another open-ended separation. Here she was, and I was thrilled to have her around.

"How could she do it? Does she have a permit to travel to the front?" the major inquired. I did not have any easy answers so I brought Marysia to his quarters. Proper charm was unleashed and the major decided not to fight a *fait accompli*. My tiny room above the bar turned out to be big enough for the two of us.

Orders came to evacuate Piolenc and move further south. The German offensive, supported by heavy air attacks, was making rapid headway. No one told us to fight. No one asked us to prepare some kind of local resistance. A sense of total defeat hung heavily in the air. We formed another column of retreating soldiers and started our march towards the sea. In one of the staff cars a seat was found for the only female in our unit. Our destination was to be the Spanish border. We soon found ourselves in St. Jean de Luze. Was this another chapter in our series of retreats I asked myself? Another journey into the unknown?

A line of abandoned cars littered the streets leading to the harbor. An ocean liner that used to carry passengers across the Atlantic and on pleasure cruises waited. Loudspeakers repeatedly announced that only uniformed personnel would be allowed aboard. Immediate decisions had to be made. Within an hour, a small uniform was secured, a spare rifle obtained and a military hat large enough to hide her hair was firmly put on Marysia's head. When the time came to embark, we formed a line with every man checked carefully by two British soldiers controlling the flow. My heart was beating so fast that I could barely breathe. When her turn came the young Brit looked at her with a smile. "This way, Madame" he simply said. And we were on our way.

The SS Batory carried a huge human cargo. There was no room anywhere except on the deck. Blankets were provided and the two of us settled in our makeshift bedroom. There was no sense of danger. No one talked about German submarines circling around. No one looked up to watch for enemy planes. There was an unspoken contract, an understanding between these masses of humanity to avoid reality. We were going somewhere to continue our fight. Nobody knew where. Nobody really cared. A beautiful sense of a world that was somewhat secured in its destiny, prevailed. When the shores of Plymouth appeared on the horizon, we cheered and applauded. We had arrived.

In reality, we had not. It was Scotland that waited for the Polish invasion. A series of small Scottish villages were about to play the role of our hosts. And those hosts turned out to be very good to us.

4

Scotland

Disembarking from the ship was not as easy as boarding her. We were separated instantly. Uniformed men were ordered one way, women, nurses, drivers and a lonely wife (mine), the other way. Men boarded trains going farther North. The women were sent to London. It was there that Marysia found herself behind the locked doors of what looked like a prison. It was there that she immediately began a campaign of liberation. Her language skills helped. Almost at once she established friendly contacts with assigned guardians by volunteering as an interpreter. It helped. Within hours she was outside, totally overwhelmed by the mere fact that she was free. Even the very short time that she was confined left deep scars inside her. The rest of the women were still inside that building, an ancient hospital long abandoned and empty.

While she was fighting her little battle of liberation, I was busy building a tent. Around us, Scotland appeared quite undisturbed and peacefully happy. The contrast was enormous. The frantic evacuation from France, seized by panic and fear of the onslaught of the German army, streets littered with abandoned vehicles, stores boarded up, all that was behind us. We marched toward our future homes, tents spread out around a golf course. And we were greeted with cheers. Cars stopped, their occupants expressing their joy at seeing us, warmly welcoming the newly arriving soldiers. Wide-open windows featured women, young and old, waving their hands in expansive welcoming gestures.

There were very few men, most of them old. The rest were serving elsewhere. The war depleted the Scottish countryside of its male inhabitants. Our arrival, a couple of divisions of young men, was an injection of energy, hope and unrestricted joy. Most of the people who greeted us had heard about the war and had felt it through separations with their husbands, fathers and brothers. But the real brunt of that worldwide calamity had not touched it as of yet. Most of the men were in uniform but not yet baptized by fire.

Could most of the inhabitants of Abington, our first camp, have been compared perhaps with Frenchmen during the *drole de guerre*, I asked myself? I soon realized how wrong I was. The Scottish mood was one of determination. The French mood was one of illusions mixed with apathy.

It turned out that it was not easy to assimilate the Scottish mood into the reality of idle tent existence.

We moved our tents from place to place, Abington, Crawford, Largo, London Links, to mention just a few. We were modern Bedouins without a desert. We pitched our tents, obediently following orders. It was so easy to be a Polish soldier fighting in Poland. It was also easy to be a soldier in France, in spite of the passivity of the people, in spite of the sense of futility. Landing on British soil, watching and participating in two major defeats, we were full of anticipation. This is where the Germans were bound to be stopped; this is where our initial enthusiasm was bound to be restored; this is where the great war orator, Winston Churchill, was going to lead all of us into the light of victory.

Under peaceful Scottish skies, untouched by enemy bombers, we kept dreaming. London, in the meantime, bore the brunt of the German assault. It was there that Marysia lived. It was there that my parents existed from one day to the next. The German Blitzkrieg was in full swing.

Their letters, however, were seldom depressing. One of them, written by Mother, stood clearly in my mind.

> It is strange to wake up in the morning with a simple sense of great relief. We were still alive. Our apartment was untouched. Tonight we will probably be once again under attack. But this is the real war. Is it? You may ask, my dear soldier-son: should we be on the front line, while you and thousands of other young men are safely in the rear? Or, maybe this is a new form of warfare? With civilians like us

forced to retreat to shelters? To sleep with masses of frightened humanity inside the London underground? What the English call the "tube." To watch a sea of fires engulfing the capital? Father and I are trying to keep calm. Your Marysia appears to be in total control of herself. Maybe this is the influence of the British proverbial "sang froid" (imperturbability). That their notion of keeping the dignity of self, remains unperturbed no matter what, is brushing off on us? The emotional and sentimental Poles? No matter, I simply wanted to let you know that we are safe, that we are alright and not to worry...

The Luftwaffe soldiers that later claimed to have never targeted civilian populations, unleashed bombing raids on London night after night. I reread Mother's letters and studied Marysia's messages, but over there, away from the terror of bombing, we were really oblivious of the enormity of the German attacks. And then came the famous speech by Winston Churchill and somehow, even in the remote camps of Scotland, we began to boil with rage and long for revenge.

Few of us - few of any on the side of the Allies - would have been able to foresee the length of the battle. Few would be able to predict the ultimate victory.

And there were tents.

Under them, the Polish officers corps was gathered. There was nobody but officers, a surplus of officers. Men and lower ranks were shipped elsewhere. After receiving a late promotion from cadet to officer - a promotion that I badly wanted - I was punished. Instead of being a part of the active elements of the army I was sent to a storage place. Instead of feeling useful, I turned out to be a member of the armed but unemployed contingent.

"Unemployed?" shouted our platoon commander, the newly promoted captain. "We will make sure that you will be fully employed. After all, the German invasion is not such a fairy tale possibility. It is real."

So we were employed. And I was one of the lucky ones. With full permission of the military authorities, Marysia joined me at one of the locations. We then faced a few logistical problems. Where to house her? How to feed her? But that was nothing, totally insignificant in comparison to getting her out of London, or of being together for a change. Within days we found a hotel room, but with no money to pay for it. A deal was struck: she would repair hotel linen and thus earn her keep. She was overjoyed and spent hours bent over a sewing machine. Every morning the Scottish landlady properly attired in a nondescript dress, would bring a pile of torn bed sheets and place them on a chair next to Marysia's workstation. She was expected, by the end of the day, to have them all repaired and looking like new. My little lady just smiled with the hidden expression of a slave. "Sure," her smile would say. "I will do it. After all I have to have a place to sleep. I have to have a place to live." As for the food, we managed to include her in our daily rations served in the camp.

What a treat.

There was endless patrolling along the beaches. Our job was to make sure to alert all concerned should German submarines or German invading divisions appear on the horizon. We walked in pairs, our rifles at the ready. Freezing winds tried to discourage us from going further. The smiling faces of Scottish fishermen brought to us the reality of the normalcy of their lives. We kept walking; we kept watching. Who knows? Maybe there will be some action? Who knows? Maybe Scotland is the next German target? We almost hoped for it. We almost prayed for it. And we kept walking. After all, we had asked for activity, hadn't we?

It was at Largo, another small village, another crowd of friendly and outgoing people, that an old castle would serve as our home. We almost danced with joy in anticipation of having a real roof over our heads. There was no need to build tents - what a relief - but the castle turned out to require a fair amount of adjustments. Bathrooms were few and far between, the water supply was limited and rooms were surrounded by heavy walls as chilly as the Scottish climate. Accommodations were cramped but they were better than tents. It was such a great improvement that nothing else mattered.

The castle proudly featured its tower. It was not more than ten feet high, with a flat top large enough to accommodate three to four people. It was there that our other wartime activities were to concentrate. Being the highest place in Largo, it was also a perfect point to watch for the incoming enemy. Nighttime was the anticipated period of greatest danger.

I liked my duty. Alone, with bright stars scattered all over the sky, there were plenty of hours to reflect, to think, to contemplate. The enemy never interrupted the peaceful existence of Scotland vintage 1940. All of us, several hundred officers gathered together to await further developments, led a life of idleness and bridge, endless hours of bridge. Cleaning our useless rifles. Keeping watch over empty beaches filled our days. Sooner or later we knew that we would be called to do some real fighting. But days turned into weeks, weeks into months, and the permanency of the Polish army's presence was reluctantly accepted by the natives as something that the war had made inevitable. Initial warm greetings turned into colder reflections. Polish intrusion into the solitary lives of Scottish war widows created resentment. The welcomed guests were no longer welcome.

The guests were bored. Wide beaches swept by northern winds no longer offered excitement. Inside soldiers' barracks and officers' billets, boredom produced friction. News from distant London, where political and strategic decisions were made, was eagerly awaited. But there was not much coming. The government-in-exile had its hands full without worrying about idle troops or a forgotten division of surplus officers corps. So we continued to drift from one day to the next, from one night spent on top of the tallest building in the village, watching for the incoming enemy assault, to another. Then the big news came and the total concentration of energy shifted gears.

The German army had invaded the Soviet Union.

The invasion moved rapidly. The Soviet Union appeared to disintegrate almost in a similar way that France did. Great Britain welcomed the new ally and we wondered how Poland, carved between the two giants, would deal with the new situation. And how we, the forgotten soldiers, would be drawn into the new shape of the war.

Or were we?

It was time to move fast. It was time to press the right buttons. It was time to finally reactivate the idle minds and idle muscles. It was time to become real soldiers again.

For me the right buttons were located in London. But instead of using them, instead of calling on Father - at that time a senior official in the Polish Government in Exile - I opted for a different route. Tired of idleness, making sure that I could become a real soldier again, I volunteered to become a paratrooper. I was not sure what I was getting into. I did not realize the tough conditions of the job. I was hoping to get into a unit that would make others and myself active members of the Polish war machine. I was also hoping, without ever facing the problem, that even among men trained in jumping and in subversive, underground fights behind the enemy lines, there would be the possibility of keeping my wife around. After all, her presence in a nearby location should not be a hindrance to my training. It was there that I sensed a chance of adventure, a good chance of action and a still better chance of learning the very real art of war. I applied. I was accepted. I was to report to a camp at Fort Williams located at the foot of the highest mountain on the British Island, Ben Nevis. It all looked promising. There was, however, one little problem, which I learned to my dismay that I had to overcome.

Marysia.

She was with me in all of the other camps. She helped in organizing a unique shop in one of the remote camps that sold Polish newspapers, periodicals and books. She was an activist. Her days were full of all kinds of ideas and actions. Her solid knowledge of English made her a natural interpreter for other mono linguistic wives, as well as men. But as usual, in the environment of confinement and limited possibilities, she was also a target of gossip. There was a degree of envy of someone who could easily shop and of someone who could easily read local newspapers and translate them for the troops. There was a rumor, spread by other wives, that she was a descendant of an aristocratic family and that she felt superior. We laughed it off, but sometimes she was hurt.

In Fort Williams, wives, I discovered, were taboo. No one was permitted to bring a spouse. The colonel in charge of our brigade was adamant about it, and Marysia and I were as adamant about not enduring another uncertain separation.

Fort Williams in 1941 was a small village, surrounded by fog, mountains and deep-seated human traditions. Inhabitants were few and far between. Older women, whose sons and husbands served in the armed forces, occupied the only cluster of homes, located about a couple of miles from our camp. Mostly, they lived alone. They were suspicious of strangers. They communicated with their God, fully convinced that He listened only to them. It was in one of these homes that I rented a room, secretly, for my "illegal" wife. Only after settling the matter with a rather stern landlady, explaining to her that I would be grateful should she be discreet about her new tenant, did I bring Marysia in and we both inspected her lodgings.

The room was on the dark side. There was one window covered with heavy curtains, a prominent crucifix hanging above a single, narrow bed. A chair, a small table and a standing lamp completed the furnishing. A copy of the Holy Book occupied an equally prominent place in the middle of the table. The message was clear. Marysia was expected to fit into the environment and behave accordingly. But we were not fully aware of the rigidity of these requirements. It hit us on the first Sunday after she moved in.

The lady of Fort Williams entered the room without knocking. Her expression was even more severe than usual. "This is God's day," she announced, "and I heard you laughing. Now I see you reading a book. You cannot do it in my house. On Sunday we rest. On Sunday we pray. We do nothing else. Your radio must never be on. Where do you go to church?"

Marysia, overwhelmed, shy and intimidated, responded in a whisper.

The landlady's expression was one of shock. "Roman Catholic? We do not have a church of that kind here. We are all Protestants, many of us descendants of Luther. All the others are devoted to our Church of England. It may be wise to think about it as long as you are in the United Kingdom."

When I arrived later in the afternoon, short of breath on my bicycle, I found Marysia in tears. "There is no way that this old woman is going to alienate me from my church. No way," she said sobbing.

At my end of our bizarre existence at Fort Williams, other clouds started to gather. My frequent visits to the nearby village aroused suspicion. It took just a few weeks before the Colonel, whose fearsome moods were known and dreaded, learned about our secret.

I was called in for a dressing down. "Yes, sir. My wife is here."

"Yes, sir. I knew about the order."

"Yes, sir. I realize that I was not following your orders. But my reasons..."

The Colonel looked at me with piercing eyes. "Okay, tell me your reasons." A brief, staccato replay of our Polish separation followed. An equally brief account of our fears of being separated again was recounted.

He listened. I waited. "If you want to continue your training as a paratrooper and become a soldier again, you must send your wife back to London. You have two days to comply."

"Yes, sir."

I did comply after the encounter with a man who later became a symbol of heroism and devotion. General Sosabowski managed to make all of us out to be a fighting unit: a paratroopers brigade that went into action, suffered heavy casualties but managed to liberate towns and cities in Holland. I was not among the fighting men. After the initial training undertaken in Manchester, England and a number of jumps to overcome the initial fear of empty spaces below, I was called upon by London to work as a civilian, temporarily on leave from the military. That call probably saved my life. Very few of my paratrooper companions survived the invasion of the European continent.

I survived, and to this day a sense of guilt sits down deep in my throat, the guilt of still being alive.

Remember the first jump, my inner voice kept saying, and your fear? It was one of the old Lancaster's planes. We climbed inside, our chutes were firmly clinging to our bodies and a piece of string put in our hands, a string that was a link between life and death. A hole in the forward part of the plane was to be our station of departure. Our instructions were clear: keep yourself erect, don't look down, look forward and as soon as you start floating downward, pull on the string. That would detach you from your plane; that would also trigger the mechanism opening the chute. Once this is done, you are safe.

Easier said than done. I looked down before my turn came and saw Mother Earth at a far distance. Instinctive fear almost paralyzed my will. Shall I jump? But fortunately for everyone around, there was no time to think. We were jumping one after another; a hesitant man would stop the entire process. Before I knew it my body was going down in a rapid pace. Then the string and the jerk of an opening chute, and a sense of supreme joy. I made it. I am floating. I am having fun. I am a paratrooper.

The sense of guilt returned with a vengeance. My buddies were jumping, facing enemy fire. At Arnhem, where the brigade suffered the heaviest casualties, the Germans had been warned. They picked off floating men the way hunters pick off ducks. Years later, I visited the place. An impressive monument commemorates Polish paratroopers. Those who perished had their names carved prominently at the base. But they are no longer with us. I still am. How did I manage to accomplish the art of survival? Pure luck or good family connections at the seat of political power? On occasion I told myself that my writing skills helped, that I was viewed as more useful to the overall war efforts as an instrument of propaganda than as a line soldier. Rationalization? Probably. But it helps; it certainly helps.

It could have been a move that was expected, or one initiated by the colonel slightly exasperated by our defying his orders, but one day, papers arrived from London transferring me to the seat of Scottish High Command in Edinburgh. That bit of news was considered good for our family life. I had already acquired a sense of what it was to serve as a paratrooper. I was no longer lured by its glamour. No longer was I ready to be dropped behind the German lines. An office job in Scotland's most beautiful city was nothing to be concerned about. Besides, we were both obsessed with the fear of being separated again. The first priority in that particular period of our military existence turned out to have been personal. Somehow, the larger goals of the war itself were pushed onto a lower rung of our priority ladder. We found ourselves in Edinburgh with Marysia working in an office, turning out press releases and texts of political pronouncements, and me, a few blocks away, working within the Scottish Command on military plans affecting the Polish armed forces.

And then another event that changed our lives rather drastically and unexpectedly occurred. On October 12, 1942, our daughter was born, a wartime baby and the fruit of thoughtless parents unwilling to face the reality of an uncertain future and the reality of a war that had barely begun. America, after all, was still churning up its underdeveloped war industry. Europe was firmly controlled by the Germans who were making rapid advances into the vast territories of the Soviet Union. And we decided (had we?) to have a baby.

She was born at home. She was big and stubborn. It took her over twenty-six hours to enter the outside world. Our friendly doctor, a colleague with a captain's rank, stayed throughout the ordeal. While the mother moaned and cried from the pain of delivery, the doctor and I tried to sleep on the floor in the room next door.

When she finally arrived and I noticed the first smile on Marysia's drained face, we both grabbed the nearest available bottle. The new mother looked at us with an expression of pride.

"It's all over," chimed the doctor.

"Are you really pleased?" I asked rather stupidly.

"And how," she whispered. "Not only that she has arrived but also, that almost until the last day I was able to be in the office."

This called, naturally, for another round of celebrations.

Within a couple of days, a formal notice appeared in The Scotsman: Maria Teresa Nagorski was born on October 12 to Second Lieutenant Zygmunt Nagorski of the Polish Army and Marysia Bogdaszewska Nagorski. The girl's weight: seven and a half pounds. The family resides at 12 Buckingham Road.

The overjoyed family in London and elsewhere decided that Maria Teresa was the most beautiful baby ever born. She was also the one that a few years later would be asking pointed questions about the unknown America.

For Marysia, a soldier's wife, companion and now a mother, a new chapter was opening up, a chapter that was to be more traditional and perhaps less taxing. For being a soldier's wife within the confines of the Polish exiled community was not a bed of roses.

I served as a reserve officer. The majority of my colleagues were professional men. They dedicated their lives to the army. It was an unwritten law that wives should be equally dedicated.

And they were. Within the garrison existence, which most of the military men were accustomed to, wives adjusted themselves to the discipline, authority and structural forms. A wife of a major automatically considered herself superior to the wife of a captain. With no visible insignia on their shoulders, army women knew their rank and seldom deviated from it. They recited songs and poems praising their husbands' branches of service. They were skilled in gossiping about the navy or the air force, considering their counterparts as inferior. A perfect spouse of an officer would be also a perfect conformist. That was what was expected. That was what she was comfortable with. A military marriage, in the eyes of the authorities, was to link two people swearing not only to be faithful to each other, but also to the branch of service they were assigned to.

The war conditions brought to the ranks of the professionals people who lived different lives, men and women for whom freedom to be different was cherished above all. Military wives, scattered around bridge tables, preoccupied with the attempt to recreate within the Scottish reality a semblance of past garrison frameworks, looked with suspicion and a degree of disdain at the newcomers. "How can they enter our ranks with their strange attitudes?" was an unspoken message. How can they be useful soldiers without first adapting to the way that the true army functions? There is no room within the army for people who defy traditions. Who questions orders? Who dares to be critical?

The first thing to do, the traditionalists opined, is to make them conform. Otherwise, we will all be lost. Otherwise, the army would simply disintegrate.

Enter Marysia, the product of a liberal education, a young woman who had a mind of her own and who, unwilling to be in the shadow of her husband, had her own ideas to contribute. Who is that person? How dare she? The other day she started an argument with a colonel's wife, which was unheard of. And then she and her second lieutenant husband decided to open a bookshop importing books, pamphlets and periodicals without checking any of them with the authorities. Does she have the right to do so?

Maybe she does. The gossip factory started churning out theories.

"She has a cousin high up in the army."

"His father is important in London and above all" – voices dropped to a whisper "she is from an aristocratic family. He is not, and according to the most reliable sources, her family strongly objected to her marrying a commoner. Is this really true?"

"Absolutely. We heard it from people who know. It is one hundred percent correct."

Marysia laughed and cried. It was both funny and painful. She wanted to be accepted, but how could that be accomplished? Should she really do her utmost to conform?

The military lifestyle continued. Our part in it remained marginal. Our acceptance by the community was limited, to say the least. Our saving grace was the strong bond between the two of us, a bond that almost made us blind and immune. We stopped observing others' reactions and we stopped listening to gossip. Instead, after I was appointed to function as the educational officer, we experienced blissful immersion in the job. It was the only job within the military structure that offered a lot of freedom of initiative and action, the only job that permitted both of us to work in unison. The garrison observed, grumbled and hoped to witness our failures, but eventually accepted the inevitable. The active twosome turned out to be useful.

It was at that time that I resumed writing.

To write is to compose. To write is to unleash hidden thoughts and hidden desires. Is this a talent? An art? Nobody can answer. But from the early days of my childhood, I had a love affair with writing and with writers. I read and reread Hemmingway and Twain. I dreamt about plots that never materialized. I tried to understand Shakespeare and failed. I attempted to read Milton and his "Paradise Lost" remained a mystery. But in my early days, I devoured Henryk Sienkiewicz, Adam Mickiewicz, Juliusz Slowacki and other major Polish writers. In some cases, I was ready to sit down and make an attempt to write like them, a young, patriotic Polish boy, born into a family that was proud of its fighting heritage. I took up my juvenile pen and started scribbling.

There was another aspect of this beautiful vocation called writing. Writing opened the door to various aspects of human existence. One of my early heroes was Stefan Zeromski, a writer probably totally unknown in the West. He wrote a book called, "Glass Houses" and another one entitled "Homeless People," a story of men and women who dreamed about having a home. A story awoke in the young reader a notion of social inequalities and a quest for social justice. Another author, Boleslaw Prus, wrote a significant book called "The Doll," once again touching on the ills of contemporary society. But probably one of the most influential books was Sienkiewicz's trilogy, which depicted, among others, Polish victory over the invading Swedish armies, a victory laced with religious undertones. The army and its dedication, the way that the church at that time performed its role as a spiritual guide for the nation, all of these factors left significant imprints on the susceptible, fragile soul of the youngster.

Therefore, it was no surprise to anyone in our household that the older boy in the family spent considerable time bent over his notebook, scribbling along.

The desk was tiny and the room also served as a dining room for the family. Next to it was father's study/reception room. He was a young lawyer, establishing himself in the newly recreated country. Mother was busy attempting to combine her musical interests with the task of running a house. There was also a maid: a nondescriptive, middle-aged woman who seemed to be permanently angry. Every time the doorbell rang, she would wipe her hands on her permanently dirty apron, and cursing under her breath, would run through the dining room towards the door. In most cases the visitors would be potential clients. In most cases her attitude was that of open rebellion. "Why do they come? Why do they interrupt my work? I have more important things to do in the kitchen." The potential client, an early victim of her rage, would then be ushered into a tiny waiting room without a word of greeting or encouragement.

"Is the lawyer in?" they would mumble sheepishly.

In the meantime, at my little desk, an army of Polish cavalry was attacking the enemy. I recreated the famous Battle of Raclawice that occurred during the Polish uprising of 1863. I was there in body and mind. I was there in spirit and in my creative mood. The maid's banging doors created for me a semblance of artillery fires. Her curses and her fast steps were a perfect backdrop for the soldiers' lives. Nothing could interrupt the young man's immersion. Did I not say earlier that I had a love affair with writing?

Where did it come from? The various theories invaded my young, then middle-aged and, much later, old mind. Perhaps genes? Perhaps inheritance? Grandfather, on my mother's side, was an accomplished writer. His column was a permanent feature in the prestigious Warsaw daily, *Kurjer Warszawski*. A well-known lawyer, he wrote about the courts, the system of justice and the way it was applied in the young Polish Republic. But in spite of the weighty subjects, he somehow added a light touch to it. His popularity soared. His influence beyond close legal circles mounted.

Was it from him? I loved the old man. He cultivated an impressive moustache. By the time I was accepted in his company, it was all white and trimmed to the size of his face. One end almost touched his ears, the other served as an elegant way for him to play with it during animated conversations. He was known for his wit and charm. He died at the age of sixty-four, a victim of the then rampant tuberculosis. He consumed two packs of cigarettes a day.

But if this was the result of genes, why had I not inherited other gifts like father's legal mind? Mother's singing voice? An uncle's engineering talents, expressed in harbors, highways and bridges? How about the other uncle, delightfully oblivious of budgetary restraints when blueprinting homes to be erected for affluent clients? He was one of the most gifted architects of prewar Poland. He was also a recognized painter. What about them? Why did I inherit so little - perhaps zero - of their talents and passions?

So? Were genes out?

The other theory was perhaps a little less complimentary. To write, to deal with intangibles and escape deep research but to touch only on the surface of existence, was so much easier. Sitting behind a little desk in the cramped Warsaw apartment, you are on your own. There is no one to check on you. You have no need of group approval and no boss. Just you and your little notebook, you and a typewriter, or you and your computer which on occasion tries to outguess your thoughts. In other words, the individual reigns supreme. The only requirement is a spark of imagination. Easy.

In those early days, when the Battle of Raclawice dominated my immature mind, the only judgment that I wanted to have was that of my parents, or perhaps more precisely, of Father. Mother was always gentle, always full of praise. But Father's severity of judgment, his cool, logical mind allowed nothing to slip by without examination. It was to him that I submitted my early manuscripts.

5

Were They My Gurus?

My Father

He was also a man who throughout my entire life served as a role model for me. I was very much unlike him, knowing that I would never be able to attain his level. My admiration, respect and unquestionable love, were sometimes tempered by a feeling of compassion. He could have been so much more successful; his talents could have been so much more in evidence, but for his total inflexibility. I felt for him and I realized that there was nothing I could do about it.

Is there a way to truly convey his personality, his strong backbone or his total commitment to the country that he admired without being a nationalist? Under his roof, the men and women of Europe who advocated unity of purpose met and deliberated. Under his leadership, a small circle of politically influential men and women formed a group dedicated to the idea of the League of Nations. That was his international dimension, supplementing international legal practice that included Stockholm as well as Dresden and Berlin. At home he was a political animal. Unable to see eye-to-eye with the socialist party that he had considered joining at one point in his life, he found his political home under the umbrella of the Peasant Party. It was a genuine party populated by equally genuine farmers. Father did not exactly fit into the landscape. I see him clearly, sitting stiffly next to a couple of substantial peasants while being driven by a horse-driven carriage through the bumpy roads of a remote village in the vicinity of the city of Lublin. He was, as usual, dressed for business. His shirt was white, his tie conservative, and his suit dark blue. But if there was any sense of doubt in the purpose of that rather awkward scene, there were no signs to that effect either in his posture or in the speeches that he was asked to deliver. He joined the ranks of the party as the only way he saw fit, in expressing his devotion to the democratic process he advocated, the only way to demonstrate his strong opposition to the semi-autocratic regime that governed his country.

In his younger days, he was mobilized and had to serve in the Russian army. Poland was partitioned by three powers, Russia, Austria and Prussia and did not exist as a state toward the end of World War I. My father was an officer assigned to the judicial branch and we were stationed in Minsk, currently the capital city of Byelorussia. While wearing a Russian uniform, he established direct contacts with the Polish legionnaires led by Joseph Pilsudski, the future Commander-in-Chief of the Polish Armed Forces. At that time, Pilsudski's units were to be found on the side of the Germans, which was the only way that they could legally exist. Their goal was clearly spelled out: the restoration of a fully independent Poland since the first partition occurred in 1776. Father's contacts led to future political connections. They also led to an offer of a cabinet post arranged by Pilsudski's forces in 1926, an offer rejected by Father. He asked for assurances that the newly formed government was to be firmly grounded in democratic principles. No assurances were given and father returned home from his meeting with the Prime Minister, saddened by the missed opportunity, but deeply concerned about the future of the nation.

That concern was not new. It manifested itself during his academic years while studying, first in Russia, then in Germany and finally in Switzerland. It was in that period in his life that he penned the doctorate thesis in German that proved to be a saving grace for his son many years later. Father's concern, as well as his talents, had been recognized as soon as the newly emerging independent Poland took her place among other nations. As a young lawyer, he was given the almost titanic task of creating a legal framework for national agricultural reform. The country was essentially rural. Its export relied heavily on produce, animal feed and animals themselves. It was also basically the very sector of the economy that provided both labor and services to the population at large. Father took the assignment seriously, forgetting about the possibility of a personal career. Concurrently, he was asked to be a member of the Codification Commission. Its task was to codify three legal systems that governed the territory of Poland during the century and a half of partition. The Austrian, German and Russian legal systems had to be fused into one. Once again, a gigantic task that he shared with a team of other young lawyers. What emerged was to form the new legal framework, essentially based on Roman and Napoleonic codes. Father's key and original contribution was towards drafting a code of civil law, a code that survived until the other war, known as Number Two, which destroyed, once again, the independence of his country.

He was a stern taskmaster. He grieved over every single unsatisfactory grade that either my brother or I brought from school. He demanded almost perfection from people who worked for him. He was also formal in his approach to others. His daily attire, identical to the one that he wore campaigning on behalf of the Peasant Party, became almost a uniform. I recalled how pleased I was upon seeing him on rare occasions wearing white pants on a tennis court. I also recalled how pleased he was that my school required a blue uniform, identical for all students. A strict disciplinarian, he equally approved our school principal's order that banned bicycle riding. It was dangerous and unequal, he thundered to me, once he learned how I had managed to circumvent the order, unequal because not everyone was affluent enough to have a bike. True enough, I agreed, but continued to cheat.

It was, therefore, almost natural that one of my first major attempts to write for publication, while in uniform in Scotland, was a piece reflecting on the differences between our two generations, Father's and mine. The date was February 29, 1942. I was at that time twenty-nine years old. What did I write?

It was a nostalgic piece and it was also a song of admiration. When I was sixteen - it began - my dream was to become an adult, fast, tomorrow. But when the day came and my maturity was legally recognized, I ceased to be satisfied, to be pleased. Something happened which was difficult to explain. I switched my vision. Instead of counting my age, according to the normal chronology, I started counting it by the age of my father.

He was getting older. And everything that was growing around me, my entire world was growing older with him. The world of ideas - touching upon social, economic, value oriented thoughts - came from him. He taught me how to look at the world, how to admire art and literature, how to judge people. He was a severe judge himself, unlike Mother whose gentleness was called upon to smooth the rough waters of Father's intransigence. The two of them created a world for the two of us, me and my brother, that provided a solid framework for the rest of our lives.
Father injected into my soul all that really mattered: love of the country, the willingness to fight for it, commitment to the idea of conspiracy - so vital during the days of foreign occupation - and total commitment to what was considered to be truth and honesty. Together with Mother, they injected into my life a joy of living, a sense of being. Mother did that through her love of music and through her songs that the house was full of.

The article, which was published on the first page of the most popular military weekly, did not stop at that. It went further. It suggested strongly that being young is not enough, that being brash and proud - the normal aspects of youth - does not allow for disregarding the past. Our fathers and mothers fought for independence. They created an intellectual climate that permitted great literary minds to flourish. Therefore, I wrote, it would be unjust and counter-productive to claim superiority of our generation.

Let us lower our voices; let us stop creating generational divisions. Let's not be so certain that we, the young, can do better than they have done. It is not enough to be young. It is a great treasure, but a treasure that needs to be cultivated as otherwise it would go nowhere. The years that we are bound to spend in exile, nobody will restore unless we use them in a productive way. Our current enemy is an innocent green table. It is around it that days and nights are being spent by many of us. Bridge can destroy minds, faster than real war can destroy bodies.

And then came a reflection on the past:

> In 1905, students declared a strike at the Warsaw University. They were expelled at once and immediately dispersed themselves all over Europe looking for other opportunities to study and at the same time to continue their fight for independence of Poland. They spent years during the war in the trenches. Instantly after the war, when an independent country emerged from the ashes of bloody battlefields, they went to work. They took over factories and university chairs. They built, with their bare hands, the new Poland. They were at that time exactly our age. How about us? Could our generation perform the same task? I fear that we could not successfully fill even two major university chairs.
>
> We are perhaps just solid branches of an old oak. That oak is still growing; its trunk has been hardened by the agonies of our century, during fighting as well as peaceful work. The trunk has been strengthened by the generations of our fathers. Let us not try to replace it. Let us not be arrogant enough to say that we are better. Maybe we will be one day. Not now, not yet. Thus, let us lower our voices; let us take a proper measure of our possibilities and our opportunities. In occupied Poland, our generation is still learning. It is being directed and inspired by the conspiracy that was started by others in the year 1905.

Congratulatory letters flooded my father's mailbox. His generation perhaps did not expect one of their offspring to pay them the supreme compliment: the compliment of having been an inspiration and a spiritual guide.

The article accomplished a number of things. It created a new bond between two generations. It also made me more comfortable with my pen.

But in addition to all of the above, Marysia, my young companion, wife and severe critic, had been exposed for the first time to a piece of my writing produced under war conditions, a piece of writing that exposed my inner thoughts, my doubts and my beliefs. It was always good to write with passion and easier for me to do than writing the scholarly pieces that were cold, distant and usually only admired in academic circles.

Not having a precise mind, not being able to think in global and deeper terms, passion and conviction helped me to compose and to create. She liked it, and in her own way, in her spontaneous manner, she passionately begged me to keep writing, to follow my urge to be creative and to continue along similar lines. I promised that I would, to the best of my capabilities. And every time that I had a chance to get my typewriter handy, I did. During the war, toward the end of hostilities in Germany, I was lucky enough to witness, to observe and to record the joy of winning, the sadness of misery and the dark side, as well as the bright side, of human nature.

Marysia

I never experienced or went through life with what she had to endure. Our paths crossed in a most unexpected way and our wedding, which followed a couple of years later, came about in an equally unexpected way. It took us exactly ten days from the moment that we decided to get married to the moment that we stood in our church, turning to the solemn face of a priest.

Marysia, whose maiden name was impossible to pronounce or even to spell by most of the Anglo-Saxons (Bogdaszewska), was born at a time when the world, into which her family lived and functioned, was crumbling. Her father, a well-to-do owner of a small estate in Eastern part of Poland, had to abandon the home at the onset of the advancing Bolshevik armies. Attempting to escape with their lives, the family - four of them - embarked on a difficult journey towards Warsaw. By the time they arrived, an independent Poland had begun emerging from the First War. The father secured a small apartment and eventually an equally small job. The apartment was located in the suburbs, but Marysia's school was in Warsaw proper. Her daily commuting trips would have exhausted the hardest working American businessman. But the little girl survived, with persistence and self-discipline.

Usually, her trip had to start around 6 a.m. Winter mornings were dark, snowy and wet. The ten-year-old plowed through piles of snow and along unpaved roads to cover her first mile from home to the railroad station. Loaded with books and other school paraphernalia, she was usually lucky enough to find a seat on that early train. The trip took about an hour, with Marysia absorbed in her assigned tasks. The battle to move forward normally started at the Warsaw end. Streetcars, by the time of her arrival, were crowded to capacity. More often than not she had to be satisfied with a small space on the running board, holding with two hands to the tram itself. She was not the only one; three or four people would be hanging in the precarious position, standing on the outside steps between the moving tram and the street below. The total time of the journey lasted close to two hours. Shortly after the evening darkness descended, the little girl returned home.

Strange as it may seem, it was as early as that time that she started dreaming about a distant land called America. It came through reading. It came through newspapers and books that she obtained from the school's library. It was almost a myth, something that probably did not exist at all: a fable, a story or a dream that stuck to her mind and never left. And when the day came, years later, to decide that her native land was no longer a choice, that dream was about to come true.

The day was February 11, 1945. The place was a small apartment in London. The evening news bulletin was just about to begin. An almost oppressive silence reigned in the room. All of us, my parents, Marysia and I, expected the worst. But there was still hope. Maybe what we heard would not come to pass. How could leaders of the allied nations be so blind? How was it possible for them not to see the danger of the Soviet policy? How could they possibly sacrifice a country like Poland, the first country to fight the German assault, then to build the largest underground army in Europe, subsequently to challenge Germany in a major uprising in Warsaw? How could they just abandon us?

Then the news came on. An impassioned BBC speaker announced the results of the Yalta Agreement.

The very next day, we requested application forms from the American consulate to obtain immigration visas. My parents refused to be rushed. It took three long years before we were invited for an interview. We passed the test in spite of one of the consulate official's efforts to convince us that we should go back to Poland. "It's not as bad as newspapers report," he pronounced solemnly.

"And America is a difficult place for newcomers."

"Thank you," I responded. "We will take our chances."

The little man sitting behind the visa window did not know, and could not have known, that the three years of waiting turned out to be some of the most politically and journalistically active years of our lives.

It took the Allies only a few months to succumb to Joseph Stalin's request to de-recognize the Polish Government in Exile, sitting in London since 1940, in favor of a group composed of a majority of men trained in Moscow. Stalin's argument that Russia wanted a friendly government on its border prevailed. At the time we knew little about Winston Churchill's attempts to persuade the newly sworn President in Washington that Russia could not be trusted. Harry Truman weighed potential Soviet contribution toward the Pacific front against concessions in Europe. The atomic bomb had not yet been tested; the United States Congress was clamoring for "our boys to return home" after the German surrender. The new president, untested in foreign policy and torn between contradictory advice coming from various quarters, decided to meet the two key players personally for the first time. All three of them, Stalin, Truman and Churchill, went to Potsdam. There, the weaknesses of the democratic system demonstrated itself to the Soviet dictator. Winston Churchill lost elections and was replaced at the conference table by Clement Attlee, another newcomer and unknown quantity. Stalin was the only remaining link between the war, victory and longevity. No wonder he felt secure. No wonder he felt as though he held most of the chips in that supreme game of vying for control of post-war Europe.

Attlee returned home, watching in deep sorrow as the real iron curtain descended on the continent.

For us, uncertain, dispirited and fully aware of the fact that the entire spectrum of our lives had been dramatically altered, a new vista of opportunity unexpectedly opened up. Yalta, Potsdam and de-recognition of the Polish London government created a political vacuum for the Polish cause. To complicate the matter further, de-recognition also meant the end of financial support for the civilian components of the government. Ministries, departments and agencies that were fully funded by the British Government had to close shop. Only the military, considered free of political bias, continued to receive diminished subsidies.

There was, however, one tiny unit left untouched by the national catastrophe. A few months earlier, just shortly after our gloomy day in front of the radio in the London apartment, I was appointed head of the Edinburgh office of the Polish Ministry of Information. In principle, it had to cease operation after de-recognition. But it did not. It simply changed names and tapped, with full involvement of the highest echelon of the Polish military, the remaining resources of the Polish Army. I was no longer working for the defunct Ministry. Marysia and I became editors, writers, distributors and promoters of the Polish Press Agency, which was located in a very fashionable part of the city called Charlotte Square. Same address, same people, just a different assignment: to keep the Polish cause alive, to bring it to the attention of the British public and to demonstrate to anyone willing to read or listen that the satellite regime in Warsaw, created by and subservient to Moscow, did not represent the country of Poland.

What a wonderful challenge. Marysia and I jumped into the wide political space that had suddenly opened. We started retooling the place, shaping it into a fighting unit. Before, it was a semi-governmental entity, cautious, secure and even sometimes placid. Now, we were given the signal to spread our wings as widely as possible. Before, the task was relatively easy. Now, we were facing a world that was determined to forget our existence. The role of our minuscule unit was to do our utmost to be remembered.

We settled behind our desks and before long were joined by two other individuals determined, as we were, to make a nuisance of themselves. All four of us were swimming against a very powerful political current. The Big Three: Truman, Stalin and Clement Attlee.

The two who joined us in that almost impossible task provided diversity and closed the generation gap. In an answer to a small ad in the local paper, a flood of applications arrived. One of them caught my eye. She was a secretary. Her last job was that of personal assistant to Lord Halifax. Now she was looking for something else, perhaps less demanding but politically interesting. "Less demanding?" I wondered. Maybe I should look at her. But - and it was a big "but"- she was sixty-three years old. Marysia and I were in our early thirties.

She looked even older. There was a map of wrinkles on her tired face. She was tiny, probably around 5'4", but her voice was firm, her curiosity about our work obvious, and her past connections impressive. Margaret MacCullogh was hired almost on the spot. We all called her our "Granny" and she proved to be a find that was better than gold.

The other addition to our team simply walked in one day and proclaimed his desire to be a volunteer. An engineer by profession with dreams of being a writer, Gustaw Sohocinski read one of my letters to the editor of "The Scotsman" and decided to enlist in our cause. We looked him over, discussed at length about the way that we wished our mission to be carried out, and decided to try him out. Since he did not ask to be paid, budgetary considerations were not involved. Gutek - as he was called by everyone around - and Margaret turned out to be a perfect match. We started our aggressive campaign in unison.

And it had to be an aggressive fight. We were alone. We were considered stubborn and inflexible. Our notion that somehow, somewhere, Poland could be saved from another foreign occupation, was viewed as an unrealistic dream. Pragmatic British politicians, and the naïve Roosveltian notion that he could trust and do business with Stalin, were combined forces that made the cause of Poland's free elections and the possibility of establishing national sovereignty, a distant illusion. Our foursome had taken on a giant. "Great," I declared. "Let us try and see how far we can go and how much we can do."

The offensive was carried on a number of fronts. The existing Scottish-Polish Society, a benign, well-meaning but rather passive body, was mobilized. All over Scotland, we flooded friendly and unfriendly publications with letters to the Editor. A daily bulletin depicting conditions in Soviet controlled Poland was initiated. Material was provided by the army, still in control of some of their sources of information, and by a private group of active newsmen working in London. We typed, edited (Margaret's job), folded, licked stamps and every day, mailed out a couple of hundred copies. At first we had a fair amount of success. The story was still fresh, human memories still retained snapshots of the Poles' contributions to the Battle of Britain: of their storming Monte Casino, of having been dropped on the city of Bredu, of their valiant battles against the forces of German Marshall Rommel at Tobruk and Marsa Matruh. Gradually, however, the passing of time blurred their memories. Instead, England and Scotland began to look inward, to count returning soldiers who could not find employment. At the same time, a powerful communist propaganda machine unleashed fierce attacks on us, the "parasite Poles," who refused to go home and work at rebuilding their native land. Anonymous letters began arriving at our office. One or two included not too subtle threats of violence. On our side, equally powerful friends closed ranks, giving us access to members of Parliament, columnists and others. But some of my own meetings with men of influence were depressing, leading me almost to the brink of resignation. One was with a prominent member of the Labor Party serving as a MP. The other was with one of the top editorial writers of the Times of London, an influential newspaper and not necessarily friendly to the cause of Poland.

H.H. Carr's office was not as impressive as I had expected. It was cramped and rather narrow with his desk facing a wall. He agreed to see me after intervention from the Labor MP whom I saw earlier. But the modesty of the ambiance was deceptive. His reputation exceeded his position. Considered to be one of the advisors of the Prime Minister, as well as influential among peers at the House of Lords and members of the House of Commons, Carr was a powerful political voice. After reading a number of his unsigned editorials, I was determined to talk to him. He was a strong advocate of building bridges to the Soviet Union. He promoted the notion, advanced and ultimately approved at Potsdam, to move the Polish frontier westward at the expense of Eastern provinces. Two major cities, both viewed as essential to post-war Poland, Lvov and Vilno, were to be ceded to the Soviet Union. Vilno, which was a bone of contention between Poland and Lithuania in the period between the two world wars, became a part of the Soviet Lithuanian Republic, annexed by the Russians at the very beginning of the war. My role was to impress Mr. Carr with the validity of our position, a position requesting the great powers to live up to their commitment to the letter and the spirit of the Atlantic Charter. In addition, I was going to share with him some of the disturbing information that came our way about Moscow's plan for the future of Germany.

It was an interesting and at the same time, strange encounter. A powerful Englishman facing a young, intimidated Pole attempting to articulate his native country's position. Carr was a polite listener, but his face betrayed a mixture of amusement and incredulity. Who is this youngster - he probably wondered - who pretends to know more about Russia than most of us? Who is behind him and why am I wasting my time listening to his stories about alleged arrests of Polish Home Army soldiers? Of deporting Soviet dissidents to Siberia and telling me that Stalin intended to create out of his portion of Germany a satellite state?

"It is often dangerous," I was informed, "to believe your own propaganda lines. We do not have confirmation about the events that you have just described to me," Carr continued in an even voice. "Besides, the allied nations are interested today in assuring a peaceful world. In order to do so, we have to make sure we recognize the legitimate interests of everyone, including the Soviet Union. Do you see anything wrong in a major power attempting to secure its frontiers? To draw on its past painful experiences? Even to the point of rewarding its smaller neighbor with a chunk of land previously belonging to the enemy?"

He got up, indicating the end of my visit. He extended his hand and with a broad smile, delivered the final blow. "Thank you for coming. I am impressed by your patriotic zeal. I am sure that Poland is going to emerge from the present post-war period stronger, better and much more in tune with the policies of her allies, including the Soviet Union. In the meantime, if I may, I would like to offer my humble advice. Do not stay in Britain; do not waste your time fighting ghosts. Go back to your native land and give a hand to the millions of your compatriots who are busy rebuilding Poland. In exile you will eventually descend to the role of a man of the past, of someone who will be a stranger wherever he goes. Only back home will you feel useful and productive."

I took his hand.

"Thank you, Mr. Carr, for your advice. Most of the men and

women, who fought with the British and other allies and went back to Poland, have been arrested, sent to Siberia or never heard from. Do you think I should follow them?" I asked.

Carr's face grew angry. He waved me out, once again dismissing my comments as irrelevant. A few days later, in one of his editorials, I discovered a faint echo of my visit.

"The remnants of the Polish army still on our soil," he wrote, "should be given access to all the available data as to the real conditions existing in their country. Otherwise, they are apt to be victims of the right-wing propaganda dissipated by some quarters."

The visit with the Labor Party MP was much more pleasant but, politically, equally frustrating. There was less British rigidity. I felt less like an intruder. But there was a wall of defiance and refusal to even consider a possibility that the Soviet Union was bent on creating a ring of satellite states controlled by puppet governments.

"We hear that type of theory only from Polish exiles. No confirmation from anyone else," he concluded. And then to make me feel that he was a friend, someone who fully understood my dilemma, he invited me for a drink at the House of Commons. I accepted and have regretted it ever since.

Margaret greeted me with a big smile when I returned home. "Three newspapers have just picked up items from our bulletin," she announced. "We are making progress."

"Are we?" I mumbled in reply.

She looked at me with a quizzical eye.

"Were your meetings that bad?"

"Yes," I responded. "Maybe it is time to go to America."

Margaret was not a quitter. "Oh really? Just a couple of lousy encounters and you are willing to quit? Is that the way your people felt when the roof was falling down on them in 1939? Was it the way you felt when you started on this lonely journey three years ago in Edinburgh? Go to America. How easy. How nice to leave behind all your hopes, all your drive, all your people who have not much else left outside of our voice from here. And, in addition, let me tell you something about America. I know it. I worked for a man who was there, spent a lot of time in Washington and came back with a lot of reflections. Let me tell you a little about that land of your dream." She was sitting opposite me, her elbows firmly set on top of my desk, her eyes piercing. I knew the expression. I learned it every time she felt strongly about something that deeply touched her inner convictions. The last time I had observed the phenomenon was when an irate young man came to our office, requesting to see me, and she stopped him, almost physically barring him from my door.

"Is there anything I could do for you?" she barked, sensing hostility behind the youthful face.

"No, Madam." There was a polite answer. "I would like to talk to the man who keeps writing inflammatory articles in our press."

"Inflammatory?" Margaret repeated with faint surprise. "How is that? Could you explain that to me?"

"I would rather talk to him, but if you insist, I'll tell you, Madam."

"My name is Margaret MacCulloch. Don't call me Madam. Haven't your parents taught you how to address people?"

Somehow, the young visitor lost his stride. "I am sorry, but I did not know your name, Mrs. MacCulloch."

"Ok, that's better. Now, what did you want to tell me?"

"Well, you see," he stammered. "I keep reading articles, letters to the editors and hearing about his speeches and I know that he is wrong. He refuses to go back to his home country and wants to live off our land. He is inflaming his own people who are still in Scotland, telling them lies about Poland."

Margaret's back stiffened and from my room, I could almost sense her furious temper coming to the surface. "Lies? What do you know about conditions in Poland? What do you know about the way that some of the former Polish soldiers who fought for your freedom have been treated upon return? What do you know about the man named Joseph Stalin? In short, what do you know to challenge us?"

This was the moment that the visitor waited for. He produced a copy of *The Daily Worker*, the semi-official newspaper of the British Communist Party. "Here it is, Mrs. MacCulloch, in black and white. Written by very knowledgeable people, published in London and based upon dispatches received directly from Moscow. Do you doubt their veracity?"

Margaret's voice was almost sweet. "Yes, I do. Why don't you crosscheck your data? Why don't you read other publications? *Time & Tide* is an excellent weekly. *The Economist* could also be useful. But first of all, before you try to confront people, make sure that you do your homework. By the way, where do you live?"

"In Glasgow."

"And what does your father do?" she asked.

"He is a unionist. He is also a regional correspondent for *The Daily Worker*."

I heard a door slammed. Margaret came into my office. "This is the only way to treat these guys," she mumbled and reached for her ever-present cup of tea.

Now it was to be my turn and I knew that she would not be gentle. Margaret must have figured out what I was thinking. She smiled, her facial expression slightly relaxed. Okay - she was probably reflecting - he remembers my outbursts and is ready for one. Let me disillusion him. But it was difficult for this product of a strict Scottish education to control her instincts.

"You will go to America and you are expecting a lot," she began. "You have told me many times that in Scotland, or in Britain, a fellow like you will never he accepted, that unless you were born around here, you are bound to remain a foreigner all your life. Maybe so, but how about the other side of the ocean? You think it is going to be different? Maybe the base of acceptance is only different? We cherish nobility of birth. Yes, we do. Over there, they cherish the nobility of wealth. Unless you enter the ranks of the rich - an unlikely possibility - you are going to be nobody. Nobody! There would be not the slightest chance that you could establish yourself as a successful missionary of a cause like you have done here. No chance!"

"I do not intend to be a missionary there," I tried to interrupt. "I will have to make a living first."

"And how will you accomplish that deal? What are you going to do there to earn that living? You will be greeted by a society that is composed of so-called self-made men. They are tough, not too well educated and devoted to the proposition that everyone is on his own. Remember how it all started? Conquering land, chasing out Indians, creating an illusion of freedom while nature ruled over every single newly minted American. They worked hard, acquired that conquered land and wrote home depicting wonders of the newly discovered place. In fact, they wanted more of their own kin to secure labor, to get help in the middle of deserts, endless plains, and barely arable soil. In Europe, impoverished, ravaged by constant conflicts, millions responded. Every illiterate peasant, every frustrated worker, saw, all of a sudden, a possibility to put some substance into their empty lives. They boarded ships and went over. But they arrived naked: no skills, no education, and no tools. And they are today forming the American society. It is a crude bunch of men. There is little sophistication in today's America. They love sports, but care little about opera. They flock to movie houses, but in small towns, or cities even the size of Edinburgh, you will have problems in finding a theater. In short, my dear friend, you will be going into what some people describe as a cultural desert."

"Margaret," I cried in despair. "What do you want me to do? To apply for British citizenship and stay here forever? To forgo all our plans? And if I do, how do you think I'll be considered an equal with someone like you who has deep roots in Scotland?"

She relaxed again.

"No, I don't want you to change your plans. But I wanted you to be aware of the dangers that lie ahead. You are not alone. You have two small children. You have responsibilities and I have been sensing, for a good little while, that you jumped into that American journey impulsively, that the Yalta announcement was enough to turn you around. But since that announcement, the two of you managed to create a tiny institution that made a lot of difference to the very cause that you thought was lost at Yalta."

I listened, and kept telling myself how much I loved that old woman.

"Let me add one little thought," she continued. "And I will leave you alone. When Malcolm Muggeridge, one of our top journalists, returned from a long assignment as our correspondent in Washington, he almost kissed the ground. He declared in his first article upon coming home that he waited for so long to look at the Westminster Abbey, to sense the cultural heritage of Britain. But I sensed that what he meant was something different. 'I came back to civilization,' he indirectly declared. You see what I mean? You understand my concern? My fear that you may be traveling backwards rather than forward?" She stormed out of the room.

The following morning, I found on my desk a copy of a letter that Margaret sent to her former employer, Lord Halifax, still serving as the British Ambassador in Washington.

> Milord,
>
> For the last couple of years, I have been working for one of the Polish exiled groups. It was not exactly the same role that I played when I worked for you. This time, the job required a commitment to a cause that I had never heard of before. Somehow, I was moved by the dedication and the enthusiasm that permeated the office. Now, the man I am working for has decided to abandon Scotland and to immigrate to America. I know that this is a foolish move, but there is nothing to stop him. I quoted some of your comments to him but to no avail. So I wonder if I could ask you a great favor? Could he call on you upon arriving there and could you help him? I know that he will be lost and probably bewildered, and a word from you could perhaps open some doors. Thank you in advance, Milord. In spite of everything, I care about this Polish lad.

"Margaret," I bellowed at the top of my voice. She was nowhere to be found. At that time, overwhelmed by her gesture, I realized little how that letter and a reply that Margaret received a few weeks later from His Lordship would influence our American adventure.

"I am not sure I can do much for your Polish friend," he wrote. "But I'll be glad to write a letter of introduction to my friend Arthur Sulzberger, the publisher of *The New York Times*. Maybe he will have some ideas."

Thus, equipped with Margaret's warning and with Lord Halifax's introductory letter, we were about to embark upon the final family preparations for our dive into the unknown. But first of all, there was a need for something rather special: how to say farewell to Britain? How to express special gratitude to Scotland for all the years that we spent there?

I decided to aim at two top publications: *The Times of London* and *The Scotsman*. But a thought crossed my mind: would Mr. Carr allow my letter to be published in his publication, the most prestigious daily paper in Great Britain?

I caught myself thinking more in Polish terms than British. The letter was published overnight and created considerable dismay within the Polish community.

"How was it possible," a prominent Polish politician asked me, "that you succeeded getting into print? Did you have some high level contacts?"

My high level contacts consisted of a stamp, an envelope and a text. What did I say? What kind of a message did I want to convey on that fateful day of December 27, 1947?

> Seven years have passed since I first trod British soil. I have been brought up to believe in the power of Britain, brought up on Lord Macaulay's words at the opening of the Edinburgh Philosophical Institution in 1846: 'and wherever British literature spreads, may it be attended by the British virtue and by British freedom.' Britain stood far above all other nations in my heart. I am leaving Britain shortly. My seven years are gone. The best of my youth is past. It was spent in Britain. I arrived here on a sunny morning of June 1940. I shall be departing from your shore on a grey day of winter. Coming as a soldier, departing as a refugee. Am I disillusioned? I think I am. But I am also sorry.
>
> I touched your soil with reverence. I looked upon you with pride. Here I am, in England, in Scotland. Here I am, a Pole thrown upon this island by the event of war. We, Britain and Poland, the world's only two people resisting Hitler. And we walked proudly in your towns and villages, displaying our white and red flashes.
>
> I learned your language. I began to read your great poets and writers. I managed even to follow your philosophers. Your great institutions, your conception of freedom, your human approach to animals, all strengthened the convictions that I brought with me. From Cromwell to Churchill, your history seemed to me equally great, and your political conceptions with regard to Europe honest.
>
> Afterwards, I passed through different stages. Many

more powerful friends and allies joined your ranks. The political game entered into the fight for freedom. We won the war side-by-side with you. But we lost this game. My stages were varied: from desperation to anti-British outbursts, from optimistic thoughts to the strong convictions that you could not desert us, from frustration to the idea of going East, joining your enemies and searching for a chance of revenge. My reverence to your country sank down almost to hatred.

It is all past. Today, I leave you to find a place where I can live and work without the horrible feeling of being a foreigner. I am sailing for the United States. And looking back over the long seven years of my stay with you, I cannot resist admiring you. I cannot resist my love of the sight of Westminster, nor the memory of the view of the long chain of mountains on a perfect summer day from the top of Ben Nevis. Nor can I forget your hospitality in the early days of the war, nor the outburst of hatred towards us as obstructers to your peace plans, or your calmness in explaining to the world that your part in dividing Europe into free and enslaved parts was done for the benefits of Europe alone.

Saying farewell to Britain and sailing out to the strange land of America, I feel impelled to quote to you the words: 'Observe good faith and justice towards all nations, cultivate peace and harmony with all. Religion and morality enjoin this conduct.' Those were the words of George Washington used on September 19, 1796 in his farewell address, which has remained the basis of United States to this day.

Evidently, H. H. Carr did not object. He might have even smiled, if he ever read the letter, reflecting on the idealistic naiveté of the writer.

And the farewell to Scotland had to be different. I had spent my days in Polish Army uniform there; friends surrounded us wherever we went. It was where two of our children were born, both at home and both attended by devoted doctors who spent long night hours by the mother's bed assisting difficult deliveries. So what did I write? And what did *The Scotsman* print a few days after *The Times* piece?

"I have memories of great days when Princes Street went mad at the sight of Poles parading in their tanks, when the Royal Family took the salute of the Polish Army at Forfar, when a Polish uniform meant an open door to every house, poor or rich, big or small, hospitable or greedy. But above all, I carry with me the memory of people who gave us their friendship, and their hospitality, who stood together with us against the whole of Europe in the darkest days of the war, and who still have in their ranks more friends than foes to the cause of freedom that we still serve."

I wrote a lot about the history of Scotland, relatively peaceful, contrasting this with the turbulent history of my native country. I wrote about the difference between the minds of highly individualistic, romantic Poles, unwilling to make compromises in life, and the minds of pragmatic, hard, practical Scotsmen. But I also reminded them of our deep historical links; Scots had gone to Poland as early as the sixteenth century and settled there as merchants. One of the most courageous and famous Polish kings, Jan Sobieski, had a granddaughter who married James Smart. They produced two sons, one Bonnie Prince Charlie and the other by the name of Henry Stuart, who became a cardinal. And finally, after the Polish uprising against the Russians in 1831, Thomas Campbell founded a literary society, *The Friends of Poland*, widely known by every school child of Scotland.

And I ended the article with a plea.

"I want to make one request. If you see a Pole walking your street, give him some thought. Think of his lost home, his lost country, his lost wife and children. If you do that, you will give him something he will prize, a smile, a friendly approach. For that he will go through fire and water..."

It was time to start packing.

SS Queen Mary, a super luxury boat, was lying leisurely in the docks of Liverpool. Equipped with cabin tickets for all four of us, presented to us with compliments of H.M. King George the Sixth as a gesture of gratitude towards Polish veterans of the war, loaded with most of our belongings, we boarded the ship for a four-day journey.

On March 3, 1948 we landed in the New York harbor, bewildered, excited but totally ignorant of what to expect. Margaret's warnings rang in my ears, 'you are leaving civilization behind.' Was this really true?

There is no question in my mind that ignorance is a wonderful privilege of youth. Walking away from one place, looking for another, searching blindly and living in a mist of uncertainty were some of the aspects of our move. Strangely enough, in the bottom of my heart, I was pleased. I was pleased that events were forcing us to make the decision. I was pleased that the events occurred. Should the political situation in Poland have turned out to be acceptable, to be free of dangers, to be more along the lines of our expectations, I would have had a major dilemma. We were set to go to the States; our doors were open. What would we do? Return to Warsaw and restart our lives in the country that still remained on the crossroads of future enemy armies? In a country that in the foreseeable future was bound to be at the mercy of other powers? Reality spared us from making a choice.

But what were we leaving behind?

We were leaving behind our European roots. We were also leaving behind a rich body of wartime experience, an experience that would be very difficult to share, an experience that would remain our very own until the day would come when facing a sea of young faces of men and women, for whom World War II was distant history. I had to open up the inner secrets of that war. For them, it was important. They listened, figuring out that twenty years from now, they would be able to tell their children of their own unique experience, listening to an old man, an original veteran of that bloody encounter.

But there was much more that we were leaving behind. There was England.

I looked back and saw pictures of the past. The first one was a view of a tent city in Abington, Scotland, an image full of smiling, welcoming faces of people who had just been invaded by strangers: men and women who looked different, spoke a strange language, wore uniforms with patches defining their nationality. The invading army was greeted with warmth and almost unlimited generosity. The second picture projected on my mental screen: a rain of bombs falling on London. A few of them landing not far from our home and I could still hear the sound of shattered glass. The third one was the final German effort to subdue the stubborn Brits to surrender, the V-2 attacks, almost more deadly, more frightening than the blitz of the earlier days. The final image was the warm, tearful farewell occasion in Scotland. Surrounded by a crowd of devoted friends - political and personal - we were saying goodbye to stability and a sense of comfort.

    The England that we were departing from was a different country than the one to which we had arrived. Devastated physically - her urban centers including such treasures as the Coventry cathedral badly damaged - depleted of financial resources, cut off from some of her traditional sources of raw materials and agricultural products, England had set out on her road to decline. None of us sensed the descent. None of us were perceptive enough to look back, when the shores of Britain started receding from our view, and tell ourselves that the next time we would see London it would no longer be the seat of an empire. We only knew that we were leaving behind a nation that stood up and decided to be counted, that, as a result, it went through a period of tough measures. England of the mid-forties coped with shortages of food and sudden surpluses of labor. Men in uniform were coming home. They were expecting to find work, to find meaningful jobs. As a result, some of them were not too pleased finding strangers in their midst. As a result, society was willing to risk a major change in the philosophy of the government. Men who were expected to manage peace replaced the victors who won the war. Clement Attlee, a rather gray, pedestrian figure, replaced Winston Churchill, whose name will enter history books along with Disraeli and other British stars. The transition from war to peace was marked by a rejection of heroes. And the people of Britain decided the transition before the job was finished. The Pacific war was still in full swing. Japan did not even consider giving up the struggle. In the midst of all that was the rearrangement of the power structure of the world: the elimination of Germany as the enemy, gradual diminishing of Great Britain as a colonial empire and the fate of a bunch of Eastern European political exiles receding from the global screen. It was, therefore, natural and inevitable that we turned inward, totally absorbed in our own fate, unable to spread the canvas of the major world's changes in front of our eyes. Instead, we enjoyed the luxury of the British past.

SS Queen Mary provided that luxury in abundance. She was our bridge to the British colonial past.

There was still much more that we were leaving behind. A continent devastated by war, our native land in the grips of another human and political tragedy: Western Europe refusing to face the reality of the Soviet threat and the Kremlin's duplicity, displaced persons camps that littered most of the European landscapes, international courts busy tracking down war criminals and millions upon millions of men and women in search of shelter and food. Was it fair for our little family to escape? To seek a safe haven in the continent untouched by war? Maybe unable to comprehend the mass human tragedy? Was it fair?

These questions were far from our minds during these exhilarating days in the winter of 1948. We were focused on the belief that England was not about to assimilate us. We rationalized freely that life for our two youngsters was to be far superior in the unknown towns, cities and villages of the United States than anywhere on the old continent. It was a dive into the unknown, a dive undertaken in spite of a subconscious feeling of danger looming on the horizon. Strangely enough, it was also the search for stability, as illusive as well as naive as it probably sounded to outside observers. But above all, it was a trip undertaken for very selfish reasons. We were tired of the continued fight. We longed for a steady job, peaceful family evenings and a sense of belonging. But we also knew, without verbalizing it even to ourselves, that the very reason we originally became displaced people was bound to remain with us.

6

New York

When we arrived at the New York port, my uncle Bohdan Nagorski, who with his family landed in America sometime earlier, was waiting for us. He took us over the Queensboro Bridge, which had never looked more glamorous. Its steel beams, covered with ice and snow, supported the bulk of this otherwise ugly structure. Below, the river was flowing slowly, with huge chunks of ice forming natural obstacles. A relatively small number of vehicles moved along. Three of us in a car driven by my uncle were glued to the windows. No one wanted to speak. We were savoring the moment of arrival.

"This is to be our start," I kept muttering to myself. Only Andrew, covered up to his little nose and lying peacefully in his basket, slept in blissful ignorance.

Our start? Where were we going? Once we left the safety of the big boat, the safety of the British crown that was still taking care of its former soldiers, we were on our own. Watching the ice floating by, carried by the current of the powerful river, I saw our little family also carried by some unknown current. That river, however, had a destination. Did we?

As if she were reading my thoughts, Marysia grabbed my hand. "We do have a destination. We do have a goal." And she pointed at little Andrew and patted the head of the inquiring girl. "They are our destination and we will make it."

I could not help but smile. My uncle, a little hard of hearing, turned towards me with a question mark on his face. "Yes, of course you will make it. Look at me. I did." He certainly did and his journey was far more dangerous than ours.

It was much earlier, just about in the middle of the war that he was asked by the Polish Government in Exile located in London to go to the States on an assignment. A specialist in ports, harbors and bridges, my uncle, Bohdan, was to investigate the availability of American expertise and funds to be channeled to post-war Poland. It was an optimistic assignment, one that assumed Allied victory during the time that the only bright star on the wartime horizon was the victory in the air battle over Britain. Europe was solidly occupied by Germany. War in the Pacific witnessed a series of Japanese conquests, and German submarines operated freely in the Atlantic waters. One of them spotted Bohdan's ship and launched its torpedoes, sending her to the bottom of the sea.

He was lucky enough to find himself, together with about thirty-five other survivors, on a rescue boat. His companion, another official emissary of the government, Zygmunt Gralinski, a man of highly visible political stature, was not that lucky. He perished together with most of the crew. Uncle and the survivors had some water and some provisions, but not much. Days were unbelievably long, nights chilly and a sense of helplessness kept drifting into the group. But not Bohdan. With his natural sense of humor and irreverence, he kept telling stories of his life and his adventures when working in the port of Danzig alongside his German counterpart. In a special arrangement, agreed upon after the end of World War I, port directorship of the free city of Danzig was to be dual. Bohdan's stories about the way that he and his co-workers drew circles around rather stuffy and humorless Germans drew cheers and laughter of appreciation.

Uncle Bohdan had another ace up his sleeve. Being a practical man, when the ship's sirens called for immediate evacuation and rescue boats were lowered on both sides, he ran back to his cabin and grabbed his diplomatic pouch as well as his well-stuffed wallet. The wallet contained a considerable amount of government money as well as his own. They were packed in five pound notes, worth at the time roughly twenty dollars and printed at that time on large, white paper. By the time that everyone settled on the rescue boat, Uncle Bohdan's monetary packet was soaked. Three days drifting aimlessly, fighting Atlantic waves, noticing that the sun was hot and a bench next to him half empty, Bohdan started his own rescue operation. He was determined to make his valuable currency dry and fully usable.

An amused cluster of men - there were no women on their boat - circled around Uncle Bohdan and his treasures. He carefully unfolded each note, smoothed it with the palm of his hand and spread it on the bench facing the sun. The other men laughed their heads off. "We may not live long enough to see them dry," shouted one.

"If we survive, are you going to share your riches with us?" called another. But at the same time, there was a grudging admiration for his optimism. Uncle Bohdan just smiled and recounted an endless series of funny stories. I never knew whether he responded to their challenge. I never knew whether he was really ready to share.

And now he was our driver into the unknown adventure, equally cheerful, equally optimistic, equally ready to share. We arrived at his modest home in Roslyn, Long Island and were greeted by his wife and one of his daughters, who both apologized for limited accommodations as we looked around. Our little family was given the use of the living room. A small crib was secured for Andrew. The rest of us had to share the floor space. Uncle Bohdan's family of four occupied the two small bedrooms located on the first floor. But we were home.

"Yes, my dear, this is America," and the six-year-old young lady went peacefully to sleep.

The two grown-ups were restless. Marysia was wondering how to obtain enough food to feed the family. I was wondering how far our limited funds, secured thanks to a wise investment in an apartment in Scotland, sold at the last minute, were going to last. Both of us fully realized that the first move must be directed towards finding a job. I fished out, from one of the cardboard boxes in which our belongings arrived, a pile of letters of recommendation and immediately started working the telephone.

I then experienced my first encounter with the different customs of our new country. In Scotland, it was perfectly acceptable to ask a telephone operator for a recommendation regarding, for instance, a place to buy good shoes. Not in America. "Should we go to Macy's or to Gimbles to find infant's clothes?" I asked innocently.

"It is up to you, sir." That was the polite answer.

"But I am new. I am lost. I need direction." A brief silence at the other end of the wire gave me the feeling that she understood and was searching for a way out.

"Sorry, sir. I am not allowed to recommend one place against another." It was the first lesson that was applied to us in a market economy (underscored later when I learned that every call of inquiry I made cost me money).

However, even more pedestrian chores had to be tackled immediately. The icebox was not prepared for the family invasion. Shopping was in order. But where to go and how to find shops? The house by that time was empty. Uncle Bohdan went to his office, Zosiu, his wife, to hers. The two girls departed for their respective schools. The only hope centered on the neighbors. They proved to be helpful. Pushing the baby carriage found in the house, and holding little Maria's hand, we trudged through heavy snow to the nearest grocery store. Then the biggest challenge stirred in our faces: choices. Accustomed to British rationing and the relative emptiness of shelves, we stood speechless trying to figure out which type of cereal we should buy, preserves, meats, even bread, that came in a multitude of shapes and names. The most difficult task awaited us regarding the baby's nourishment. Once again, we learned that having choices is not always the easiest way to live.

Back home, exhausted by the two-mile trip through difficult terrain, I resumed working the telephone. My first concrete contact suggested lunch. I was elated. Lunch? Maybe he has something concrete for me. Otherwise, he could have suggested a visit to his office. I corresponded with him, he knew my background and he was well placed to do something real. After all, you don't get to be one of the senior editors of *Reader's Digest* unless you have decision-making power. Robert Littell suggested the Oak Room at the Plaza Hotel. Armed with clippings of articles and letters testifying to my journalistic talents, I took the train to Pennsylvania Station for the first time in my life. Our new life in the U.S. was about three days old. Somehow, and to this day I have no explanation, I sensed excitement. My first outing to the heart of the city was for me an exhilarating experience.

The Oak Room, with its dark walls and deep leather chairs occupied by men - and only men - who looked both serious and important, was a strange introduction to American abundance. I looked around, somewhat intimidated, somewhat unsure of what to do with myself or how to find my host. I kept my heavy portfolio close to my chest, fully aware of the inquiring glances of the assembled customers. I probably looked more like a salesman of nondescriptive merchandise, than an aspiring journalist. My English suit was slightly crumpled, my tie was narrow and out of fashion, and my expression broadcast uncertainty. "Can I help you, sir?" I almost jumped at the sound of that voice. The maitre d' looked me over. "Are you, by any chance, meeting Mr. Littell?"

How did he know?

Bob Littell looked more like an Englishman than an American. Immaculately dressed, speaking with a slight New England accent, he extended his hand, suggested that I put my files under the table, helped me in selecting a meal off of a menu that made me feel lost after being accustomed to skimpy Scottish choices, and settled down to business. A career in journalism is not an easy task in America, especially for someone for whom English is his second language. Not everybody is a Conrad. He smiled broadly. Nevertheless, he was ready to help. An avalanche of questions followed. He was deeply interested in my war experiences and equally probing about my family, children and plans for the future. At the same time, he was ready to advise and to warn.

"It is difficult in the America of today to be concerned about Europe. We have our own problems," Littell continued. "There is going to be a shortage of energy and steel, the two key ingredients that are needed for the economy to prosper."

He grilled me about European conditions and was obviously well informed himself. Then, realizing that I would also like to hear a little more about my own prospects, he changed the subject. "You want me to tell you how to begin? Okay. I will. I realize that you have been moving in rather high circles. Forget about that here. You must start at the bottom. Journalism and writing in this country is a tough profession. Take any job, if you want to penetrate various barriers. You must learn how to write here and learn how people read newspapers and periodicals. Learn the American habits, which include a considerable degree of superficiality. A book in America has a very short life span - a few months - then it disappears to the extent that it is no longer available at bookstores. It is a depressing situation for writers, who often lower their writing standards. But a book is not yet in your vision," he smiled. "In the meantime, take a job, any job offered to you by a respectable newspaper, even as a copy boy." I later learned that most of the copy boys carry copies and serve coffee to numerous writers and editors.

A rather important looking waiter brought our check. I did not even dare to look at the bottom line. My host barely glanced at it before signing. I was introduced to the credit phenomenon. I never witnessed it in Scotland.

"Let's meet again. We may want to put our heads together to figure out how to write your resume, a summary of your accomplishments, and then think about a series of introductions to open some doors for you."

A good listener, he must have seen something of value.

"Why don't you try your hand at a piece for the Digest?" he added as an afterthought. "It ought to be simple, not too lengthy and as personal a story as possible. We are a very human-related magazine," he explained gently, "and a human story of the kind that you have just told to me may have appeal."

I left the Oak Room flying. Where is my typewriter? How soon can I begin writing? How soon will I feel like a journalist again?

After the moment of self-generated illusion passed, other thoughts invaded my mind, thoughts more disturbing, more reflective and more down to earth in spite of the momentary exhilaration caused by the friendly and helpful manner of my new acquaintance.

How are we going to fit into this affluent, self-confident society? How will I earn a living without having any easily marketable skills? After all, my entire life so far had been divided between military service on one side, and writing on behalf of my native country on the other. I was a lobbyist of sorts. I was a fellow who had lived on the margin of British society. We crossed the big water in order to escape that margin. The Oak Room gave me a glimpse of the American world I would like to belong to. Was this a dream? An illusion? How could I be that naïve? My legal training back in Poland would not serve me here. And I kept looking around, walking briskly along Fifth Avenue, trying to read faces, guess people's positions in life, see the two of us entering the melting pot of America. Rich America. Overwhelming America, where masses of pedestrians are surrounded by equal masses of tall and impenetrable buildings. Behind their facades, thousands of men and women work. Behind their windows, hope lurks for people like us, that perhaps one day we would have such a window next to our own desk. Maybe one day.

In the meantime, let's start on that piece for the Digest. Maybe they will even pay me. Maybe I will earn my first paycheck in America.

Little did I know that America was ill-prepared to issue that paycheck or how poorly I was prepared to deal with the reality of our new land, a reality that we knew so little about and understood even less but were determined to plough through, the American reality of the year 1948.

Robert Littell said something else, which reverberated in my head, about the way that I operated in Britain at high levels with important people. Now he wanted me to start at the bottom. Good, solid advice but what about the assignments that I received upon departure? What about the documentation regarding the Soviet Katyn massacre of Polish officers that I was given personally by the man who had a national defense portfolio in the now defunct Polish Government in Exile? Or the request to establish a unit representing Eastern European journalists and pleading their cause at the United Nations? If I start at the bottom of any profession, will anyone be willing to talk to me? To listen to my plea about a country that probably was not too high on their political agenda? A clear, sharp conflict between the basic needs to secure a job and an economic foothold, and the requirements of a much higher nature, confused my mind.

Basic needs prevailed. I continued knocking on people's doors.

The experience was revealing. People's attitudes reflected the spirit of the country built by immigrants like us. Not once did I encounter hostility. Not once did I feel unwelcome. And yet, the road was bumpy, the goal on occasion appeared almost unattainable and my optimism was challenged more than once.

"What is America, Daddy?" The question echoed in my head. I will tell you later. I promise. In the meantime, there was somebody else who helped me answer her question.

7

Arthur Hays Sulzberger

The offices of the publisher of *The New York Times* would overwhelm anyone from the outside. I came clutching, once again, my portfolio of numerous credentials and was ushered in by a friendly and graceful black doorman into the presence of the man himself. Arthur Hays Sulzberger stood up and shook my hand. He must have been in his late fifties or early sixties. He greeted me with a broad smile, asked about Lord Halifax (it was our link) and settled down for a chat. It turned out to be more of a monologue than a conversation. After stating my case, looking for a spot in American journalism, I just sat there and listened, almost incapable of uttering a word. The surroundings, the man himself, the mere fact that I was sitting in the office of the publisher of the most influential newspaper in the world, made me shy, silent and unsure. Sulzberger must have sensed my uneasiness. His voice was soft, his posture relaxed. But his message was as clear and as crisp as any other that I had received during my travail.

"It is not the best of times to search for a writing job," he started. "We at the Times decided, not long ago, not to hire people from the outside. We promote individuals from within the organization. Besides," he looked at me sharply, "how much do you know abut America? How much have you studied our history, our political system, and our social and economic structures? We could not hire anyone whose elementary knowledge of our country is lacking. Sure, you are well versed in the European situation. But we already have a number of European experts, a number of correspondents located in Europe. That is where we keep them. Not here." He stopped for a while, as if awaiting my reaction. He got none. I was still mesmerized by the situation, still numb and too shy to respond.

"Let me give you another piece of advice," he continued, "avoid New York. This is not the place to learn about America. Try to find a location somewhere else in the country. In the provinces, your experience, your knowledge is bound to be unique. In New York, there are plenty of people similar to you. In addition, it is bound to be a learning experience for you. What about looking for a lecture agency? That would give you an opportunity to travel around, to acquire first-hand knowledge about the country, to meet people from all walks of life. An experience of that kind would give you a chance to decide what you want to do and which way you wish to proceed."

There was once again a sharp look of expectation answered by my total silence.

"Why don't you think it over and come back to see me in a week or so."

I finally regained my voice.

"Would you be willing to give me a letter of introduction to a provincial newspaper that I might work for?" Little did I realize that at that very moment I was opening a door to the South.

Sulzberger did not say no. He would think it over.

"Let us talk again," he said.

The same elegant, black man, who escorted me in, appeared noiselessly to escort me out. The most important meeting of our initial days in America was over.

It was back to the streets of New York.

These streets fascinated me. They were a kaleidoscope of people, colors, noise and chaos. I watched faces, most of them stern, with their eyes fixed inwardly, avoiding contact. What were they saying? I am busy; don't bother me. My thoughts are on my next appointment, on my next deal, on my immediate problems. I cannot afford to be involved, not even to be aware of a stranger's presence. I know that they exist. I touch them, brush by their moving bodies on the streets and avenues, but they cease to exist the moment I pass them. I am who I am. I cannot do much else. It is a city that demands total commitment to oneself.

Shall I join these faces? Should I also become an anonymous pedestrian refusing contact? I guessed I had no choice.

My next date led me to Wall Street.

Bankers Trust Corporation was located on one of the top floors of an impressive skyscraper. Inside the elevator, going full speed, similar faces failed to make eye contact with me. They were, like the others, internally centered. My host, sporting the impressive title of "Vice President," greeted me warmly, asked about the health of a friendly Scotsman who wrote to him about me, and promised to help. He suggested approaching a publishing company on whose board he served. I walked out of his office, after a ten minute interview, admired the Italian marble used for the elegant floors, reflected briefly on the wealth and ostentatious decorations all over his office, and sensed, almost certainly, that I would never hear from the Vice President again. I never did.

What was next on my American agenda? A hell of a lot.

A series of meetings with British correspondents accredited to the United States. One of them suggested *Voice of America*. A great idea until the day that I was told that to work for the government, you have to be an American citizen. Five years to wait and too long to remain hungry.

The New York Sun appeared to be a busy paper. The advertising director kept me waiting for half an hour then sent me to the assistant managing editor. No luck.

Next stop: a very elegant apartment belonging to a well-known columnist. I admired the Flemish tapestries, French furniture and exquisite china displayed in various cabinets. The distinguished writer was busy. He was ready to write a note or two. The meeting lasted less than ten minutes. Out you go, his eyes declared.

How about the School of Journalism at Columbia University? The wait was two hours before the dean was ready to see me. Sure, come next September, we may want to enroll you. But it is not cheap. Could you get $3,000 to pay for tuition, room and board? Three thousand dollars? Our total worth amounted to about $9,300 after selling our Edinburgh apartment. But we had to live on it, all four of us. We needed a car. In America, you could not function without a car. And what about rent? Maybe our Polish-American contacts will be generous enough to lend us that much?

A strange misunderstanding led me to an unexpected meeting with Edward R. Murrow at CBS. I was looking for Edgar Mowrer, a writer and someone to whom I had a letter of introduction. I was not sure where he worked, but somehow I assumed it was CBS. As I sat in the waiting room, here came Edward Murrow with his eternal smile, the ever-present cigarette dangling from his lips, a cheerful approach and an expression that indicated full understanding of my situation. Then he started to explain that he was no longer involved with personnel, but would see what he could do. We sat in the waiting room for about half an hour and I left uplifted. He promised nothing concrete, but would start inquiring at once. Obviously, he understood how badly I needed help and support. His attitude made me feel so much better. It was great to move from one illusion to another. Years later, observing him on the television screen during the McCarthy period, watching him destroy one of the most dangerous demagogues in contemporary America, I realized how lucky I was to have had a chance to meet him in person.

In the meantime, the search had to go on. Strange ideas, suggestions from friends and newly acquired contacts kept piling up. One of them outlined a great opportunity to invest a relatively small amount of money in a local bakery: $2,500. A small amount? I almost shouted. It was a fortune. But our friend, Marysia's former boss from pre-war days in Poland, was ready to invest the same amount of money to start us off. The outline of the proposition was simple: after the capital is raised, my job would be the deliveryman, while Marysia would remain in the office, taking care of books. At once, our wonderful ability to dream and to project went into high gear. A successful bakery, a small house not far from Columbia University, a car to move around and enough money to pay for tuition at the School of Journalism. How about it?

Are the two linked? The bakery and continued contact with Sulzberger? How can I dare compare them? To even think of them in the same breath? Stupid. But both mind and body were tired, with the mind beginning to wonder whether the decision to cross the Atlantic was a correct one. Doubts were not acceptable. Just be tough, patient and strong.

Easier said than done.

The date of another meeting with the powerful man at the *The*

New York Times was approaching. Burned so many times, fearful of jumping into another dream, another illusion, another false feeling of progress, I racked my mind for various alternatives. The problem was that the pile of introductory letters was getting thinner and thinner. The problem was also my total focus on finding an economic base and inability to look at a larger spectrum of the American reality. How was the national economy doing? What was the level of unemployment? Were the forthcoming presidential elections apt to influence future events?

I had the limited vision of a newly arrived immigrant who was unable to absorb anything not directly related to his fate. Prior to the next visit to *The New York Times*, I wondered whether I should beef myself up with basic data on the American political and economic scene. But there was no will, no incentive, no power of concentration to do it. And yet, had he not asked me how much I knew about the country that I chose to emigrate to?

In the meantime, less important events absorbed our minds. A fellow Pole was to give me an address where one could buy an inexpensive suit. Another Polish exile, who managed to penetrate the high level of the American political ladder, promised to give me a letter of introduction to the presidential press spokesman. And my friendly dentist kept warning both of us against taking any sales jobs. "They are dead-end streets. They dehumanize people. They put you at the bottom of social respect."

Finally, the day arrived when the second visit to *The New York Times* was to occur. My initial shyness lessened. I walked through the impressive corridors without being overwhelmed. I greeted the official, welcoming man with a friendly smile of recognition. I even walked into the office of Mr. Sulzberger without feeling like a supplicant, a representative of a lost cause. It was a strange transformation. With previous encounters, my hopes were high, my expectations naïve. This time, I was almost resigned to the likelihood of another polite conversation, another promise of future contacts and not much more.

He once again rose from his seat to greet me. "Tell me, what have you been doing since we saw each other last time?"

My shyness gone, I launched into a brief monologue. He listened with a polite smile on his face. Was he registering or just acting? Was a man in his position capable of understanding a young man at the bottom of the ladder attempting to find the first rung? Fortunately, my host gave me every indication he not only listened, but also understood. When he spoke, that impression turned out to have been well grounded.

"I cannot even consider finding a place for you at *The New York Times*. There is, however, another newspaper where I could perhaps make an inquiry for you. Would you risk going to a place in the South? To the state of Tennessee?"

I just sat there mute. Would I consider? "Yes, sir," I mumbled.

"We do have a connection in Chattanooga. Their daily paper, called *The Chattanooga Times*, may be a little more receptive. Let me see."

The secretary was to connect him with the editor in Chattanooga. While waiting, he picked up a book, opened a page and started reading aloud. *Tragedy in Europe* was the title, he said. I looked up at him. "Oh, I'm sorry. I should have told you what this book was about. It is a collection of wartime editorials from *The New York Times*. Charles Merz published it in 1941, edited and with an introduction. The first editorial dealt with the invasion of Poland, published on September 2, 1939. Listen to this: 'The first feeling of a heartsick world will be the sheer inability to believe that the thing long feared has actually happened, even though the evidence is spread before your eyes. Here is war, not in distant Africa or Asia, but war in the heart of Europe, war with all its terrible possibilities for the involvement of the whole world in an immense catastrophe.'"

He stopped, almost overwhelmed by the words he had just finished reading. Then, he continued.

"'If ever war was made by one nation on another deliberately, without cause or justification, it is this undeclared war that Germany has made on Poland. The claim of the German Government, that it had no alternative in the end save to meet force by force, is belied by the facts in the record. Poland had not refused to negotiate with Germany a settlement of any dispute between the two nations. It had merely refused to enter into negotiations which demanded that one party surrender on a vital point to the advantage of the other party, in advance of all discussion.'

"You see," the publisher turned again to his listener, "this is how we reacted here to the attack on your country. And two years later, on September 1, 1941, this is what we wrote.

"'Two years ago this morning, the Nazis lit the fire that has been ravaging an ever-widening area of Western civilization. We do not know whether or not they expected their invasion of Poland to bring on a general war. History may say that the British and French governments should have gone to war sooner, on the clear issue of the violated Munich Agreement, or that they should have waited still later, when their fighting strength had been brought to a peak. But history, if it is written by free men and not by the lick-spitless of triumphant dictators, will certainly say that the Nazis offered the Western world the single choice between war and slavery, and that sooner or later, the war had to come... For two years, the American people have watched this disaster. For two years, they have been torn by conflicting emotions: on the one hand, a deep and passionate hatred for all that Hitler represents, and a profound sympathy for his actual and intended victims; on the other hand, an equally deep, equally passionate reluctance to spend blood and treasure in a quarrel not unanimously accepted as their own.'"

My host stopped, emotionally drained. Silence descended upon both of us as he reflected. I was deeply impressed by his willingness to share his emotions and his time. The ice had been broken. I no longer felt as though I were a stranger, a supplicant or an unwelcome visitor.

The telephone rang. The secretary reported that the Chattanooga editor was not available. He should be back in his office in a few hours.

Arthur Hays Sulzberger bade me goodbye. "Call me at around 3 p.m.," he said. "I will have an answer for you."

I got up, ready to leave.

"Take the book," he added.

I took the book. Inside the front page there was a dedication:

To Zygmunt Nagorski, with the hope that he may find in this volume and in this country all that he is seeking. Arthur Hays Sulzberger. March 16,1948.

It was a joyous return home. It was a smiling Marysia and noisy children that greeted my return.

"Three o'clock," I said. "Three o'clock," I repeated. How about finding Chattanooga on a map and inquiring a little about the state called Tennessee? But we can always wait until three o'clock.

The waiting was longer than anticipated. It took a couple of days before word came from the publisher of Chattanooga Times, suggesting that I should look elsewhere, that an European journalist, accustomed to writing editorials, would probably be lost in a provincial, Southern newspaper. The only crack in the message received through Sulzberger's secretary was a comment that should I insist on trying, they would be glad to see me for a couple of days.

Marysia watched my reaction. "What will you say?" she asked. "How do you explain Mr. Sulzberger's willingness to assist a stranger? To put his reputation on the line by recommending an unproven writer to a friendly, but obviously independent, newspaper?"

The question, which had not occurred to me before, opened up a new vista of reflections. Could I put myself in that man's position? Could I really understand his willingness to give me his time, his interest and his direct help? Was this rooted in the American tradition to view newly arriving immigrants as potential contributors to the American dream? Or was this his personality that called for understanding and compassion?

I concluded that it must have been both. Born into a comfortable Jewish family, married to the daughter of a prominent newspaper publisher, Arthur Hays Sulzberger inherited a zest for accomplishment as well as a sense of duty. The former allowed him to build the best daily paper in the world. The latter gave him the human ability to relate and to comprehend. Suddenly, I remembered how during the long march from Warsaw to freedom in France, I was looking for both, people who would relate and people who would comprehend. I was able to find some in the most unlikely of places.

One was in former eastern Poland, now occupied by the Germans and populated by the Ukrainians, who were hostile to the Poles. Our group of former soldiers consisted of twenty-six young men. In one of the Ukrainian villages, which we approached with considerable apprehension, we were housed and fed by a Ukrainian family. It was a dangerous gesture on their part. The rest of the village was all set to kill Poles, whom they considered oppressors. In addition, the village was poor and the family that put our group up - opening a large attic covered with hay - had barely enough food to feed themselves, and yet they shared their bread and their milk with every single one of us.

Compassion? Understanding? Why did this incident come to mind after meeting my newly discovered American angel? He was not in danger. He was not hungry, but somehow he managed to put himself in the position of a nearly lost, young man, desperately looking for support. He was so unlike my father's friend in Budapest whose bell I had rung, introducing myself and telling him briefly about our escape. He listened, offered me a cup of tea and a cookie, never asking what I really needed. It so happened that I was hungry and penniless, too proud to ask and too disappointed to admit that I was hoping for understanding. The two encounters - in the Ukraine and in Hungary - flashed through my memory, comparing, reflecting and thanking God for having the opportunity to link the Ukrainian poor family with a compassionate, sensitive American.

Time was up for reflections. A decision had to be made. Shall I take the challenge and go to Chattanooga in spite of the serious reservations of the people involved?

Of course I will. What were some of the other alternatives open to us?

Chattanooga, it was. My train was waiting. So was the little family, anxiously awaiting for the father's return from his pilgrimage.

8

Chattanooga

It was just about three weeks since the SS Queen Mary docked at the New York harbor, three long weeks, full of discoveries. New York streets were full of men and women so preoccupied with their own inner thoughts that they swam through each day without noticing anyone around them. Business people attempting to be helpful and making it as fast as possible, newspapers full of job openings with no job to be found for someone like me. A volatile political scene, fascinating, and at the same time distant and unapproachable. One President dead, revered by many and hated by a lot. And a new President, an unknown quantity, an average fellow from the state of Missouri, assuming the most powerful office in the Western world. 'Was America in turmoil?' we were asking ourselves. Or is this country resilient enough to absorb the change and sail with it into the unknown future? Little did we know, little did we realize that the post-war years would be the most productive, offering the most opportunities for all who were ready to grab them. Homeowners flocked to Levitt Towns where houses were available for veterans with no down payments. Farmers received federal subsidies that made them one of the most productive producers in the world. Colleges bursting at their seams with an influx of students armed with Government stipends, allowing them to study any subject they wanted.

Little did we know that we had arrived at a time that America was on the move and that we were silent, passive witnesses of that dynamic change. Little did we know and, at that time, little did we care. Our goal was survival. Our other goal was integration. It took time, growth and maturity to make us, the newly arrived immigrants, see the bigger picture.

It did take time. In the meantime, the train to Chattanooga was going peacefully through famous American towns: Washington, then Richmond. I watched, talked with strangers and inhaled the new air of the American South. Where was I going? How much did I know about my journey? Was the unknown the key attraction? Or was this simply the only opportunity offered to make a living and maybe, who knows, to get accepted as someone desperately in need of that acceptance which eluded us in Scotland?

Enough of reflections. The obviously well fed and well-paid conductor announced that the next station would be mine. He made sure that I heard him. He came to my compartment, obviously intrigued by my Eastern European accent, asking what I planned to do in Chattanooga.

"Writing? About what? How can you write, fresh from the other side of the Atlantic? Do you know about our Negroes? About their culture? Their past? About people like me, born and educated in small towns of this region? I wish you luck," he concluded, extending his powerful hand to me.

The train stopped with its locomotive breathing heavily. My travel companion, a young, 19-year-old pianist from Israel named Moshe, bade me a warm goodbye. We had talked about our respective lives. He was born in Poland and this was our immediate link. His father, a textile manufacturer from the city of Lodz, escaped to Switzerland shortly after my friend was born. In the middle of the war, the family obtained American visas and came to New York. His father reentered the textile business; his mother, a seamstress, obtained work in one of the sweatshops on 34th Street. Within a year, she was able to quit. The family somehow established their own little shop manufacturing evening attire. They hired a tailor, also an escapee from Poland, and started their own business. By the time Moshe was ten years old, they had enough money to purchase a used upright piano. It was all that the boy wanted. He played continually, practicing in spite of the loud - and sometimes violent - protests of various neighbors. At the age of sixteen, he was admitted to a prestigious music school on a full scholarship.

Moshe was on his way to his very first concert. Invited by a Jewish group, active in the artistic circles in Miami, he was to perform solo. Moshe was scared, shy and unsure of himself, like me. The two of us, a generation apart, suddenly felt bound together by the origin of birth and the danger of the new American experience.

We promised to keep in contact. We promised to write to each other. We promised to share our pain and our joy. But we both were naïve to think that time and preoccupation with daily life would permit us to keep our promises.

I never heard from him again.

Southern heat engulfed me the moment I left the train. Was the station in Chattanooga heated? Just twelve hours ago, I had left a snow-covered New York. I emerged from the building to discover that even in March, a temperature of 88 degrees was nothing unusual. I looked around, searching for the hotel where I had been directed to go. I stood rather helplessly clinging to my small suitcase. "Can I help you?" a voice came from nowhere.

I turned toward it. "Yes, sir. I am looking for the hotel where I am supposed to stay."

The friendly policeman, his moustache freshly waxed and his dark glasses firmly sitting on his nose, pointed his finger. "Is that the one?"

I looked, compared it to the name I had written down, smiled and thanked him. My hotel was facing the station. It was about a two-minute walk.

The room was small but clean and airy. I stripped, took a cold shower and immediately went out to explore. In front of me the impressive bulk of the railroad station served as a constant reminder of my journey. I looked closer. There were two entrances: one for colored, the other for whites only. The reality of segregated America invaded my consciousness with brutal force. How would I explain that reality to my little girl? How would I retract my comments made while we were still in Scotland? A comment suggesting that she would be able to play with a black American boy?

In the meantime, Chattanooga's streets absorbed my immediate attention. They were colorful to say the least. Flowery shirts, mixed with equally loud blouses, dominated the streets' profile. I was struck by the youthfulness of the crowd, by the mixture of blacks and whites, and by the relatively slow movements of individuals as well as groups. Accustomed to the swift currents of New York's rivers of pedestrians and fast moving vehicles, I watched with fascination the relaxed way that men and women of this newly discovered southern city lived. It was much too early in our American experience to draw any conclusions, but was Chattanooga, Tennessee a little like Edinburgh, Scotland?

My mind and imagination started racing into the unknown. Maybe what fate prepared for us was the best solution. Moving from one environment, where we forged a perfect niche for ourselves and where we earned friendships and respect over time, to another where we must start all over, was just about right. Similar challenges were awaiting our little family. Similar opportunities?

Before I dived into the luxury of dreaming, I knew that I had to listen to another voice, the voice of logic and reason. That voice reminded me of a different reality. 'In Scotland, you were crusaders for the cause of your motherland. In Chattanooga - or wherever you end up - you are going to be a working journalist. Being crusaders, you and Marysia attracted people who felt like you and who were addicted with the same missionary zeal. Here, you will be called upon to earn the respect of your peers. The only way to get there will be through learning, learning how to write differently. Not propaganda pieces, but solid news items, and learning the techniques of the journalistic trade. In short - my other voice was telling me - it is to change your personality. You are no longer a writer whose creativity will be called upon. You are now a craftsman. Learn your craft as fast as you can.'

I hated that voice. I buried it deep in my mind. I escaped with delight into a world of fantasy.

In the meantime, I continued walking. It was so much fun to window-shop. Still accustomed to the scarce supply of basic commodities in Scotland, I observed with fascination the rich displays of meats and vegetables, dairy products (eggs were still rationed in Britain) and compared prices. They were definitely lower than in New York. My Marysia will be really pleased.

I stopped again. How do I know that she will come here? 'Let's not jump too fast,' my inner voice of reason once again asked to be heard.

To my considerable surprise, I found an envelope waiting for me in my room. It was from the managing editor, Jim Jarvis. He just wanted to have a drink with me. What a great welcome. What a wonderful way to make a person feel at ease.

Chattanooga 91

The editor's home was rather modest. His furniture simple, his decorations, especially paintings, indicated a certain lack of sophistication. We sat at the two ends of a flowery sofa. His rather substantial wife brought tumblers of drinks that proved to be potent, and after the usual meaningless chitchat, Jim started his investigation. "I would like to know you better," he began softly. "Since this is the first time during my tenure of office that we have come across an European newsman who wants to work in our town." He sounded genuinely interested.

What a chance, I thought. What an opportunity. Finally, there was a possibility to tell the full story about the war, the exile and the work of a forgotten and betrayed country, to talk about the desire to enter a new place, to be accepted and integrated.

It took less than five minutes, barely starting with my journey from Warsaw, for me to notice Jim's almost total concentration on his drink. He asked for a second one and by the time I was at the Hungarian frontier, he could not endure it any longer. "It's great that you managed to do all these things. But tell me, have you ever worked for a daily paper? Kept deadlines? Written headlines? Reported from a police beat?"

"Not really," I mumbled. "But I was a war correspondent, kept deadlines, filed copies, wrote editorials, reported from war ravaged Europe towards the end of the war, and was published widely in such newspapers as *The Scotsman, Edinburgh Evening News* and even *The Times of London*."

Jim Jarvis grew impatient.

"In that case, maybe aren't you better suited for *The New York Times* than for us? Did you tell all this to Mr. Sulzberger? Does he know of your world-wide talents which may be wasted in a provincial paper like ours?"

"Yes, I did. There was no opening in New York and he thought that perhaps..."

"We could train you? Bring you down to the reality of the pedestrian, boring existence of a working newsman in a place like Chattanooga? And once you learn the tricks of our trade, he may take you back?"

I wasn't sure whether he was serious. But he was. I was flustered.

"I don't think so, I really don't," was my barely audible answer.

"Okay, okay," he noticed my discomfort. "I didn't mean to be rough on you. But I am just very curious why you came to us. Why you have abandoned the big city where there are so many opportunities in preference to a place that probably is going to be as strange to you as you are to us?"

Should I tell him the truth and confess that no such opportunity was available? That I had just heard for the first time in my life the name of Chattanooga? That I had not the faintest idea what a copy desk was? That I grabbed the straw that was offered to me and undertook the journey in spite of all the warnings?

I did not reveal any of my thoughts. I just sat there mute, emptying my tumbler.

Jim finished his third drink. He stood up, smiled broadly, suggested a test and promised to give me a fair chance during the next few days.

"After all, you came to test the waters and see how you would fit in here. We plan to do the same, and then we will talk. Before you leave, why don't we see what we can do to make you look more American."

I left loaded with a couple of shirts and a nearly new suit that fit me perfectly. Jim explained, pointing at his expanding belly, that the suit was now much too tight for him and that it was simply wasted hanging in his closet.

I accepted his explanation without an argument. It was much later in our American journey that I understood his gesture. It was a way to say thank you for what I had done as a soldier in spite of his impatience with my long-winded life story. It was also an instinctive way that people in my newly adopted land responded to other people's needs.

The streets of Chattanooga smiled at me once again. I could not wait for my first test. It would start the very next day and would be the perfect occasion for putting on my new suit, to try the blue shirt and to become an American journalist.

Dinner with Ruth Golden and her husband was to be held the following day. While Jim's house was on Signal Mountain, a good, fairly affluent district, Ruth's house was on Lookout Mountain, the most prestigious and expensive Chattanooga suburb. She also informed me that her mother, Emogene Sulzberger, was visiting them and would join us for dinner. Great, I thought. Maybe after my first swing at reporting she would be able to report good news to her husband.

How wonderful it was to continue dreaming.

The Chattanooga Times newsroom received me with a mixture of curiosity and bewilderment. It was populated by men and a few women, most of them natives, most of them well rooted in the local customs, slang and activities and who seldom met total strangers. I was one of these strangers, entering their professional lives and pretending that I could be their equal. Numerous pairs of eyes turned in my direction. A number of green shades, which many men wore, were lifted for a second or two only to be swiftly lowered.

I was given a chair at the copy desk. It was a semi-circular table with the slot man, a big, husky looking fellow who turned out later to be a wonderful friend, and who extended his hand in a welcoming gesture. I sat next to a young, tall man whose curiosity about his new colleague was written all over his face. Around the table, six other individuals nodded their heads, acknowledging my presence. In a brief, machine gun style, Gary, the slot man, explained the rules of the game. Then he pushed in my direction a sheet of paper with brief explanations. Each headline had a number; each number indicated the type of head to be fitted into a prescribed number of letters. It looked like a puzzle to me. Gary gave me time to absorb the instructions. By the time I was just about ready to try my skills, I was called over by the city editor, an older, distinguished looking man whose desk was a few feet from mine.

"We have a little assignment for you," he said smiling. "There will be a meeting tonight at the University of Tennessee. A representative of the State Department is going to speak about a new idea that is being currently implemented by the government. It has something to do with the economic assistance to Western Europe. It is called the Marshall Plan. We would like you to go there and write a news story."

I nearly hit the ceiling with delight.

The large meeting room at the University was nearly full. I looked around. Students were few and far between. Most of the audience consisted of adults. It was difficult for me to guess. The president of the University chaired the occasion. A tall, rather impressive looking man started to speak. The idea, he pointed out, was to make Western Europe economically sound and politically strong. The danger of communism is there. The Soviet Union has not given up on its concept of conquering the rest of the continent. Communist parties in France, Italy and other countries were actively promoting the notion of close cooperation with Moscow. It was in the interest of the free world to provide a safety net, to make Western Europe truly democratic. America was ready to invest its resources to achieve that goal.

Loud applause. I was unable to resist and promptly forget my role as a reporter, who should be objective, neutral and impassioned. I stood up and shared with the audience my own experience, my own knowledge of Soviet domination and of the fate of Eastern Europe. I sat down, pleased with a separate round of applause directed at me. I was even more pleased when the president thanked me for my contribution. I was too preoccupied with the whole procedure and too immersed in observing the reaction of the audience to notice a surprised look on the face of one of my colleagues from the newsroom. I later learned that she was asked to accompany me on my first assignment, just in case it would require a substantial re-write.

Nancy was an older woman, probably in her late forties, who had been working at the Times for over a decade. We walked back together and she warmly congratulated me for my comments. Now, let's write the story. It was an interesting meeting and ought to be communicated to our readers. Why don't you try your hand at it?

There was nothing I wished to do more. My typewriter was waiting, my copy desk crew was watching. My city editor was expecting the piece within an hour. I sat down, full of impressions and satisfied that America was finally being awakened to the danger that the Soviet Union represented. And I wrote accordingly.

My copy violated every newspaper rule.

The opening paragraph was full of praise for the speaker. My second graph described the political danger that Western Europe was facing. The story was not a news item; it was a mixture of editorializing, reporting and congratulations addressed to the

Department of State. I knew that the story would hit the editorial page of the Edinburgh Evening News. The problem was my new location. I was no longer a contributor of opinions; I was no longer in Scotland. I was a reporter of a Southern American daily, not an editorial writer, not a contributor of thought pieces. But internally, I had not yet made that transition. And pleased with myself to no end, I produced my article in less than an hour and I handed my copy to the city editor.

He glanced at it and silently handed it over to Nancy. Not a word passed between the two of them. She simply sat at her typewriter to do a re-write.

"A meeting held last night at the University of Tennessee featured a representative of the State department. The subject evolved around the new American approach to the economic revival of Western European countries. The speaker..."

I suffered. I bled. I sensed not only my own failure but also what I perceived to have been a failure of the paper to see the essence of the Marshall Plan, to be more interested in the dispassionate, pedestrian technique of writing than in the substance of the message.

The report appeared in the next morning paper under Nancy's byline.

I had, however, three more days of a trial period to try out my writing skills. "Writing skills?" I asked myself, "Or the ability to adapt myself to a different journalistic culture and a different role into which I must fit?" My mind was clouded by a deep sense of potential failure when I was finally able to put my head on a pillow. Merciful sleep arrived. It was devoid of dreams, problems and thoughts, a few moments of total detachment. Who was it that said sleep is the brother of death?

The next day, I was to start my copy desk try-out late in the afternoon. I found an invitation for dinner on my desk. Ruth Golden, whose desk was five feet from mine and was the daughter of my benefactor in New York, thought that I might enjoy some of her friends. But how could I do that? It was my working night. I walked over to my boss Gene Carter, the slot man, asking for help in resolving the dilemma. There was not the slightest hesitation from his end. "Of course you go to Ruth's dinner. It is important for you to meet people. It is important for you to get to know Ruth and her husband. They are influential members of the team."

Their house sat on the top of Lookout Mountain, with a breathtaking view of the valley, and was filled with English antiques and had a few Civil War paintings. I spotted a fascinating sculpture of a galloping horse, only to be told that it was an original Remington. The assembled group consisted of a young couple - neighbors living in one of the adjoining houses - an equally young man who turned out to be a reporter from the Times, and an elderly lady. I did not catch her name at first, but it was she who appeared to be especially interested in my history. It took me a good hour before I realized that I was talking to Ruth's mother, Imogene Sulzberger herself.

It was Ruth who focused the group's attention on her visitor. "Tell us," she suggested gently. "What brought you to Chattanooga? How did you manage to survive the war in Europe? How did you meet my father in New York? In short," she laughed, "we would really like to have your life history before we sit down for dinner."

There is nothing that pleases a person more than the interest of others in his story. Forgetting the possibility that a mixture of politeness and curiosity prompted her series of questions, I plunged into a monologue. There was the beginning - the Polish war, the blitzkrieg in France, the bombing of London...

A head with a white scarf appeared at the dining room door. Ruth nodded. The signal was clear, but I was oblivious.

It was Claude, the neighbor, who came to everyone's rescue. "We also had a test of war in Chattanooga," he interrupted me in mid-sentence. "Twice, we had to descend to our basements. Twice, we had air raid alarms. Twice, our sirens woke us up in the middle of the night. It was not at all funny. We were in real danger."

I stopped, suddenly deflated. Ruth seized the occasion and chaperoned all of us into the dining room. I was seated next to Mrs. Sulzberger. Ruth's husband, Ben, proposed a toast welcoming the newcomer to the Times and to the city.

"But how much do you know about our Chattanooga? About the South? I don't live here," Mrs. Sulzberger said, "but since this is where the newspaper career of my father began, I learned a lot about it. It was here that the birth of both the Times, New York and Chattanooga, took place. But *The Chattanooga Times* is older. It is the father of *The New York Times*. Did you know that?"

Of course, I did not.

"And as far as the city itself is concerned," chimed in Claude. "Let me tell you a little about it. I was born here. My father started a factory manufacturing cardboard boxes. Now I run it. I went to school here. I graduated from our university. It is a great place to live, to learn, to work, to educate children. I hear you have two. Great. We will do our best to help you once you move here."

"Hey, hey. Not so fast." Ruth interrupted. "He may not like it after his adventurous and exciting life. He is here just for a few days, testing the waters." She was subtle enough not to mention that I was there on probation. That everyone, including herself, was looking me over.

"Thank you, Ruth." I whispered to myself.

But Claude was not to be deterred.

"Now let me tell you a little about our city. This is where three of the most important battles of the Civil War were fought. The time was 1863. The Union army was at first routed by the Confederates. A bulk of the fighting took place here on Lookout Mountain as well as Missionary Ridge. Then the fortunes of the war were reversed when the Union army received major reinforcements. At that very moment, General Hooker, commanding the Union forces, decided to attack Lookout Mountain, a very risky undertaking resulting in stalling the attackers. Once again General Grant, who commanded the operation, ordered his troops to capture the western foot of the ridge. They did so and proceeded to the top, catching the Confederate army by surprise." Claude stopped, trying to judge the effects of his impressive knowledge of history.

"This was the third major victory of the Union Army. The first was in Gettysburg, the second in Vicksburg, Mississippi." He stopped again.

"Today, Chattanooga is growing, developing, making huge steps forward," interrupted Ben. "And our metropolitan area tops 200,000 people. Isn't that impressive?"

I listened, totally absorbed in what I heard. This was a long journey, I mused to myself, from Warsaw to Chattanooga. It was a long journey from World War II to the Civil War in America, from 1863 to 1939. What am I doing here?

Imogene Sulzberger gave me a hug goodnight. Unaccustomed

to this type of intimacy, I added my own cultural bias. I kissed her hand to the delight of the entire company.

It turned out to have been a great evening. I thanked Gene for letting me off my copy desk chores for the night. But the chores were waiting for me with all their intricacies, traps and the occasional feeling of satisfaction, very occasional.

There was, however, another encounter that put me squarely on notice. Toward the end of my first visit to Chattanooga I was invited by the publisher, Charles Puckett, to the final debriefing. Jim Jarvis was there, too. The message could not have been clearer. "We will let you come back to Chattanooga. Everyone was impressed with your enthusiasm and your readiness to take on a very difficult task. But there is very little chance that you will grow and very little chance that we will be able to move you from the copy desk to the editorial page where you really belong. In short, this is a limited opportunity. Furthermore, it will take time for you to adapt to the Southern culture, language and customs. Are you sure that you want to try? To risk? To plunge into the unknown?" Charles rhetorically inquired.

"And one other factor you must keep in mind," Jim Jarvis chimed in. "In case of staff reduction, you will be the first to go. We operate on the principle of seniority. Who ever comes last, goes out first."

I was listening, but not hearing. In response, I simply smiled and repeated to my newly acquired friends, that I considered this a very unique opportunity for someone like myself. If you want me, I would wish nothing better than to enter the Times family.

They stood up, shook my hand, not really surprised but somehow a little impressed.

"The fellow," Jim whispered aloud so that I could hear, "obviously has guts."

The fellow also had no other alternative.

Two people were high on my priority agenda once I returned to take up a more permanent job. One, obviously, was Jim Jarvis, the managing editor, who reigned over the newsroom, peering from behind a large glass partition that divided the ants from their king. The second was my immediate neighbor sitting next to me at the copy desk. I assumed correctly, as it turned out later, that I must satisfy both of them.

Jim Jarvis, a short man with the figure of a boxer, was a product of the newspaper profession, a down-to-earth, no-nonsense fellow, apt to be profane and a straight shooter. Jim looked me over with the eye of a coach assessing a new player on his team. He was skeptical and, essentially, opposed to my even coming on a trial basis.

"What are we going to do with a guy straight from Europe? How much time will I have to invest into making him an American journalist?"

So when I appeared at his office, he was hardly able to constrain his reservations. "Are you sure that you want to work here? Let me tell you how I reached the level where I am at today."

Born in Athens, Georgia, Jim went to the local public school before his father, a grocer, decided to move to Chattanooga. By the time he graduated, his father needed him at the store. He spent a year bagging groceries, ordering supplies and making himself useful. Bored by the work, he looked around and an ad caught his eye. The local paper, the Times, had an opening for a copy boy. Jim applied and got the job to the great distress of his father. But the initial pay of $15 a week was a fair amount during the Depression. He was able to save about $5 to help his father. His mother died earlier and Jim hardly remembered her. Brought up by his father, a strict disciplinarian and religious man, Jim inherited two principles. One was that a job, any job, required total commitment. The other was that God was watching over everyone and was the ultimate judge. The two served him well and, within the family of the Chattanooga Times, his principles were recognized, his devotion to work appreciated and he steadily climbed the ladder. When the Japanese attacked Pearl Harbor and all able-bodied men were ordered to report to the nearest recruiting centers, Jim dutifully went, was declared fit to serve and wore his army uniform proudly for the next four years. Somehow his unit, stationed at Fort Bragg, was never sent overseas. Jim was asked to run an information bulletin, later transformed it to a daily paper serving the entire division. Demobilized at the end of the war, he went to the Times to reclaim his previous position of city editor. Instead, the publisher asked him to take the top job. Jim installed himself immediately behind the imposing glass partition. His father, still struggling to keep his store solvent, boasted about his son's success. Above the cash register, the most prominent place in the store, a photograph of Jim in his army uniform was to be, from then on, a permanent fixture.

Jim looked at me expecting a reaction. There was a passing moment when I wanted to reciprocate by giving him a short summary of my life story. But it passed as fast at it had appeared. The memory of Claude comparing his wartime tribulations in Chattanooga with my reflections on London helped kill the initial urge. So I just sat there listening, genuinely absorbed in what I heard. Jim was the first Southern American I was exposed to. The others, whom I had met at Ruth's, were not ready or willing to open up the way he was. Jim, for reasons that escaped me at that time, somehow felt an affinity with me, the stranger, an affinity that must have developed after we met. Before that, he was both distant and critical. "Now, just go back to your desk," he dismissed me gently, "and good luck. You'll need it."

I stood up to leave.

"Oh, one more thing," Jim added. "There is a very strict policy at the paper. You can't drink on the premises. You can do it outside but never, ever at work. Do you understand?"

I looked at him in disbelief. "Of course, I do. But I don't drink much, socially from time to time but it is nothing that I would consider a habit."

Jim winked at me. "Sure, sure. Me too."

I walked across the room, greeted Ruth, who was busily writing another film review, and sat down next to Chuck, my colleague and fellow headline writer.

Chuck, a lanky young man, was well equipped for the job. A graduate of one of the journalism schools in Tennessee, he was well versed in all the technicalities of the profession. He was also a local boy who knew the environment, the personalities playing important roles in the community and, after spending over a year on the copy desk, was considered a seasoned writer. My hopes centered on him. My desires were aimed at learning from him and convincing him that by teaching me, by being my role model, he would enhance his own self-respect. He was about ten years younger. He was also, for the first time, exposed to a European trained individual.

I was to learn rather rapidly that training me, tutoring a stranger, were thoughts that had never entered Chuck's mind. Instead he, and a few others, resented my presence. Oblivious to that, I repeatedly asked for help, unaware of the fact that every time I asked, I gave Chuck more ammunition for the argument that I should not have been hired. I continued living with my illusions until the day that Chuck asked me to stay after work and have a talk. "It has been now several weeks since you came aboard," he started. "Most of the pieces tossed your way by the slot man come back. They're incorrectly done. The simplest headlines, number eight, now routinely go your way. Everything else must be handled by the rest of us. It took you forever to figure out that we do not write Chamber of Commerce in a headline but simply C-o-C. You probably will never be able to write heads number 18 or 22, where there are even more strict limitations on typewriter's symbols in each line and on the number of lines allowed."

Chuck stopped awaiting my reaction. There was none.

"Okay," he continued, looking at me with stern expression. "How much are you being paid?"

"Seventy dollars a week."

"Seventy dollars? That is unbelievable. I have been at the job for over a year and I am making thirty-seven fifty. Is this just? Do you think that is fair?"

"I did not ask for any amount," I mumbled. "It was what I was offered."

Chuck's anger was barely contained. "And why did they offer you that much? What was the reason you were jumped over most of us? Because the big boss from New York ordered it. That's what it was. And you came, not knowing what to do, not having the slightest idea about journalistic technique and took the job. Why don't you ask the publisher to take you off the copy desk? To make you write, if you are capable of doing that, which I doubt. But don't spoil our record and our work here."

He looked at me and softened his voice. "Look, we all like you, please understand. But you do not fit in. This is not a European newspaper. Should I find myself in London tomorrow I would be as lost as you are here, so don't take it too seriously. I wanted to be your friend, and friends must be honest with each other."

He grabbed my hand in a reassuring gesture and was gone.

I stood there alone, crushed under the weight of a reality I neither anticipated nor welcomed.

In the meantime, the two of us searched for a place to live, trying to decipher the mystery of that new city where fate had sent us and to figure out the best way to connect with the spirit, ambitions, dreams and thoughts of men and women who were to be a part of our lives.

The learning process continued and the price paid for that learning proved to be rather high. My first major mistake was to apply Edinburgh's experience to Chattanooga. In the Scottish capital, we used our meager resources to put a down payment on an apartment that quadrupled our investment within two years. Why not do the same here? We had a few thousand dollars left and I was to have a steady income. Why not invest? The rented room, without our own kitchen and paying more than we could afford, was just a stopgap arrangement.

We bought a house. It sat on a hill, had a small backyard, and the total price was $8,500. We took a mortgage from the owner, put down $2,000, which almost depleted our capital, and signed a promissory note to pay $50 a month toward the principal and interest of the mortgage. We were in seventh heaven, on our own. I had a job and our children had space to play. The fact that the house was more of a shack than a solid structure, that my job was not at all secure, never entered into consideration.

Our neighbors came to welcome our arrival and the mailman started delivering our mail. Our girl was enrolled in her first American school. Was this the beginning of our American adventure, the beginning of the fulfillment of our American dream, a dream that Marysia nursed for years, ever since she was a child reading and thinking about a distant land called America?

We discovered our new world gradually, more by direct experience than by study, more by contact with people than by reading about them. Chattanooga, in 1948, was a deeply Southern city and was also a segregated city. It was a city where the Ku Klux Klan functioned openly and was considered a group of men whose presence was almost a natural social phenomenon.

We were blissfully ignorant of all of the above.

Somehow, it was both difficult and painful to change gears, to switch from the Scottish-Polish world, limited but greatly satisfying, to the normal, pedestrian but necessary world of a working American journalist. The problem that I was to discover later was that I was not prepared, ready or trained to be one.

My mind was still elsewhere. I was dreaming about bringing my father to teach at the University of Chattanooga. I was searching for places where other Polish exiled academics could work. I was submitting, to a rather bewildered editor, letters to the editor reminding Southern readers about Eastern Europe. I read with excitement the news item indicating that a group of congressmen was introducing a resolution requiring Washington to denounce Yalta and Potsdam. I suffered no end reading about familiar quarrels that divided the Polish exiled community over the selection of individuals to form a delegation to go to San Francisco to witness the formation of the United Nations.

Winston Churchill, at the same time, approached a group of Polish exiles in connection with a conference to be held at The Hague. One of the invites, Stanislaw Stronski, representing the right wing political spectrum, turned them down. Others went, but left without finding a way to agree on a common stand. When the time came to consider an unofficial attendance at San Francisco, Winston Churchill, according to all the available data, was so frustrated with the Polish inability to find a unified voice, that he left others to negotiate with his difficult clients. It was at that point that my father's name surfaced as a possibility to be one of the delegates. But he was well known for his hawkish approach toward the Soviet Union. In speeches and writings, he strongly opposed Soviet territorial demands on Poland. At that time, a faction favoring cooperation and compromises with Moscow headed the Polish Government in Exile, no longer recognized by the Allied nations. Stanislaw Mikolajczyk, with whom Father openly and vocally disagreed with, and who was ready to discuss territorial adjustment with Moscow, would not even hear about the possibility of Father's inclusion. The final group that went to San Francisco was acceptable to all quarters and as such, its presence had no impact.

I read about all these events in between my inept attempts to write proper headlines for various articles submitted to me by

Gene. There were days that it took me hours to figure out the proper headlines. Other days, I would write five, or four, or two. The flood of returning articles weighed on me heavily. I could not sleep. I could not bear the air of disapproval that surrounded me in the editorial room.

Could I write something about the events in the Near East? Fights between Arabs and Jews who are attempting to create their own state? About the growing threat from the Soviet Union?

I was listened to, but few heard me. I was considered slightly outside the mainstream of local thinking.

"It would be great to have readers interested in the great world," one of my co-workers noted. "But why don't you write about something affecting us here and not men and women in a distant land?"

Still in a state of mind drifting away from Chattanooga, I could not understand the question. Everything I was proposing sooner or later would have a direct effect on everyone concerned, irrespective of geographic location.

"In the meantime, how about writing a juicy headline," Jim interjected. "About the woman who divorced her third husband and plans to remarry shortly? She is a prominent citizen here, ran for office twice and has a son who may one day become mayor. You could say for instance, "Woman's Dynamics Work," and it would fit into the easiest headline ever."

A burst of laughter greeted Jim's comments. I wasn't sure how to take it so I laughed along with the rest of them.

But it hurt. And it continued to hurt. In one of my diary entries, I wrote a sentence reflecting a sense of despair.

'How could I get into a wider world?' I wrote. 'How could I get out of that little dead-end street, that at first I considered a God sent retreat? But I am not equipped to do anything else," I wrote. 'Psychologically, I am a wreck. I lack basic intelligence, talents, education and everything else that would be needed to widen my horizon,' I mused. 'What am I complaining about? Why am I being hysterical about our fate? Am I not covering my ignorance by attempting to be a journalist? A writer?'

Jim Jarvis must have sensed my mood and decided to help me the only way he knew how. A bottle of bourbon and a six-pack of Coca-cola awaited us in his car.

"We never drink on the job," he reminded me, "but the parking lot is another proposition."

It took us a good two hours to finish this particular job. I don't remember how I got home or how I drove through the tunnel leading to Red Bank. I only learned later that Marysia was sure I had suffered a heart attack. I also learned the next day that there was no way I could go to work. Jim Jarvis was surprised.

"Is he sick?" he inquired when my wife called.

I was not sick, just depressed and nursing a killer headache, almost unable to think or even anticipate the future. How many more sessions awaited me in Jim's parked car?

There were none. But there was a lateral transfer that gave me what I thought was a break. I was transferred from the copy desk to the city desk. That meant reporting. That meant writing. Elated, I went home proclaiming a new era, a better chance, and a distinct possibility that I would make it after all. In retrospect, thinking about the move, I knew better. The city editor, an older man, sweet and gentle, was persuaded to take me in, in spite of serious reservations. The Times team, fair and devoted to doing everything possible to give the stranger a chance, realized that I would never be a successful copy editor. Let him try something else. At the same time, word went back to New York that there was a distinct possibility that the newcomer would fail. Could Mr. Sulzberger consider taking him at *The New York Times*?

I knew nothing about the way that the reflections on my fate went from bad to worse. Unconcerned, I found unlimited pleasure in playing with my baby son, in writing long articles about the Soviet Union and its control of Eastern Europe and in analyzing and denouncing the Yalta Agreement. My pieces were long and ponderous and they were returned with one rejection slip after another.

Marysia, my young wife thrown into the unknown, into a complex and different lifestyle, coped with our domestic life. It was not easy. She was alone in a sea of strangers and a stranger herself. Accustomed to moving among friends and people in tune with our own fate, Scots and Poles alike, she bore her isolation with cheerfulness and courage. Our little son Andrew helped by demanding full attention. I added to her chores by asking for advice, support and editing my freelance pieces that never saw the light of print. We were both half-convinced that Chattanooga was not ready for us, nor were we ready for it. Only half-convinced, after all, there was still plenty of room for illusions. There was still plenty of room for hope.

My deep reflections were interrupted by an unexpected and sudden meeting with the local nature. I looked through the window and my blood froze. Andrew, with an angelic smile on his face, was playing with a snake. I knew little about snakes, but knew enough to recognize a rattler. In a rapid move, I snatched the boy, kicked the snake that did not bite. Exhausted, we both sat perfectly silent. Only Andrew was totally nonplussed.

"Can I have my milk?" he cried in the only language he knew.

The milk was served, the story about the snake circulated widely inside the editorial room and for a while, Andrew was labeled as a potential snake charmer.

"He could make much more money in that profession" commented Jim Jarvis, "than you will ever make as a writer."

I believed him entirely. Another rejection slip waited at home. Inside the Times, my writing efforts were scrutinized carefully. Once again, the old habits of producing editorials, of injecting my own feelings, opinions and thoughts, hampered my otherwise genuine efforts. I was learning. I was learning about stories that I never knew I would tackle. I was also acquiring a taste for researching and distaste for constant re-writing.

But how could it be otherwise? In the middle of one of the night shifts, the rather distressed voice of a man, speaking with a distinct black accent, informed me about the death of his father. Could I, please, insert, an obituary item into tomorrow's paper?

My answer was duly subdued, duly attempting to share his grief. Of course we will be ready to print the text. Could you dictate it slowly?

A steady stream of names followed. There were easy ones like Tom Washington and difficult ones like Herman Copperfield. There were cousins, parents, sons, daughters, granddaughters and grandsons. The obviously emotional man grew impatient with my steady requests for spelling not once, but at least twice. Mortified by the possibility of misspelling strange names, with mispronouncing when repeating his words, I put down the telephone after close to a half-hour of listening and taking notes, totally exhausted. Carefully, repeating aloud to myself every single name and first name, I proudly handed the copy to the slot man. He checked it for length, number of words in each line and put it through. I felt proud of myself. The feeling did not last long.

A message from the city editor awaited my arrival the following morning. He reported an irate call from a member of the family of the deceased. How can a respectable newspaper, like the Times, have such sloppy copy editors? Half of the names in the obit dictated to me were misspelled. Several were mangled to the extent that some grandchildren turned out with the first names of their parents. Will the paper correct the entry by the next day? Will the responsible man at the end of the telephone wire be properly reprimanded?

Both requests were granted.

Leaving the editorial room on special assignments was viewed at this point as a saving grace.

The assignments had proven to be the best and the most exciting parts of the job. No matter that almost every copy I produced went through a re-writing process and no matter that in each case - with one exception - what I considered to be the most brilliant points were usually softened and brought down to a pedestrian level. I was elated with the chance to learn directly how this distant, strange and unknown world, lived, functioned and developed its own customs, its own values and its own way of dealing with diversity of the local population.

There was a meeting convened by the Chamber of Commerce to discuss the Negro health and housing contest. The purpose was to create a better standard of living for a small area located in the southwest part of the city. Twenty-five families - all of them black - lived there as renters, as well as a large number of children. Sanitation was inadequate and next to the building were four empty lots unofficially used by a number of downtown stores as a dumping site. The meeting, attended by several women leading the movement to improve conditions in the entire city, the fire marshal and a man in charge of publicity, stressed the need to educate tenants as to their responsibilities and convince owners that once investments are made in the buildings, the tenants will be responsible for keeping up the improvements. The fire marshal, speaking on the necessity for fire prevention, said that more black people each year die through carelessness with fire than from any other accident. Two educational films, *Crimes of Carelessness* and *The House Fly*, were also shown.

Exposed for the first time to a rather typical American self-help project, I ran all puffed-up back to my desk. The puffing up was promptly eliminated from my copy. The enthusiastic comments barely survived. On the other hand, all of the names of the participants and all their utterances - whether weighty or not - were left untouched.

The next trip, looking at the other side of the racial issue, was much more exciting. I was asked to observe, cover and write a piece describing the initiation of the newly elected members to the Ku Klux Klan.

What a strange turn of events. I remembered vividly reading about the Klan and looking at the pictures of several hooded men as a teenager in pre-war Poland. I was petrified, almost physically sick with fear. Was there any chance that these people would ever come to Warsaw? To my house? Why do they look so fierce? So angry? Totally ignorant of the principal goals of the Klan in my youthful imagination, I pictured them as somebody to fear, to escape from and to avoid at any cost. And now I was going to meet them face-to-face, maybe even to talk to some of them and perhaps even shake their hands.

The old fear was reborn with a vengeance. The little Polish boy reentered my soul. I drove slower and slower. Don't be silly, I told myself. You are no longer that little boy.

A wide-open space, a meadow lying between two walls of tall trees, was roped off. Inside, a number of men were busy arranging the area. On the side stood a number of hooded horses. Two large crosses dominated the scene. Both were covered with what turned out to be flammable material. A fairly large crowd of onlookers formed a circle. I flashed my press credentials and was allowed to stand close to the rope.

It was getting dark as the ever-blazing sun hid behind the forest. Promptly, when the hour struck eight, a line of men, their faces covered with white hoods, emerged from nowhere. They marched in a loose formation, stopped in front of one of the crosses and waited. The crowd watched in total silence. Within a minute or so, the Grand Wizard of the Klan walked slowly towards the cross and took a position facing the men. He spoke briefly to them, outlining the difficult but imperative task of keeping America white. He reminded them of the oath about to be taken, swearing them to total secrecy. He talked about the danger of mixing races and of the total dedication of the Klan to keep Negroes separate from humanity at large. He evoked God who knew perfectly well the reason why He created different colors of skin. He reminded everyone, within earshot, of the fact that both Adam of Genesis and Jesus of Nazareth were white and that - to the best of his knowledge - there was not a single Saint mentioned in the Bible who was colored.

"It will be your sacred task, men, to keep that tradition. To make sure that you and your children remain faithful to the principle of white people's superiority."

He stopped and the first hooded man stepped forward. The Grand Wizard put his hands on the man's covered head and recited the oath. The man bowed, repeated the oath and returned to his place. He was now a full-fledged member of the Klan.

Others followed. When the entire group of roughly twenty-five new recruits went through the ritual, the horses were brought in. The men mounted them and started, first slowly, trotting and finally galloping, circling the two crosses. The Grand Wizard, with a theatrical gesture, lifted a lighted torch and touched one of the crosses. Instantly it was covered with flames. The hooded men on hooded horses kept circling, and the onlookers watched, with an occasional excited woman's voice piercing the silence.

The onlookers began slowly dispersing. A couple of elderly people, their arms around each other, reflected in whispers on the total dedication of the Klansmen to their mission. A group of teenagers walked away in silence, followed by their parents and grown-up cousins. There was no way to judge their reaction. In the crowd, there was not a single black face. I figured that it would have been dangerous for me even to try and sneak a look.

The two crosses continued to burn. The Grand Wizard was still there watching, sitting stiffly in the saddle of his horse. The newly anointed freshmen watched him for a sign indicating that the ceremony was over. Mesmerized by the entire spectacle, I was the only one left outside of the meadow.

My piece, written with passion and reflecting my earlier fears of hooded men, went promptly to the rewrite man.

"Another meeting, accepting a group of young men into the family of Klansmen, took place yesterday in the outskirts of our city," read his opening paragraph.

My text had read differently, "A fascinating ceremony, featuring excited newcomers, burning crosses and stern promises to keep America white, unfolded in front of several hundred curious spectators. Some applauded, but most just watched the entire bizarre procedure in silence. For one, lonely European present, the scene appeared not only bizarre, but almost surrealistic."

Mobilizing all the courage that I had, I approached the city editor. "Was there anything wrong on my lead? Anything inaccurate?"

He looked at me with a smile of understanding and tolerance. "Not at all. The lead was fine. But it was a story written by someone for whom this entire event was a big novelty. It is not for our readers. We witness these initiations at least twice a year. It is a rather uneventful piece of news. And had to be treated as such."

"Why did you send me there?"

"We always have a reporter when the Klan gathers. You never know what might occur: violence, protests, an attempt to lynch. Who knows? Besides, wasn't it a good reporting lesson for you?"

I went back to my desk pondering, thinking and becoming more and more depressed. Would I ever make the grade?

9

A Baseball Game

Unexpectedly, the time came when I was a hero for a day. Out of all of the paper's departments, there was one department that I never expected to write for. The sports editor had a question. Did I know anything about baseball? Had I ever played? Observed?

The answer was "no" to all of the above. Buss Walker, a large man, with a warm smile and a very Southern approach, handed me a pass to the press section of the stadium. "Go and write what you see. Don't try to read up on the rules. Don't ask anybody any questions. Just observe and come back with a story. I will give you my column for a day."

So I went and the piece that emerged was in the form of a letter to an imagined friend in Europe. I used the first name of my newly born son, hoping that when he reached the ripe age of seven or eight and would be ready to start playing, he would read my piece with proper reverence.

The column's headline was written by Buss himself. It read: "A Pole Sees First Baseball Game," followed by a brief explanation: "Zygmunt Nagorski, Jr., an ex-Polish army officer, saw his first baseball game Sunday and described it in a letter to a friend on the other side who has never seen one. Nagorski left Poland in 1940, spent seven years in England and Scotland doing newspaper work and helping the Free Polish Government. He landed in this country on March 3, and is a member of the news staff of the Times."

There was, I thought at that time, an interesting omission in the introduction: not a word that during the entire seven years I was a soldier, not a word about my days in action, not a word about the fact that I found my wife on the other side of Europe and that we both were in Chattanooga. Buss knew what was of direct interest to his readers and his colleagues: my newspaper experience. How many of his readers - I asked myself - knew about the Free Polish Government?

No matter, I was finally published on my own. I was finally left untouched by the re-write man. What a triumph.

> May 17, 1948
> Dear Andrew:
> I started to see my first baseball game early in the afternoon. A boy directed me to the parking lot. I had to walk for a while until I reached the stadium, which is like any stadium in the world. The only difference is that it is privately owned. Can you imagine that? What about starting the same business in Europe and making nice money? But nobody, so far as I know, had ever thought of owning a stadium.
>
> The crowd needs description. Crowd of the American South, colorful, with girls dressed in the latest new looks and men partly undressed owing to the climate. It looks more like a European public watching a swimming contest. The men are sitting with their legs high in the air and their hats on. I still cannot trace the tradition of the much-used American custom of wearing hats inside, hanging your coat and proudly displaying your braces. But I suppose that one day I will find out all about it.
>
> Before climbing the steps to reach the press box I went to the office. There, I was able to see how interesting the sport profession can be - money, big money is being counted. And once more I would stress to you the importance of owning a stadium.
>
> Press box is nice, but I was a little shocked seeing it behind a solid piece of wiring. Later I was to discover that it was for the protection of the pressmen against the ball and not - as I feared - of the public from the occupants of the box.
>
> The game was about to start. It is a semicircle with four bases. This will explain to you the name of the game. One is

A Baseball Game

home base. Another number one, two and three. You have to run from one to another as quickly as you can. It is really a game of race. But you race against the ball. You have to be faster than the ball. Don't get excited - it is perfectly possible. I also thought at first that these fellows have undertaken an impossible task.

And the game. I see already how impatient you must be. You want to hear about the baseball and I keep writing about everything else. But remember, Andrew, all these details are part of the game, of its atmosphere, crowd reactions, surrounding.

Players - Nashville against Chattanooga - are dressed blue and white respectively. What is that? Three solid men dressed in navy blue, which from my end look like black - are solemnly marching into the home base. Two players, one from each side, join them. They seem to talk about something very serious. Undertakers? A stupid idea crossed my mind. Or maybe like at duel places in the old Champs Elysee in Paris? Witnesses of the crime about to be committed? Slowly they moved into three corners of the play. One, the nearest to me, put on a masque protecting his body with heavy bumpers and the game was about to start. Oh, yes, I forgot to tell you about the players. They were there all right, standing around in a circle, nine of them. In the middle, on the soft piece of ground, stands one man only. His task is to throw a ball into the home base. His fellow player is the catcher. His idea is to catch the ball. Sounds easy? Wait. The ball must be above the batter's knees and below his shoulders. Who is batter? He is the guy who prevents the ball from being caught by the catcher. The batter tries to hit it. So you have these three men around on whom the main interest is focused.

Once the batter hits the ball, he runs to the first base. If he is there before the ball - which in the meantime is being caught by some other fellow from the pitcher's party - he is safe. If the ball reaches the base first, the man is out. I mean out for the round. If he is first - I was just about to write that in this case the ball is out - then he makes one step towards the goal. Goal is scored when one man makes the complete circle and comes back to home base. Do you follow? I doubt it.

And one more detail to make things look more complicated. If the batter does not manage to hit the ball for so many times, while he is supposed to do so, he is out. You follow the idea? All Blue players want to get rid of one White who is the batter. Oh, yes, another detail, if the pitcher does not score right, the batter moves automatically into the first base. Another player from the White party takes his place in the home base. You see? I bet you don't. Neither do I, yet.

Crowd watches with restrained excitement. Some people shout, and I suppose they have to. Others sit quietly. But when the ball is hit over the high wall surrounding stadium almost everybody is on his feet shouting. This was the score. And the Blue men who are on the run score their goals easily until the ball is returned. I know what you would say now: why not build the wall closer and make the whole game easier? I would not dare mention even your wild idea to my American friends.

With the game proceeding I start feeling strange, after all, this is my city. Chattanooga go ahead. Don't slow down. Just one more score. And it is my first baseball game in my life. You must win. Hey. Hit that ball fellow cries spectator with blue face of anger, equally blue pair of pants and fantastic hat adorned with pictures. Hit it, fellow. I almost follow his lead. The ball goes wild, our man runs from the first base to the second and throws himself on the ground, touching the base with his feet. Got it. One split of a second. We are leading the game.

Young pitcher tries to use psychological tricks. He almost hits the batter. The batter protects himself with his club, or what they call here, the bat. Someone whispers to my ear that this is a good move. Now he will be scared. I don't blame him. I would too.

I brought them luck. Chattanooga won the game 9 to 4. What that means? You should be ashamed of yourself not realizing it after my clear, business like explanation. It mean that Nashville made only four times the round trip from home to home, while we did it nine times. I really hope that you can go now to any baseball game and feel like an old player.

By the way, do you know that it pays to be a player? Players, I was told, make a thousand a month. Figure that for a year, ten years or longer. Supposing you take up this letter, make it published in European papers, get together men willing to earn decently their living in America, train them - along the lines of my instructions - and then apply for United States visas for them, they will get them. How would you feel about it? The first team can be composed of unemployed university professors who cannot manage to get entry into America. Try, however, to choose younger ones. It is not a very difficult game. But the ball is heavy and the club pretty rough to handle.

Yours very sincerely,
Zygmunt

Fifteen minutes of fame followed. The piece traveled around the newsroom, and a flood of congratulations suddenly descended on me. Readers - at least some of them - were amused, delighted and wrote to that effect. There was even one very significant letter that I cherished to no end. An unknown lady declared that finally someone had the courage and the ability to explain baseball in simple, understandable terms. I almost framed her note.

After the great and unexpected fifteen minutes life in the newsroom and around the copy desk resumed its normal pace. I was out on assignments. I was also sensing more and more that I had neither the ability, nor patience to continue trying. While still in the field - and the paper gave me every opportunity to find a niche for myself - I was busy writing letters and making telephone calls looking for an out. At one point I made a call to an Army colonel who commanded a unit stationed in the outskirts of Chattanooga, inquiring about the possibility of enlisting. The man at the other end of the line was gentle, understanding and ready to explain to me that both my age, 36, and my lack of citizenship would preclude any chances of wearing an American uniform.

A sense of desperation permeated our household. We were both full of mutual reassurance, repeating to each other how fortunate we were to secure a home, a job and a place from which we could eventually climb to higher and better lifestyle. Marysia, absorbed by endless details related to the household and children, maintained a smiling exterior. Only the two little ones, oblivious of anything outside of their own horizons, appeared as happy as any child could be. What else do you need outside a little piece of ground where you could play? Outside of a mother who feeds and cares for you?

During one of the long mornings with Marysia on leave from the kids, enjoying her dentist appointment, and me in charge of the little fellow making a mess of himself, I ran into an interesting passage written by Epicurius in the third century B.C. I copied it down; somehow it fit nicely into our moods.

> Nothing satisfies a man who is not satisfied with a little. It is common to find a man who is poor in respect of the natural trend of life and rich in empty fancies. For of the fools, none is satisfied with what he has, but is grieved what he has not.

Thank you, dear Epicurius; you brought me back to reality.

That reality translated itself into peaks and valleys of my continued attempts to make the grade as a reporter. Driving home one evening, I spotted a major fire. Jumping out of the car, I took copious notes, secured names, ages and addresses of people affected, and had a full story ready, only then to be told to turn over everything to a more experienced writer.

I was then appointed on a temporary basis to review films. It was a fair amount of relief to spend time inside movie theaters rather than inside our rather gloomy editorial room. I wrote a few fair reviews, experienced special attention from theater owners and was asked once again to return to the home base.

The next assignment at first made me bubble with excitement. I was to write a major story on the Tennessee Valley Authority, started in 1933 and which was faced with a huge task of examining the entire valley area for the planning of its numerous projects. The Authority, in order to approach the matter, created a survey branch and special maps. I was to do a two-part article outlining the history of TVA and the role that the branch was to perform.

The initial enthusiasm was quickly extinguished. The first draft was full of stupid grammatical and spelling errors. It took me several weeks of interviewing, writing, re-writing and witnessing what I considered to be beautiful prose, but butchered by others. Finally, the two articles appeared under my byline on August 22, 1948. But it was really not my piece. It was a fair description, but not my decent journalistic piece of work with emotion. Flares of "creativity" and the enthusiasm for an exciting project were considered superfluous and eliminated.

Without my realizing it, the day of our departure from Chattanooga was drawing closer. Absorbed in our own efforts to escape, immersed in observing the world scene - the Soviet threat to Berlin and Yugoslavia's refusal to become another Soviet satellite - we failed to notice the growing sense of impatience with me as a member of the Times' staff. At the same time, it must have been a great disappointment for my powerful protector and supporter, Arthur Hays Sulzberger. He was the one who sent me South. It was now up to him to return us to New York.

It was a perfect Sunday. Marysia was busy cutting grass; my role was reduced to some weeding. Our little girl, full of energy and ready to play, took the garden hose and sprayed both of us with streams of cold water. Our little fellow, barely able to express himself, kept grabbing the hose from his sister and making a mess of himself. We all laughed, filling the air with family noises. Anyone looking at us or listening to us could have easily concluded that he was witnessing a perfect picture of happy Chattanoogans.

There was no question that a sort of temporary happiness surrounded us. Inside, unseen by either children or strangers, we were both eaten by deep anxiety. We had dived into the unknown. I had responded to a call from the man who saw a glimmer of possibility when talking to a budding journalist searching for a professional home. Had I a more realistic approach to the situation at hand, I probably would have declined. But how could I? There was an emptiness within the New York City orbit. There was a very limited number of dollars in our pockets. And there was the glamour of the unknown. It has always been one of my problems - right up to old age - being attracted by the unknown, digging deep into secrets of a potential adventure, deaf to warnings and to voices of reason.

The piercing ring of the telephone in the kitchen interrupted our playtime. Charles Puckette, my ultimate boss and publisher of the Times, was calling. He inquired about Marysia and the children. He also asked if I could stop by his office early in the evening. Mr. Sulzberger was in town visiting his daughter and would like to have a chat with me.

Marysia and I looked at each other. What does it mean?

It meant a lot.

The meeting lasted no more than twenty minutes. My New York patron and friend was obviously concerned; he was concerned how we would fare back in the East without the safety net of a pay check. He was slightly embarrassed facing Charles Puckette upon whom he had hoisted an unqualified person. Facing the two men - both of whom tried their very best to smooth our American entry - I felt inadequate and terribly sad. It was not that I was losing the job; it was not that the day finally came when we had to cut our Chattanooga links. I felt the weight of a major failure.

The two men stood up and we shook hands. Just before I walked out of the room, Charles Puckette casually mentioned that I would be paid until the end of the calendar year. The meeting took place close to my birthday around September 27. The generosity of the two men was unprecedented.

It was time to start packing.

"What is America, Daddy?" It is a land of unbelievable possibilities, my dear, young lady. It is a place where disasters can be met with the full sunshine of hope and where people around you cherish your successes more than your failures. It is a place where surprises meet you at every street corner and every morning you wake up. It is a place, in short, where life bubbles endlessly.

Leaving the South, we also left behind a short, but rich experience. Was there really a big race problem? Yes, indeed. Was there really a sense of being a stranger like it was in England? Not at all. We were strangers upon arrival and continued to be looked upon as newcomers, but so was everyone else. But it did not matter. What mattered was that we came and all the previous newcomers expected us to join them in the famous melting pot. They looked upon us as a seasoned sailor would look upon a novice climbing a ship's plank. There was neither animosity, nor huge expectations. It was rather a feeling that we were another arrival, another member of the crew that one-day would be able, capable and willing to be a full partner.

"How did you come to that conclusion, Daddy?"

I smiled to myself, recalling my little daughter's original inquiry. How did I?

Six months in the American South provided a painful lesson and a lifetime experience. We observed a part of the continent that lived in the past. Segregation was a way of life. Marysia's innocent move to take a seat at the back of the bus caused consternation, angry stirs and reluctance on the part of the bus driver to proceed. The status quo was, seemingly, accepted by both races. White women, involved in the development of the new housing project for blacks, were proud of their charitable - not social - work. The two most affluent areas of the city, Signal Mountain and Lookout Mountain, were entirely white. Somehow nobody considered the situation unjust, improper or cause for people to think differently. And the two of us had neither the sophistication, nor the concern even to ask questions.

Years later, little Andrew was to be one of the freedom riders during the civil rights movement. His parents, absorbed in their total preoccupation with making a living, adjusting and surviving in those early days, were oblivious of the social challenge that would eventually engulf Andrew's young mind.

Chattanooga also gave us, a couple of displaced Europeans, a new sense of freedom, freedom to cover miles of space without frontiers, without fear, without passports, without a sense of being lost. But above all, the Southern experience opened to both of us appreciation of the American society.

How else would one define the treatment that we received from Arthur Sulzberger? How else could one define a gesture of the local Ford dealer offering help to bring my parents over from England, or an extended arm of assistance by Marysia's tennis partner to hire me as a foreman in his small factory, after learning that my job at the Times was to be terminated?

The South, in addition, provided us with a brief insight into an elegant, very civilized way of life. Inhabitants of Lookout Mountain - old, affluent Southern families - retained and promulgated grace and panache. One of the homes, in that distinctly upper class and almost aristocratic neighborhood, belonged to a colleague of mine. Ruth Golden, probably the only Jewish owner of real estate in that enclave, worked at the desk adjacent to mine on her father's paper. It was in her home that we experienced that Southern way of life so distinct and so much more to our taste, than anything we would encounter later in the East. From the way that people dressed, to the way they addressed each other, to the quality of silverware, furnishings and - most importantly - seeing how Ruth, her husband and her children treated their black servants almost like members of their family.

Armed with unlimited optimism, reflecting upon all that we had learned since our arrival in New York six months earlier, without a job, without a place to go and without the slightest idea what to expect, we packed the kids and a couple of suitcases and drove to Florida, not to work, not to contemplate but to play, swim and explore the beaches. In my notes from those days, I observed that my life companion looked like a schoolgirl on vacation, full of joy and totally unconcerned with the future. She knew that we were bound to muddle through.

The four day long escapade into the world of illusion was a great adventure. Our trip, undertaken by a 1947 Hudson acquired from a Polish-American friend for a sum of $1,700 that depleted our resources considerably, was a discovery and a revelation. Colonial architecture, the sight of fields that displayed the remnants of corn and no indications that either potatoes or wheat were ever planted there, gave us pause and comparative reflections. In Poland, there would be no corn. In Poland, fields would have displayed bare sticks of harvested wheat or remnants of potatoes plants. Large, screened porches and impressive columns supporting equally impressive villas paraded in front of our bulging eyes. From time to time, we noticed a group of black men and women, with their white aprons tied around their vests, working with brooms inside and with pitchforks and shovels outside.

An army of tall palmettos held out their arms when we crossed the Georgian frontier and entered Florida. Marysia was driving, proudly pointing to this exotic flora and attempting to draw our daughter's attention. The young lady was busy arranging a new outfit for her newly acquired doll. The little fellow was fast asleep. The sight of St. Augustine, the oldest city in the United States, well preserved and proud of its unique place in American history, captivated our attention. We stopped, walked around and decided to proceed. There was nothing that would distract the children from their basic needs. Andrew, obviously ready to be taken out, watered one of the palms, leaving behind faint Polish footprints. About an hour later, noticing a set of "tourist courts," an institution completely foreign to our European eyes, we rented a tiny cottage sitting on the beach, that included all that was required for our family. The place where we parked was called Daytona Beach. The daily rental rate was seven dollars. Clad in swimming suits, our family ran toward the ocean.

They not only ran, they galloped. Marysia, in her yellow swimsuit, chased her daughter, attempted to build sand castles and looked like a twenty-year-old. I just sat next to Andrew who seriously contemplated eating samples of sand, and watched this scene of ultimate happiness.

Minor car troubles gave us another little surprise. A local mechanic, who arrived promptly upon our distress call, reacted with a broad smile when he heard Polish. He was also from Poland. Not only himself but there was a group of Polish immigrants who settled not far from Daytona Beach in 1928, brought there by an agent who sold them land and promises of tourism bonanza. The mechanic insisted that we come with him to a place called *Korona* (Crown), settled entirely by the Poles. No one spoke English in that little enclave. No one asked us any questions. The assumption was that we were part of the community. The houses reminded us of Polish villages, with the men and women dressed the way that Polish peasants had dressed twenty years earlier. Even the stray dogs reminded us of similar creatures wandering around the Polish countryside. The only hotel in the community was called, "White Eagle," the Polish national emblem.

It was 1948, exactly twenty years since the group of Polish farmers decided to look for a better life in the distant land of America. Upon arrival, these Poles recreated the village from which they came. Instead of grabbing new opportunities, or immersing themselves in the purely American way of life, unable to adjust, they took what looked like the easier way, continuity rather than change. Physically, they moved, undertaking a painful, difficult journey. But without realizing it, they stood still after that journey.

We looked at them with a sense of compassion and pity, of people who took a different route. Maybe even felt, for a moment, slightly superior. And then a few reflections flashed through our minds. And almost instantly, upon return to Chattanooga, for the last couple of weeks on the Times' job, I ran, as usual, to the nearest typewriter to register these reflections. Was there much difference between the people in *Korona* and us? Who chose the better road? I wrote in a diary:

> At 35, I am starting my life again. At 35, I am nobody, as so many other people are. Being ambitious, overly ambitious, full of plans and ideas, I came down to earth with a big bump. The bump is still painfully vivid in my body and soul. But was it a bad and negative or a good and positive bump?
>
> To begin with, why is it that a man of my age had to restart life? War, one would answer. Foreign soil, would add another. As usual, many more uncontrollable reasons come to mind in order to free myself from responsibility. But let's take it calmly, slowly looking inside and asking the fundamental question: are we all blameless for creating the circumstances that appear to be beyond our control? Of instantly giving up a possibility - even as remote as ever - to, if not to control at least to influence events?
>
> I left home on the last day of August 1939. I was then 26 years old. I had my university degree, brief legal practice at my father's office and a lot of fun behind me. My studies were worth very little. I was a spoiled brat. Not being stupid I managed to stick to books for several weeks before the final examination. Before and after, my days and nights were

full of fun. Suppose that everybody has to pay for pleasure. In money and in kind.

It was a long letter to posterity, a lengthy self-examination attempting to understand the failure of our first exposure to the American reality and to tell myself that maybe the fact that I was a misfit behind the copy desk of *The Chattanooga Times* was part of the penalty that I had to pay for not being diligent enough in the earlier days. But what was most painful in the experience was a sudden realization that I may be failing my little lady who asked me such penetrating questions about our newly discovered country.

"Daddy, where are we going?"

"Back to the big city, to New York."

"Why do we have to go? I like it here."

"Well, my dear, maybe people down here don't like your daddy so much." The eyes opened wide, very wide.

"I can tell them that they are wrong. Should I?"

"That would be just great. But in the meantime, why don't we all think about that great city of New York."

"Great city, Daddy? I thought you did not like it at all and that was why we came to Chattanooga?"

I looked at her and marveled at the logic of that small, developing mind. How could I explain to her the key dilemma that we all encountered in this newly chosen road for the family?

Her initial question, asked while we were still in Scotland, came back to me: what is America, Daddy? 'What is it,' I kept asking myself. Do I know the answer? Would I be as perceptive looking at that vast continent and as clear in my analysis as Alex de Tocqueville? I started laughing aloud. What a comparison, his mind and mine, his time frame and mine, his wide horizon and mine, limited for the time being to the outskirts of a medium-sized Southern city.

Be realistic, an inner voice whispered, don't fall into your usual trap of dreaming.

I always needed the inner voice. I always cherished its sudden appearance when I really looked for it. But often, pushed by what many considered an almost unlimited energy, I would plunge ahead with dire consequences to follow.

Chattanooga was such a major plunge.

It was, however, important to observe and to remember the new American mood.

The big war was over; unprecedented opportunities were about to be opened to veterans. But before they did unemployment among returning veterans soared. The full capabilities of the nation to switch from wartime to peacetime production had not yet been tapped. Applicants besieged employment offices. In the newspaper profession, editors and publishers were looking for young men and women, fresh from school, willing to work long hours for minimum pay.

Customs and the way of thinking were rooted in the tradition of immigrants who went through difficult times, discarding those who did not make it and rewarding, royally, those who did. Outside of the recognition of an individual's capacity to work hard and to climb the ladder, there was also a well-grounded belief that God was on the side of the industrious, energetic go-getter. Religion, the element that seldom surfaced in Scotland, was a strong, motivating factor. There was a proliferation of churches, with Baptist denomination usually leading the pack. Not unlike our native land, where the stronger attachment to one's church meant the less tolerance towards others. Conflicts developed, with the old Christian attitude of 'being your brother's keeper' losing its meaning.

The American South also offered a glimpse into the proverbial gentility of men and women born, educated and formed in that part of the continent. What was sometimes difficult to comprehend was that gentility crossed the race line, that it was visible and used by both blacks and whites. Observing the strict lines of segregation, talking with the few blacks that we had access to about slavery - not so distant from their families' memories - we expected anger, rejection and an occasional burst of hatred. Instead, a decade and a half before the civil rights movement engulfed the South, we saw a different mood. It is plausible that we just looked at the surface, that the boiling kettle of frustration was still hidden from casual observers. It is also possible that being such strangers, so detached from the Southern way of living, we were oblivious of its structure. Whatever the reason, whatever the justification, we left Tennessee not too well prepared to articulate the cause of black Americans. And it was a wake up call when upon returning to New York, with

Tennessee license plates on our car; we were jeered by a group of black teenagers driving alongside. At first we were puzzled, but it took only a couple of minutes to realize that we had been taken for people from the South.

10

New York, Once Again

America, my dear young lady, had given us a number of opportunities. We walked along the streets of a Southern town. We observed the new habits and a new way of life. We were received with warmth and understanding, with some critical comments and with a touch of resentment.

She looked at me with her eyes wide open. Did she pretend to listen?

I knew that she did not have to; it was much too early in her young life. I was just talking to myself, convincing, persuading and attempting to soften a sense of not belonging, of being bypassed, of feeling like a stranger. Didn't we cross the Atlantic in order to lose that feeling?

The streets of New York welcomed us back. They welcomed us with all their anonymity, impersonality and toughness. Marysia stayed home, immersed in the daily chores of a young mother. I commuted to the nothingness of the big city.

In reality, it was wrong to define it as 'nothingness'. Each street offered new possibilities. Each passerby could have been an important contact and every office building housed institutions, groups and organizations that I was convinced could have used me in all kinds of capacities. The problem was how to jump the barrier of non-recognition, how to convince the army of gate keepers to allow me to talk to the principals, and once in front of a principal, how to sell myself.

Sell myself? Did I really use this type of language? Am I a commodity, a piece of merchandise to be peddled around? Or am I getting more and more accustomed to the way that potential employees see themselves entering the American labor market?

I commuted day in and day out, knocking on closed doors, sneaking into the presence of all powerful receptionists who sometimes with anger, more often with understanding, talked to me about the scarcity of jobs and my obvious handicaps, lack of experience or having too many qualifications for entry positions. How can you ask someone with a master's degree to be in charge of a mailroom?

There was a middle-aged woman at the Encyclopedia Britannica who received me with a big smile, friendly and warm attitude, and suggested an application for a sales position. No, there is no salary. No, there is no guarantee of continuity, but there is a lot of pleasure in meeting all kinds of people. Britannica, I was told with a very stern expression, caters to the literary public. The cream of the crop.

At the American Committee for Émigré Scholars, an institution created shortly after Adolph Hitler came to power in Germany, Miss Elsa Standinger, herself an émigré, pointed out that journalists did not qualify as scholars. At Newsweek, there were no vacancies and would probably never be for writers with English listed as their second language. Catholics at the New York Diocese and Protestants at the Council of Churches were encouraging, pointing me in all kinds of directions. Lecture agencies were looking for celebrities. At the *Voice of America,* there was hope and almost a thrill. I was asked to take a test in writing, voice delivery and language. The Polish desk was considering a possibility of using me as a freelancer. I passed all of the tests and was informed that I would be called when needed. The call never came.

But there were still office buildings. There were still untapped receptionists and unlimited inner-faith that somehow, somewhere, there must be a landing path.

The New York Times featured a small announcement:

JOURNALIST, 35, publicity man, political writer, lecturer, excellent knowledge European, international affairs, wide experience in organizing, planning; held chief executive positions, employed, seeks responsible post with prospects, future where initiative and energy not objected; highest references, Z6158 Times.

I considered myself employed as long as *The Chattanooga Times* kept my salary going.

Two inquiries arrived promptly. *The American Exporter*, a trade magazine, sought and lost interest. *The Editor and Publisher*, where my initial contacts led me straight to the editor, asked for an article. But nothing materialized.

Great start and wonderful moments of continued illusions. From time to time, dark clouds of inner-despair kept descending upon all of us. But at that very moment, Marysia got a job. A job? An elderly gentleman collected stamps; he needed a secretary and somehow we got connected. He was marketing his stamps as a rare commodity. He was willing to pay $25 a week for almost a full-time commitment.

The job lasted two weeks. It was finished abruptly when Marysia got one of her severe hypoglycemic attacks.

We left Chattanooga early in November. December came and Christmas was around the corner. The deadline approached when I was to receive the last check from the Times and there was nothing on the horizon that could potentially fill the gap. From London and Edinburgh letters, dispatched by my Polish friends and companions, urged me to do my utmost to awake Americans to the dangers of Soviet communism.

"It's just too bad," wrote my successor at the Polish Press Agency in Edinburgh, "that you have to waste your time working for American newspapers instead of continuing the type of activities that you were involved with here."

What a great idea.

There was another ad in the paper that invited my answer. Within a week from responding to it, I became a kitchen utensils salesman, successful salesman and someone who knew nothing about cooking but was suddenly transformed into a cook, a baker and a presenter of the most advanced and most health-oriented way of cooking, a salesman who, in spite of himself, made a major sale on the first day of his job. A salesman who was cheered by the unruly crowd of men dedicated to the profession, unable to understand the luck of the newcomer.

This lasted just about four long weeks, but it brought a couple of hundred dollars and enough to feed us for a month.

It was just about the time that the first sale was made that I decided to take a day off from searching, inquiring and getting deeper and deeper into a sense of hopelessness.

My little girl and I went out together to have fun and to try, once again, to answer her penetrating questions. New York City, with all its fascinations, was to point us in that direction.

The long trip tired the young lady and she dozed peacefully while I watched a parade of unbelievably tall buildings passing by my vision. Pennsylvania Station instantly opened a vista of crowds and of the fast moving life of busy people. It also gave us a glimpse of the poverty hidden behind the facade of shops, drug stores and other establishments. Men in rags, unshaven and unwashed, asked for money. I took her little hand firmly in mine and we walked briskly toward the main street. Fifth Avenue, starting above 42nd street, gave us a sense of glamour. The Rockefeller Center the skating rink captured my little girl's imagination. Could I one day do what they do? Could I get skates and learn? Before I realized that dream I plunged into the different type of adventure.

It was time to think about a gift for Marysia, the occasion was another of our wedding anniversaries. So I stopped in front of a store, whose name Bergdorf Goodman meant nothing to me, and walked in. Smiling, an eager young lady approached me with a traditional question, "How may I help you?" I explained to her that I was looking for a gift for an important wedding anniversary. It was to be exactly ten years since Marysia and I were married.

Within seconds she produced a tray full of diamonds, gold and rubies. And with an equally short amount of time, I picked up a gold necklace and said to her, "How much?"

"Two hundred dollars," a fortune to me. Sheepishly, I asked her if I could pay in installments. She responded, "Of course."

"Could you also engrave our names and the names of our two children?"

There was again a positive answer.

I picked up the necklace two days later, my down payment was twenty-five dollars. I was not asked any questions regarding my identity or credit references and I walked out with a two-hundred dollar gold necklace in my pocket, engraved, with only a promise

New York, Once Again   131

to pay twenty dollars a month as was required. Marysia still wears the necklace today and we still compare people's attitudes to each other in 1948 and the beginning of the 21st century.

An upward voyage to the top of the RCA building creates sensation in the ears and offers a breathtaking view of the city. "Look," she pointed to a forest of buildings below. "They look like doll houses. Don't they? Maybe they are?"

Wide terraces on the upper floor permitted a leisurely stroll, with tiny dots of humanity below reminding us of ants running in all directions. Like ants, the little dots below move with a purpose. Like ants, they probably reflect some inner calls or instructions. And maybe, like ants, they also obey other ants, other dots control and regulate their lives.

We go down using the fast moving elevator. "Someone blocked my ears again!" screams my young companion with delight.

It was Saturday afternoon, the middle of winter, yet it was warm and sunny. We plunged into the moving masses of ants and were immediately absorbed by them. Looking up, I saw the imposing structure of St. Patrick's Cathedral. How about stopping there? Showing my little Maria the inside of a church the size of which would probably overwhelm her. At first she just looked around without any visible impression. All of a sudden, I felt her hand pulling me in the direction of the main altar.

"There is a wedding here," she whispered. "I have never seen one before. Can we stay? Please, please..."

"Of course we can."

The bride, in a white dress, was escorted by an officer of the American navy. They were tall, handsome and beaming with joy. "What is this priest telling them, Daddy?"

"He explains to them that this is a very important moment in their lives, that they must respect and love each other. He is also telling them to be good to people all over, and to bring up their children as good Christians."

There was a moment of silence. "How does the priest know that they want to get married?"

"They told him some time before."

"You mean to say that they saw him before, told him about their plans and then went home and put on different clothes?"

"Not exactly. But yes, they informed the priest what they wanted to do."

More silence, another look of extreme curiosity. "What does she do with her wedding dress once she becomes a wife?"

"She will keep it and hopefully give it to her daughter when she will get married."

"Really? So my mother will give me her dress?"

"I don't think so, my dear. To begin with, she was married in a white, very beautiful suit. But even that suit is gone. The big war, during which you were born, took away all that your mother and father had. Including her wedding suit."

At the altar, the final ceremonial act was about to begin. Wedding rings were being put on the bride and groom's fingers. "What is he doing, Daddy?"

"Wedding rings are shared to make them feel that they belong to each other. It is important for people to wear them all their lives. When you get married, you will also get a ring. But first, you select someone whom you would really like."

The little face lit up. "You or Grandfather. I don't want anyone else."

And we both laughed a little too loudly. Heads turned into our direction. We kept walking. The replica of Michelangelo's Pieta and a group of worshipers surrounding it made us stop. Men and women bent and kissed Jesus' feet. "Why do they do it? Wouldn't it be nicer to kiss him on the mouth?"

It was high time to leave the cathedral. It meant not only re-emerging into the bright sun on Fifth Avenue. It also meant bringing my thoughts and my worries back to the realities of our, as yet, unsettled existence.

11

Benjamin Franklin

I always believed in our luck. I also believed in attempting to open what appeared to be doors, forever closed. One of those doors led me to an obscure lecture agency on Lexington Avenue. The staircase was not very inviting. The office was small and looked slightly abandoned. The man who greeted his unexpected guest introduced himself as Benjamin Franklin. It sounded familiar. I asked him the obvious question and he smiled with understanding. No, he was not related. No, he was not a descendant.

Was there anything that I wanted to talk to him about?

There was indeed.

With fervor, which I tried to soften as much as my enthusiasm permitted, I described the types of lectures that I had given on the other side of the Atlantic. I told my newly acquired listener how well topics, related to the conditions behind the Iron Curtain, had been received all over Scotland. At one point in my presentation, he interrupted. "Do you think that you would get the same reaction in Topeka, Kansas?"

"I don't know. I've never been there. But why Topeka?"

"Because that is where our headquarters are located. That is where I am from. That is where real Americans live."

"Real Americans? Are you suggesting that in New York, people are different? Or in the South, where I spent my last six months?"

"You are very perceptive, young man." Ben Franklin responded. "Yes, indeed, in this city there is a real melting pot. People like you, immigrants from all over arrive and settle. They don't move any further. They still live in their respective "countries," speak their own languages, worship their own God. You were lucky to have a taste of southern American culture. Most of the others don't. They create their own little enclaves, their own little ghettos and live happily ever after. Is this what you want?"

Intimidated by the lecture, I was determined to state my position. "No, sir (I learned my lesson how to address important people). My wife and I both came with the firm resolution to immerse ourselves in American life, to integrate. As a matter of fact, I was offered a scholarship to enroll at the Columbia School of Journalism and turned it down. For one, I could not afford it, but two, the condition of the scholarship, offered by the Polish-American Congress, was that I would work for the Polish language newspapers upon graduation. This was not acceptable to us."

Ben Franklin looked and listened. "Okay," he said, "would you be willing to deliver a lecture to one of our Clubs free of charge? We would like to see how you will be received and then decide. We will pay your expenses, but no fee."

"Of course," my immediate reply jumped out of my mouth before I had a chance to think about it.

"What topic would you like to address?"

"There appears to be a fair amount of interest in the way that Communists mold the minds of young people. How about 'Education in the Soviet Union'?"

"Pretty exotic subject for your average American," Ben Franklin smiled. "But let's try. We will let you know where and when shortly."

This was the beginning of another chapter in our American saga, a chapter that permitted me to visit the majority of states, facing mixed American audiences in small and large cities, and learning about the way that the country was turning. Large and formal dinner meetings, radio and later television appearances offered wonderful opportunities to immerse myself in the "real" America.

It was much later that I learned a little about the network of clubs that I was about to enter. It was also much later that I learned that Ben Franklin, the owner and the initiator of the idea, was in New York only one day, the very day that I knocked on his door.

There were several hundred Associated Clubs scattered all over the country. They served a multitude of people for whom a meeting with an outside speaker was the highlight of the year. There were some real celebrities like Randolph Churchill, some comedians of national fame and others, like myself, who filled gaps in scheduling. An average audience consisted of a couple hundred people, most of them local merchants, lawyers, doctors and a large contingent of elderly women. They paid annual dues to belong and they were also charged for meals. But all of that was considered worthwhile. This was their link with the outside world, to political and cultural events, and to the men and women with whom otherwise they would never be connected. That was the genius of Ben Franklin and his associates; they built bridges from small, often isolated towns and cities to the large spectrum of decision makers.

They succeeded beyond anyone's expectations. And I was lucky enough to be included among the list of selected speakers.

My fee, after the initial trial appearance, was to be $50 per lecture plus expenses. As a special gesture of generosity, Ben agreed to finance the purchase of a black tie outfit, which I would not have been able to afford on my own.

The first test was Laconia, New Hampshire, where Ben Franklin dispatched me. It was an experience that would be difficult to forget.

I took a bus from New York, tugging along the newly acquired tuxedo. A tall, smiling, friendly man met me at the bus stop and we drove in a rather impressive car to his home nearby. The trip was short but he managed to crowd into it some essential data on the town and his position in it. He owned a funeral home, as well as a drug store. He was also one of the major shareholders in the local hospital. The previous year, he had run for mayor, but was defeated by the well-oiled and well-financed political machine of an opponent. That cured him of political ambitions. Now, he was totally devoted to his business and felt that he made a difference for the people of Laconia.

The rest of the family was as friendly as my host. During lunch, we talked about the way he was able to combine health care with arrangements for final departures. The wife, a pleasant woman in her mid-thirties, expressed regrets that there were no customers on the first floor where men and women were usually prepared for burial.

"They come here, often disfigured by pain, looking much older, much more scarred by suffering than what they looked like when alive," she explained to me. "Then we start working, and by the time we are through, they look younger, more cheerful, their smiles are genuine and the relatives can part from them in a different mood. It is simply amazing what we can do to prepare them for their eternal journey."

I listened and wondered. I was relieved that no customers were around. And I continued to learn, more and more, about another phenomenon of the American culture: a cosmetic approach to the dead. Evidently, even for the dead, appearances meant everything.

My evening lecture went swimmingly. The topic was received with wide applause. After all, what I was depicting to them was a nation molded in one pattern. It made my audience feel so much better, so superior. They loved me dearly for giving them a sense of greatness. Their children were given choices. Their schools were free of political indoctrinations. And here was a refugee from a communist controlled country, telling the inhabitants of Laconia how grateful they should be for what they had.

Ben Franklin received full endorsement for his new speaker and I was at the receiving end of a list of dates throughout the winter of the 1948-49 season. They ranged widely from North to South and East to West. I was overwhelmed by the geography, choices and responsibilities. Our household erupted in happiness and joy. Daddy had finally found his niche, his independent way of making a living.

I looked over my initial itinerary:

January 3 - Fairbury, Nebraska.
January 4 - Grand Island, Nebraska
January 5 - York, Nebraska
January 6 - Sheridan, Wyoming
January 10 - Cody, Wyoming
January 11 - Missoula, Montana

The list continued. There were dates in Texas, Oklahoma, Kansas and Ohio. At one point, there was a jump from Mexico to Montana in one day. The more dates, the more money I would make, and in my ever-unlimited optimism, I never thought that my physical or mental capacities would falter. After all, I was young and I was strong and I loved to lecture. In addition, I had a wonderful chance to learn about this new continent of ours.

The chances of discovery presented themselves, often under various circumstances. In a tiny village of Nebraska, I was able to test people's interest in foreign policy. In Powell, Wyoming, I discovered real Native Americans and the people who lived among them. What better opportunities could have been offered to a recent immigrant from Europe to learn about his newly selected country?

Maybe now, upon my return home, I would be able to answer more fully my daughter's questions about America.

My fascination centered on Wyoming, a huge state (96,000 square miles), tiny population of 300,000 people (in 1950) and a Mecca for tourists. I noticed my first authentic Indian on the streets of Powell. I wasn't sure that I was seeing right. A question, directed at a passerby, elicited a strange look and a terse answer. "Indian? Yes, he is an Indian. And if you are lucky, you will see some of them riding horses. They still do. Not as many as in the past, but tradition and habits are maintained."

After my dinner lecture, I asked one of my hosts whether I could use my extra day by going into Indian territory. The request was considered to be a compliment to the local culture. My wish was immediately granted and a young man, the manager of one of the local shops, was assigned to guide me into the interior.

We left early the following morning. I watched him prepare himself for our relatively brief journey, about 50 miles. In addition to a pair of heavy boots, he loaded his car with sleeping bags, blankets and snow shovels. "You never know in Wyoming," he explained, noticing my surprised look, "what you might encounter in the middle of winter. We will be driving along deserted roads and it is not unusual to be hit by a sudden snowstorm from behind the mountains. The storm has its own characteristics. It turns every single snowflake into a blinding weapon. It creates white powder that settles on every object it encounters. Driving becomes impossible. The only way to deal with it is to close all windows, cover oneself with blankets, crawl inside the sleeping bags and be patient. Every year, there are a number of fatalities when people, unaccustomed to the changing moods of Wyoming weather, fail to take precautions."

We drove without meeting the "enemy," and we arrived at

a small, more civilized part of the state. The highway was wider and permitted our car to navigate between frequently encountered herds of cattle led by cowboys on horseback. From time to time, a colorful bird - which turned out to be a pheasant - escaped from the wheels of our car. My guide said there were brown bears and cougars in the mountains. The place was full of animals and birds, a great hunting area and tourist attraction.

At the end of the side road, a small, white house was to be our arrival point. Two large dogs greeted us with appropriate noises. Before we had a chance to stop the car and get out, an old man, beautifully crowned by a full head of white hair, opened the doors and greeted us with a warm smile and extended arms. I never learned his name. He never volunteered an introduction. Instead, the minute we entered the house - a kind of mini-museum - he began pointing at various objects explaining, describing and obviously delighted to have an occasion to talk about the people he lived among and the mementoes he acquired.

The old man, 78, was the local minister. He drifted into this Indian settlement a number of years ago. One of his professors at an eastern university suggested a research project: the Life of the American Indians. Upon arrival he found wigwams, Indians speaking their own dialects and a fair degree of contempt toward the white men. The year was 1901. It took him a good while to be accepted. It took him even longer to persuade them to consider wigwams as fairly inadequate protection against the weather. He built his own house using logs, instead of twigs and branches. It was the first solid structure erected in the village.

"Now," and his pride was distinctly visible. "I have this house and I have those precious items." A saddle that was given to him by the chief of White Ravens and a special carry-on bag for tobacco belonging to one of the chiefs from another Indian tribe. With enthusiasm and the energy of a much younger man, the pastor painted us a colorful canvas of the past. When he arrived, only a handful of people spoke English and only a handful were interested in learning how to read and write. Mothers treated their sick children by applying charms. Shoes were almost non-existent.

"Now," he pointed to a row of solid houses, to men and women walking with shoes, "things are different, better, more adapted to the climate and to the general improvement of the quality of life."

The man bubbled with pride and brimmed with happiness at being a witness of progress without attempting to bring himself into the center. He was just someone who started the process; the rest was the natural progression of human development.

"But let us go into the village," my guide suggested. "Let me show you some real people, real Indians whose lives are simple and yet fulfilled.

Running - he never walked - between whitewashed homes, he knocked on one of the doors and we found ourselves facing a family. A father, in his early forties, his wife and three children, for whom we were probably more of a curiosity than they were for us. When he informed them that I was from a distant European land called Poland, their facial expressions betrayed a mixture of disbelief and excitement. 'Where is that land?' the widely opened eyes were visibly asking.

The father, Don Deernose, his face reminding me of the color of autumn leaves, was not easy to converse with. The old minister tried his best, but it was rather obvious that my presence was an intimidating factor. He was looking at me the way one looks at exotic species. The children's eyes were focused on the stranger. In turn, I started feeling uneasy. Maybe we better leave, I thought. Then I noticed on the wall a color photograph of our host in full Indian regalia. His head was adorned with impressive feathers. His jacket, or rather his shirt, displayed richly woven gold patterns. Before I had time to ask a question, Don Deernose volunteered the explanation. "Once a year, we have a rodeo and we dress the way our forefathers dressed. And once a year we feel like real Indians."

"You really do?" interrupted our pastor. "On the day that you perform for white men, for tourists?"

Deernose almost blushed. "You are right, sir." he responded. "This is for a show, but I really feel the way that I described. By the same token we dress the same way on some Sundays and some special holidays. My wife," he pointed to a silent female observer crouching in the corner, "never wears white folks' dress. She is always an Indian woman."

Deernose regained his confidence and the story of his life followed, a story that I could not at first believe. The family owned a sizeable plot of land, large enough to sustain fifty heads of cattle. Don was born here and his father was a simple, illiterate rancher. But he was lucky enough to have a mother with high ambitions for her son. She was also limited and never learned English, having spoke an Indian language all her life. But somehow, somewhere, her ambitions led her to the decision to send her son away. "Where did you go?" I asked.

"To Harvard." Don answered, almost apologetically.

Upon graduation he was showered with job offers. Instead, he decided to return to his roots. The man from Harvard found in a tiny, remote corner of the state of Wyoming, and the old pastor, who after years of dwelling with the Indians probably thought more like them, remained in my mind as vivid examples of American reality. Both men were devoted to the ideal of giving anyone equal opportunity. Both chose the way of life that suited them best. Both, in my own interpretation, were missionaries of their faith.

I was leaving Wyoming with two thoughts in mind. One was the ecstasy of true discovery. The other was that I would be able to tell my little girl that I met and talked to real Indians, people who came to America first, long before white men invaded their territory.

Nebraska provided me with a different experience.

It was in York, a modest town located somewhere around Lincoln, not far from Grand Island, that I was scheduled to speak. My hosts, Mr. and Mrs. Robert Crooks, suggested almost at once that we - the family traveled along - should stay with them rather than going to an impersonal hotel. Our first meal at their kitchen table evolved into a full-scale discussion. We learned more about the way of life in a small American community. They asked not so much about the subject of my talk but much more about the way that we had managed to escape the ravages of the war and reunite the family. Marysia and my two youngsters felt at home within a few hours of arrival. Would that have been possible in Europe, we both asked ourselves?

The local club must have been a terrific magnet since about two hundred people assembled at the banquet hall in the local hotel.

As usual, the audience listened politely, gave me a warm round of applause, asked a series of fairly knowledgeable questions and dispersed well after 10 p.m. There was one rather frail lady who obviously had a problem with my Polish name and addressed me as Mr. Nagasaki. But another person came with a bright idea. "Do you think that after your visit here people may be a little more interested in American foreign policy? In events that only indirectly touched their daily lives, indirectly or not at all? Like the fact that young people in the Soviet Union are so deeply indoctrinated through their educational system?"

"How about doing a survey?" Marysia asked. "A public opinion polling using the local paper? We have a few days free before the next date."

Ruth Crooks jumped on it. "Great. I will call the editor. He is a friend of ours and he was at your lecture. Let's do it."

The series of questions printed on the front page. They were followed by an editorial, under my byline. York responded with the full force of suddenly unleashed energy and creativity.

'Yes, it is important to look outside,' came back a chorus of replies.

'No, it is interesting but not vital to our lives. We have enough to worry about in Nebraska,' responded a vocal minority.

"Is the educational process that you have observed in the Soviet Union not an element of learning about human nature?" one of the respondents asked. "Youngsters enrolled in the ranks of Octobrists, later entering another rigidly regulated group of Komsomol, are obviously apt to be molded the way that the system wanted them to be molded. Would we react differently in America to a similar situation? Or are we all adaptable enough to be responsive to whatever system is applied at our early age?"

At dinner tables, at local bars and even at the well-equipped bowling alley, the men and women of York thrashed out in arguments for and against. And the two of us, Marysia and I, watched delighted, proud and a little concerned about the little storm we were instrumental in unleashing.

All of them, on both sides of the argument, manifested to us the fallacy of pre-conceived notions. Men and women in a place like York, Nebraska were probably more receptive, more open to new ideas than individuals absorbed and overwhelmed by big city complexes, and often less than satisfactory existence.

The American plains, Nebraska and Kansas, were left behind. Montana, covered with snow and ice, extended its wide horizon of mountains, rivers, tall trees and almost deserted prairies. Then there was Utah, overwhelming visitors with its red rock formations that looked like forgotten temples from ancient times. Salt Lake City, featuring a very contemporary temple housing the headquarters of the Mormon Church, displayed architectural beauty combined with mystery hidden behind the upper chambers. On the streets and along the various roads where my journey took me, there was plenty of time to talk customs, religion and politics. Why did Harry Truman win? How do you explain the miracle of recent presidential elections that brought back the very man whose demise was loudly proclaimed by most of the newspaper pundits? My taxi driver was not at all surprised. "When things are going well, who wants to change horses? Foreign policy? What are you talking about? Yes, we heard that Harry was pretty tough on the Ruskies, but who cares? He promised to bring a number of federally financed projects to our state. That's what matters. But still Utah is and remains a solid Republican state. We are religious people. We are bound by tradition but we are also independent thinkers. Nobody in Washington can tell us how to live, how to work or even what kind of taxes to pay. Nobody."

We drove the rest of the trip in silence. The driver looked me over and probably decided at one point that I was a hopeless proposition. Besides, I was a foreigner, and not even a Mormon.

I was fascinated with the religion that created almost a welfare state for all its followers while on the outside of the church it propagated a conservative creed. Each Mormon, I was informed, donates ten percent of his pre-tax earnings to the church. In return he was fully covered with health and life insurance, private schools and even Brigham Young University. The elders of the church, led by a select patriarch, run the entire structure. Their decisions are shrouded in secrecy and are seldom, if ever, challenged. And the church is considered to be one of the most affluent religious institutions in the country. It all started with Brigham Young's journey.

It has continued uninterrupted for several decades with a steady flow of young, devoted missionaries replenishing the ranks of the faithful year after year. Mormons, I was informed, acted with discipline under orders from an authority they respected. They moved in groups, settled the land in groups and farmed in groups. Their prosperity depended entirely on each community. Families, not just men but also by women and children, paved their history.

There were other, rather fascinating aspects of this branch of Christianity that I was about to learn. The Church, through the teaching of Brigham Young, decided to build itself a political and territorial base. Salt Lake City was just the beginning. Later, around 1879, the Church issued a call to settle the area around Montezuma Creek, which was in danger of being settled by non-Mormons. The result of that call - to which Mormons dutifully responded - was the San Juan mission, later to be known as Hole-in-the-Rock expedition. Historians of the period outlined the danger of the expedition and of the heroism of the Mormons. Eighty-three wagons carrying the household goods of forty-six families, 107 children, some of whom were infants, over one thousand head of cattle and hundreds of horses, comprised the caravan. In some cases, men and women had to build roads they would drive over. But at the end of the mission, Mormons settled the land.

While I was admiring the impressive structure of the temple, I was totally oblivious to not only the past heroism of the members of the Church and their inbred obedience, but also of the imposed exclusivity of the church. Neither women nor blacks were considered worthy of membership. It took years before the temple doors cracked opened just barely wide enough for those "lesser" human beings to enter. But I still stood there, impressed, admiring the deep faith and deep devotion, thinking even about my own Roman Catholic Church and asking myself why it did not adopt a similar generous attitude towards its own flocks.

The learning experience during the stopover in Utah remained with me for years to come.

It was, however, time to leave. The next lecture was to be given in Mason City, Iowa. My Utah host drove me to the airport. "By the way," he mentioned when saying goodbye, "I am a bishop of my church. It was wonderful to notice your interest."

The bishop wore blue jeans, a cowboy hat and a brownish, tired shirt. I shook his hand, amazed, slightly put off and puzzled to no end. Was this an example of theological democracy?

American surprises awaited me all over the States. My journey took me to places where waitresses wore belts and pistols, where bartenders ordered their customers to stop drinking, where emotions ran high about the unwritten, but highly debated contest between Chico, California and Lafayette, Louisiana over which one had the oldest and highest oak tree. And when I finally arrived to my first stop in Port Arthur, Texas, my mind was barely able to keep up with stories heard from my hosts and audiences about the wonders that this particular state offered. Overwhelmed by the size of the ranches, by the pride of Texans and their disdain for other, smaller and "less developed" states, I traveled from Port Arthur to Loredo to Brownsville, and was greeted everywhere with the identical attitude.

On my way from San Antonio to Houston, we stopped in what looked like an empty spot. My host, a native Texan who knew his history, wore his boots and his ten-gallon hat with pride and whose face was etched with traces of both sand and sun, just looked at me. "What do you see?" he asked.

I looked around. In the distance I spotted a couple of houses. Behind them was a spiral indicating a church. Otherwise there was nothing.

My Texan friend said nothing. He put the car in gear and drove another quarter of a mile. Then he stopped facing a sign indicating the name of the settlement. In perfect Polish it said, "Panna Marja" (*Virgin Mary*).

"How come?" I exclaimed.

"It's a long story," he responded, obviously pleased by my astonishment.

In the middle of the last century, a Polish priest wandered into Texas. Somehow, he managed to come as far as San Antonio. He was amazed how well people lived, how easy it was to survive, and, remembering his own peasant roots and his family struggles in the poverty of the Polish countryside, he sent a message home. The essence of it was simple: 'I found a country of milk and honey. Come over. I am awaiting your arrival.'

And they came by the hundreds. They sold their farms and their belongings, and landed somewhere along the Gulf of Mexico. There was no other way to reach the priest but to walk. And they walked hundreds of miles. Their ranks were decimated by thirst and hunger and many perished after encountering venomous snakes. But many of them, maybe a hundred or less, met their priest here. Exhausted, hungry, in rags but full of gratitude to God for allowing them to get to the promised land, they settled and built this church. The priest, whose name was Moczygeba, watched, helped and officiated the first mass. How they managed to live, to finance the building, no one knows.

"Here we are, young man. And one day you may also want to build a church thanking the Almighty for bringing you to America."

I stood there with my eyes fixed on the portal of that unbelievable temple. Then I walked in and, in the total silence of the empty church, I offered my private, almost too emotional to describe, thanks.

The time was approaching for my return trip home. I covered over twenty towns and cities, delivered that many lectures, a number of radio and newspaper interviews, and participated in various private dinners, luncheons and breakfasts. My Topeka sponsors were clear in their instructions: never turn down an invitation. You are an important visitor. In addition, they pay for you. Be generous, otherwise they may not want any more of our speakers.

So I was generous, often exhausted but always fascinated by discovering the true America. This was not New York where most of the immigrants stop and settle. This was not even Chattanooga where we were isolated from the rest of the commonwealth. I looked at the vastness of the Texas plains, I marveled at the industriousness of small town entrepreneurs, and I inhaled with delight the air of friendship that awaited me at every stop, every dinner, and every home that opened its doors wide to a stranger.

We had traveled the length and the width of the continent, delivering a message from the European part that was controlled by a solidly entrenched foreign totalitarian regime. And you know what was a big surprise to us? They listened. They asked questions and they seemed to have been genuinely interested.

I could now answer my little girl's question with full conviction and knowledge.

"What is America, Daddy?"

America herself was also unsettled. The big war left major scars. Returning GIs were busy rebuilding families. Lonely wives attempted to accept back men who in some cases had become strangers. The national economy, having been fueled by the war machine, had to retool itself. Housing became a big problem and a new phenomenon. Homes available to returning soldiers with no money down revolutionized the market.

The newly elected president, whose humble roots made him a man of the people, was faced with the growing threat from the Soviet Union. Domestically, Harry Truman had to deal with considerable unemployment and the fear of inflation. Americans from all walks of life sensed the uncertainty of a peaceful future. Few of them were optimistic enough to foresee a possibility of a tremendous economic expansion. Even fewer were able to look into the crystal ball of the American role in the world. The war was won and the price paid by everyone extremely high. Truman, surrounded by a group of close advisers including Dean Acheson, General Marshal and others, made a bold decision. In order to rebuild devastated Europe and stem the flood of Communist ideology, a mass injection of American money and American technology was voted on by the United States Congress. The initial offer was extended to both Western and Eastern Europe. The Marshall Plan was born, the Plan that not only revitalized countries like France and Italy, but also provided large numbers of jobs at home.

For people like ourselves, this was a sign that the never-ending struggle to free our native land was entering into a new phase. Moscow vetoed any assistance to the Eastern European part of the continent. Washington was getting to the point of seriously recognizing the newly emerging danger in the postwar European continent.

The Cold War days were unfolding themselves in all their ugly colors. Men and women in Western Europe, tired of the war, dreaming of stability and personal security, looked across the Atlantic for both. After all, the reasoning went, America was an untouched continent. There were no ruins, no destroyed cathedrals, no bombed out cities. What can the Americans do to bring about an assurance that no more wars were on the horizon? What can they do, in addition to their contribution to the defeat of Germany, to make our lives livable? The newly initiated plan for economic revival was great, but how about the new threat from the East? How about working out some kind of an accommodation with the Soviet Union? How about it?

The Communist parties of France and Italy picked up the chant. There was nothing to fear from Moscow. The Kremlin had initiated the most powerful voices calling for peace. It was indeed there that international peace movements were born. It was in the Soviet Union that massive youth festivals calling for peaceful resolutions of international conflicts were organized. In the minds of millions of Western Europeans a thought was planted that the real obstacle for a peaceful solution was in America.

The exiled community of Eastern Europeans watched the spectacle in deep despair. In their homelands, where communist parties took over power and where Soviet generals were in charge of Polish, Czech and other armies, the mood could not have been more different. While in Western Europe, red flags were paraded along the main avenues of various capitals, in the East underground movements, dismantled after the German occupation, started coming back to life.

It was time for us to get re-involved.

12

Two Lives of a Salesman: Pots and Pans, and Ideas

It had to be a totally different way of involvement than what had existed in Scotland. There, running a press agency and working for the Polish Government in Exile combined working for the cause with making a living. In our newly selected land, of what we viewed full of unlimited opportunities, the two had to be totally separate. There were no subsidies available. We had to earn our keep. And yet the inner voice, strongly enforced by outer voices coming from Poles still living in Great Britain, called for an attempt to combine the two. The first opportunity occurred when I was appointed as representative of the newly created International Federation of Free Journalists. I was to fight for a status as Non-Governmental Organization accredited to the United Nations, and to keep the name of IFFJ alive.

The appointment came exactly at a time when I kept bread on the family table by learning how to cook, how to serve and how to convince my innocent, potential customers to buy waterless cooking utensils. What a great double challenge.

The challenge was met with mornings at the United Nations temporary headquarters at Lake Success in Long Island, and late afternoons and evenings cooking, baking, selling and cleaning someone else's kitchen. What fun and what satisfaction to convince the Chairman of the U.N. Sub-Committee on Freedom of the Press that our Federation should have a voice and then later sell a set of pots and pans.

The Chairman was a very nice and friendly Chilean. He was obviously on our side, but he was also an official of his government and a person given special responsibility by the United Nations.

We were friends outside of the meeting room, yet distant acquaintances when facing each other across formal gatherings.

The point person of the other side was the Yugoslav delegate. The man was smooth, articulate and well trained in the Marxist vocabulary. The days of his country's split with Moscow were still very much in the future.

"Well, Mr. Nagorski, you are suggesting that people like yourself are true representatives of free press in Eastern Europe, he told me. "If this is really correct, what are you doing in America? Why are your headquarters in London and not in Warsaw, or Budapest or Prague? You assert that the governments of your countries are not representative, but the people elected them. Why don't you go back and fight your battles on the home grounds, rather than poisoning the atmosphere of international bodies like ours?"

There was a movement of chairs among the delegates. There were exchanged glances between some of them. There was also an air of expectation. What is he going to say? How is he going to refute the basic accusation of being people without courage to fight their battles where the true enemy was?

The problem was that the same Yugoslav delegate was himself fighting a battle, a battle to keep me silent, to refuse permission for someone representing nobody to speak.

"His federation - his so-called federation - does not have any status. Why should we waste our time to listen to his tirades?" he continued.

In the manner that turned out to be a typical compromise for most of the international groups, the U.N. Subcommittee on Freedom of Information decided that I could submit a paper outlining the IFFJ position. But I was not allowed to speak and not allowed to partake in the deliberations.

I dutifully submitted a paper, I dutifully attended meeting after meeting, and I dutifully kept mum. And during the breaks, coffee hours, luncheons and cocktails times, I kept buttonholing delegates.

Some listened. Some were glad to share a drink. But most saw me as a missionary of a lost cause. And I felt like one.

To my surprise and relief, I found consolation during my evening activities of selling pots and pans.

Figure 1. Zyg and Marysia.

Figure 2. The Polish Army in Scotland during the war.

Figure 3. Maria, our firstborn, and I in Chattanooga.

Figure 4. The snake-charmer, Andrew, in Chattanooga.

Two Lives of a Salesman   153

Figure 5. The Foreign Service in Cairo.

Figure 6. Our "extended" Cairo family.

Figure 7. The Lumumba Saga and the convertible.

Figure 8. Marysia and Zyg in Korea.

Figure 9. Marysia (right), the tennis champion.

Figure 10. Our daughter, Terry, holding Andrew's firstborn.

Figure 11. The Hudson Institute in Vietnam.

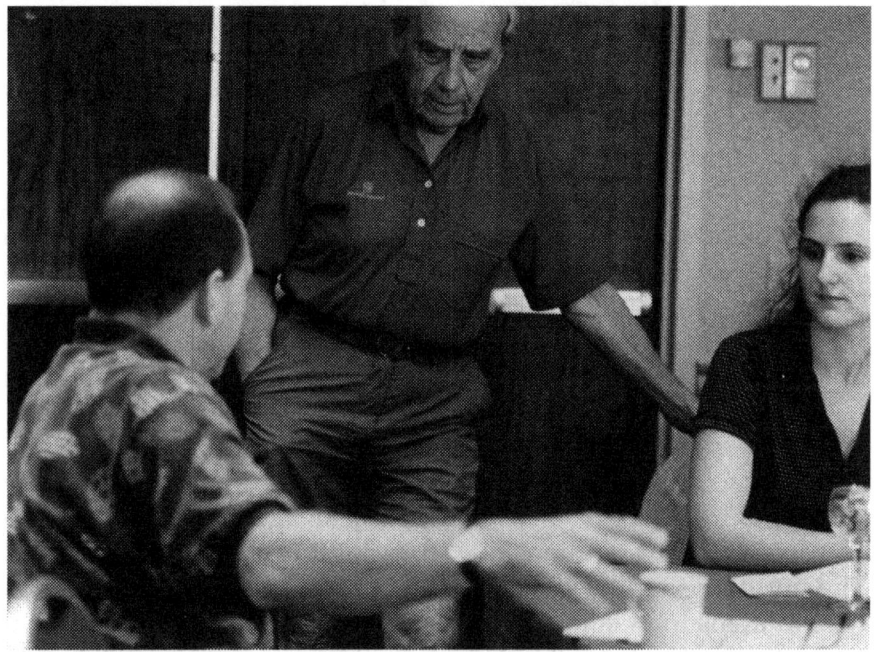

Figure 12. Our Center For International Leadership.

They were fun and there were discoveries. Fun in entering a modest home on the outskirts of New York City, fun in observing how carefully the hostess would prepare her table, put out her best china - usually from the local 5&10 store - and her carefully selected silverware. It was a relief to listen to the conversation of the guests - quite a few of them invited to a free dinner - talking about family, children, limited budgets and plans for long awaited vacations. They all sounded genuine. The artificiality of the diplomatic chitchat permeating morning gathering was missing. Men in corduroy pants and women in flowery dresses were addressing issues that affected real life. Others were paid to be just actors on a seemingly larger scene.

The two worlds, populated by similar human beings but molded by the society in different shapes, provided the newly arrived immigrant with powerful learning tools. Which one would I like to be? Which one would I like my children to grow up to be?

I did not know the answer. There were essentially two: one purely intellectual and the other emotional. But neither was to be rejected.

By day, I kept attending the Lake Success meetings; by night, I kept cooking dinners in strange homes. The contrast of these two exposures kept my mind sane, my body fed and my sense of purpose intact.

But at the same time doubts kept creeping into our minds, doubts focusing on the possibility of combining the two to remain faithful to the principal reason for choosing the exiled existence and to integrate us into the mainstream of the American life.

The two stages of that journey led to a third one. The first one was to attempt making a living by being an agent of a London outfit specializing in sending food and clothing packages to Poland. The outfit, created by an old friend, allowed relatives and friends to ship items to Poland, that were in very short supply there. In a tiny office on 42nd Street in New York, Marysia and I went to work. An ad in a local Polish language paper did the trick. Americans of Polish origin were eager to help. For the following six months or so, the tiny percentage of money invested in the project, supplemented our otherwise very meager income.

The second to provide Western media with uncensored and untarnished news from the countries that found themselves barred from the outside world by what Winston Churchill described as the Iron Curtain.

And the third one, emanating from the previous two, had us entering the ranks of American civil servants.

One of the highlights was a speech that I was invited to deliver at the Seventeenth Annual Convention of the American Newspaper Guild. The occasion took place in June 1950 at the Hotel Statler in Washington. I acted as an official delegate of the International Federation of Free Journalists. It was there that the credentials of the Federation were not only accepted, they were venerated.

The ballroom was packed. The usual theatrics of a major American convention were all in place: booths selling books and artifacts, placards announcing future events, men in funny hats and women dressed in seemingly native costumes. Observing the scene, I felt butterflies fluttering in my stomach. Within the next few minutes, I was expected to take the platform and the microphone and address the mass of humanity.

There were at least seven to eight hundred people awaiting my performance. I had a message, didn't I?

The appearance of the representative of the exiled and voiceless journalists from Eastern Europe was sandwiched between two rather major speakers. A Canadian newsman, pleading for Canadian representation within the Guild, spoke just before my turn. He deplored the existing conditions in Canada, different organizational problems in Toronto and Montreal, and lack of cooperation between the two.

Aren't they lucky? Being able to have problems of that kind?

Harry Martin, President of the American Newspaper Guild, introduced me in glowing words. He praised our Federation, describing it as a fighting unit. He was a friend and a committed supporter.

"I give you Brother Zygmunt Nagorski, delegate to the International Federation of Free Journalists."

A sea of faces turned in my direction. I slowly walked up to the podium. 'What is America, Daddy?' flashed through my mind. This is it, an America that is willing to listen to your daddy.

"I am bringing to you greetings from a group of twelve-hundred men and women, all of them your professional colleagues. My words probably evoke in your imagination pictures of editorial and composing rooms, parking lots with cars awaiting photographers and reporters, and a huge classified ad department. You are wrong. The greetings that I am bringing to you come from a man who used to be a nationally known reporter but who today edits, sets and distributes, all by himself, a duplicated sheet in a displaced people's camp in Germany. Greetings from a woman who only recently was employed as a copy reader in a busy Hungarian daily and who fled her country searching for the lost freedom of her profession. Greetings from a man who is too old and too sick to work and who lives on potatoes and black bread and his thoughts are about his past, crowned with a very successful career as an editorial writer.

"Why did I come to you? Our people at home expect that you, having in your hands the most effective means of public information, a newspaper, will go on a crusading mission. That you will not stick to flat, pedestrian stuff, killing the interest of your readers in anything else besides their own immediate circle. That you will act not only as educators but also as guardians of American democracy. That you will come into the open, fiercely exposing these forces which have already conquered and subjugated twelve independent countries of Europe, bringing to them the darkest regimes of dictatorship and complete control over the body and the soul of man."

There was a thunderous applause. I basked in it, never for a moment realizing that I was asking my American colleagues to transform their papers into something they are not: advocates of a political mission. I learned during my Chattanooga days that two could co-exist and that I also learned that there was a big difference between the mission of the *Polish Press Agency* in Scotland and the reporting for *The New York Times* or *Kansas City Star* or any other American newspaper. Fortunately, my audience, members of the Guild, gave me a reception, which in my mind blurred the difference.

To follow the Canadian call for recognition was not as challenging as to be followed by the President of the United States. It was almost at the last minute that I was informed about the President's timetable.

Harry Truman arrived almost unnoticed. There was a flurry of preparation, a call for attendees to vacate the room prior to his speech, but nothing to compare with the pomp and fanfares that FDR liked and preferred. Sitting in the second row, I had ample time and a clear view to listen and to observe.

Followed by a couple of assistants, the President walked briskly to the podium. His steps were springing, his focus on the audience which he obviously wanted to appraise before speaking. Dressed in a gray suit and a blue tie of nondescript design, Truman gave the impression of an ordinary, modest and simple individual. And he was all of the above. He was also not a great orator. In his speech, which he read carefully without attempting to add a little fire into rather descriptive text, he talked about the role of trade unions, about the way that the communist regimes control labor and about the way that American money and know-how, exemplified by the Point Four Program, helped to eradicate hunger and misery in the third world. He cited Northern India. It was there, in the Terai district that malaria forced people to leave the land; one hundred and four villages were totally abandoned. The World Health Organization's malaria control team arrived and sprayed the area with DDT. A year later, no infected mosquito was to be found. Villagers went home and revitalized the region.

Then he talked briefly about the war in Korea and unprovoked communist aggression. But his key issue was the American concern for the human misery in Asia and Africa. I was waiting for a word or two about the European fate in our part of the continent, but there was just silence.

The audience arose and applauded. The President left and so did I. Leaving the convention hall, I kept hearing Canadian voices still pleading their cause. I was wondering what kind of reflections Harry Truman left behind. After all, he was pleading the cause of free trade unions and telling the assembled newsmen about the good news of America feeding the hungry world, reminding them of a struggle going on between the forces of democracy and communism. How much of his message, I wondered, the listeners would retain among the steady diet of much more mundane messages: pay scale, collective bargaining, and even home rule for Washington, D.C. And would anything that I had to say be rescued from the flood of speeches and declarations?

But here I was, a refugee, an unknown quantity and a young

man desperately looking for a job, walking out of an occasion that permitted me to be on the same platform with the President of the United States.

"What is America, Daddy?"

13

South America

It was shortly thereafter that somewhere and somehow an idea was born in someone's mind to send me on a voyage. Our home life still evolved around daily chores. Our attention span to the little ones was steadily interrupted by the urgent need to earn a living. Marysia thought about getting a job and I kept hunting. In between, I also kept writing, an escape from the tough reality of adjusting. Deeply immersed in the Polish syndrome of anti-communism, my writing centered on life in my native land. I knew a fair amount about it, we both were fed a steady diet of news from Eastern Europe and the habit, acquired in Scotland to keep voicing our concern about the Soviet Union, prevailed.

The Christian Science Monitor developed into my principal outlet. It was widely read at that time, the 1950's, and some of the articles caught the attention of a man who was in charge of North American Newspapers Alliance. A call from NANA, as it was known in the profession, came out of the blue. "We are interested in investigating communist influence in Latin America. This is a continent where poverty, illiteracy and unjust distribution of natural resources create a perfect climate for Marxist ideas to flourish. How about going there? How about writing a series of dispatches from the key countries - Argentina, Brazil, Peru and Chile - and uncovering the reality of the political climate? Talking to people from all walks of life? Interviewing some of the major Communist activists?"

I listened in disbelief. I had never been to the Southern continent before. I didn't speak Spanish or Portuguese. How was I going to manage?

I did not know. Neither did my editor nor my wife. But the lure was too strong to be a working journalist again, to explore totally new territory, to earn enough money to muddle through the next couple of months and be assured of an outlet in print.

It was indeed new territory, a fascinating possibility to explore the *terra incognita*. What did I know about that vast continent lying to the South of us? I knew so little that I could indulge in the luxury of letting my imagination run wild. That imagination provided a canvas of rather primitive people, desperate living conditions and a number of isolated islands of prosperity. But I also saw in the corners of that imaginary canvas dark forces looming on the horizon, ready to exploit misery, ready to establish the same system that was earlier superimposed on my own native land. What would be a more challenging, a more daunting task for a fellow like me, who knew so much more about the real nature of the communist regime than anyone in an atmosphere of relative freedom?

I jumped into the assignment with the zeal of a neophyte suddenly transformed into a role of a writer-missionary. It was fortunate that my editors were not privy to my thoughts, that they could not read my imagination. Peacefully, they sat behind their desks in New York City, convinced that they had acquired a new reporter.

The first stop was Chile. It was there that the Nobel Laureate poet Pablo Neruda towered over the entire Marxist establishment. Around him gathered the cream of the crop of the intellectual elite. On the fringes were workers organized within the powerful trade union dominated by the Communist Party. I knew all about that before I landed in Santiago. The trip was long. It also offered the unique excitement of going by air. Air travel was not as yet fully developed. The thrill of flying at 20 thousand feet was overwhelming.

Little did I know that the thrill of flying was bound to be overshadowed by the thrill of discovery, discovery of a new continent and its political convulsions and discovery of Polish footprints left all over that continent. I was traveling as an American journalist. The natives quickly perceived my European roots. The combination of the two opened more doors than I ever expected. The key door was the one with a huge label: *Latin America*. The other one was centered on the Polish Diasporas scattered all over the continent.

My assignment was rather narrow in scope, although I perceived it as vast. My editor saw the Southern part of the American continent of limited interest. But there was one aspect of it that caught his imagination: the communist influence. He knew about my obsession with the subject and he saw in my previous writings a passion and a dedication. They were there, no doubt about it. What neither of us, the editor and the writer, stopped long enough to analyze were the roots of the movement in Latin America. I saw it through the eyes of an Eastern European exile, unable to return to a home controlled and occupied by the party that was a tool of the Soviet Union. The editor, a Midwest American, saw it differently. First, he saw a story. Then he saw an opportunity to capitalize on the anti-communist crusade that was in full swing in the States. My articles were reprinted from coast to coast. The mere fact that I was not an unbiased observer was not obvious to the readers. I was sailing on the wave of popular trend. The other fact was my own inability to dig deeper into the socio-economic conditions that led people to embrace Marxism and to have a blind eye observing lights and shadows of communism in practice. Moscow could do no wrong as far as Chileans and Peruvians were concerned. After all, the Soviet Union was run by working people, there was no unemployment and on the surface, there was no large discrepancy of income. Pablo Neruda, the national poet and treasure of Chile, proudly carried his party card. He was a social communist, offended and grieved by conditions under which his own countrymen had to live.

Chile was where I met three remarkable people: two priests and one poet. The priests were both Polish. The poet was Pablo Neruda. Let me start with Neruda, the very man who captured the imagination of young and old alike, and whose romantic poetry earned him global fame. The very man whose voice, on behalf of the poor and disenfranchised, made him a man to follow, whose political affiliation with the communist movement was much more a voice of a prophet than that of an agitator. Unable to find understanding of his message among his country's Christians groups, he wrapped himself in the red flag. But it was not a flag that was catching the wind of the Red Square in Moscow. It was much more the only flag he found at his disposal, also a flag that he saw defending Spanish democracy.

Neruda witnessed the Spanish Civil War while living in Madrid. It was there that he wrote his remarkable book, *Espana en el Corazan* (Spain in My Heart). It was remarkable not only due to its content but because of the way it was produced, in an old monastery that improvised as a printing shop. There was a shortage of paper pulp; therefore, any kind of material was good enough, including enemy flags or the bloodstained shirts of Moorish soldiers.

He was gracious enough to receive me. But I went there not fully realizing neither the strength of his personality nor his power as a poet. The year was 1956, two years after his return to Chile from his diplomatic post in Spain, and thirteen years before he entered the political arena as a presidential candidate. I faced him with a set of naïve, probably stupid, journalistic questions related to his communist affiliations. Faithful to my trade and my mission, I failed to realize that I was facing a giant. I later read some of his poems translated into English. I saw a film depicting his relationship with ordinary people, called *The Postman*. Even later, in my life reflections, accounting for accomplishments and failures, I judged the meeting with Neruda to have been a massive failure.

Years later, I bumped into his own reflections on poetry.

And it was at that age... poetry arrived
in search of me. I don't know, I don't know where
it came from, from winter or a river
I don't know how or when,
no, there were not voices, there were not
words nor silence
but from a street I was summoned,
from the branches of night,
abruptly from the others,
among violent fires
or returning alone,
there I was without a face
and it touched me.
I did not know what to say, my mouth
had no way
with names

my eyes were blind,
and something started in my soul,
fever or forgotten wings,
and I made my own way,
deciphering
that fire
and I wrote the first faint line,
faint, without substance, pure
nonsense,
pure wisdom
of someone who knows nothing,
and suddenly I saw
the heavens
unfastened
and open,
planets,
palpitating plantations,
shadow perforated,
riddled.

A poem of a man searching, searching, searching...

The two priests were more like two Apostles, preaching and practicing Christ's gospel. They did it in their own, peculiar way, one through warnings and the other through pure, unadulterated charity. Both decided to devote their lives to what they considered to be the highest goals of a modern, developing society. The warning focused on the danger of communism. The charity was focused exclusively upon lonely and abandoned children. The two common denominators linking the two men were their professions and their nationality. Both were Catholic priests. Both were born and educated in Poland.

The Rev. Michal Poradowski, educated at the University of Warsaw and at the Sorbonne, drifted into Santiago six years earlier. He spent his first two years learning about the new country. His conclusion was that Chileans were in desperate need to be educated about the true nature of communism. They had illusions, which were far from Soviet reality. They were dreamers. They had to be awakened to face the danger.

Through unbelievably hard work and minimal resources, Poradowski had initiated a quarterly publication, "Studies of Communism." Within a year, the publication earned itself the reputation of a serious and a unique contribution to the issue. The priest, in order to survive, secured himself a professorship at the University of Valparaiso, a three-hour commute with a forty-dollar a month salary. His aim, when I met him, was to secure one hundred dollars a month. "If we get that much, our work could be really effective." He looked at me as someone coming from a real, affluent world of North America. 'Could you help?' his eyes were asking.

"Do you understand that the Soviet Union has an army of people whose job it is to convince Chileans that their future lies with the system that rules in Moscow? That America and the free market economy are the enemy?"

I stood there, helpless, impressed, convinced and at the same time, fully aware that the crusading priest will have to continue his crusade alone. I am just a reporter. I responded to his silent plea, just an observer who will certainly communicate his plight to whoever will be reading my dispatches. But this is all I can possibly do and a wire went out to my New York home to send at least the first hundred dollars to my newly discovered friend.

Another one also waited for my visit.

He was short and chubby. His clerical garb had seen better days. He was constantly on the run, looking, searching and discovering. After his escape from his native Poland and settling in this far away Latin American country, father Szymon Wojcicki made a shocking discovery one day. The steady flow of refugees from Eastern Europe brought to Chile were men and women without skills, without professions and, naturally, without Spanish. They were lost, and unskilled jobs were few and far between. Whatever they were paid was barely adequate to feed a family. Those who suffered the most were children. Desperate parents, hoping that strangers would take pity on their offspring, abandoned them. Walking at night, the priest noticed tiny human beings clinging to each other in a desperate gesture, calling for help.

There was very little hesitation; he took them home to be fed and sheltered, and to have, for a little while, a sense of belonging. Gradually, our priest's gesture turned out to be an avocation. Most of the children were Polish. Most of their parents were eager to get them back once they secured a decent earning. Father Szymon and his actions became a symbol of hope. Reclaimed children provided parents with tangible proof that they were not alone, that somehow, human kindness and human love prevailed. In a country where life was extremely hard especially to new arrivals, the sudden appearance of this apostle of supreme charity lightened up the horizon.

I left the country leaving behind all three of these apostles, each one different but each one with a mission.

I was determined to observe their way of living. The City of God, the very name that would offend God Himself, lay on the outskirts of Lima, Peru. An overcrowded bus took me to that very place. There was an almost abrupt end to the city. No more regular, individual homes, no more apartments; instead, on top of sandy, almost desert-like terrain, strange structures caught outside observers' eyes. Constructed between several bamboo sticks, the ground covered with dirty, nondescript pieces of rugs, no running water, no electricity or gas, the structures housed Lima's poor humanity. The area around and in between piles of foul smelling garbage covered with flies, served as playgrounds for masses of children. They were half naked, their limbs looked fragile, as if they were the dried and brittle limbs of a dying tree, their tummies stuck out in the telltale signs of hunger.

It was named the City of God to indicate that mortal humans are either unable or uninterested in getting involved, and that only God could help the inhabitants. I was informed that several thousand similar structures had been erected. Each housed a family and, when translated into numbers, it was easily calculated that on average, between five and eight people shared every one of these "homes." There were no schools, no government assistance or medical facilities. Children born in the City of God had little chance to escape poverty during their lifetime.

The City of God was a perfect setting for radical ideas; it was also a breeding ground for communism. But was it similar to the party faithful in Eastern Europe or to the French left wing, composed of two hundred and thirty-five recognized 'intellectuals'? To Americans impressed by Joseph Stalin? I immersed myself in that island of forgotten humanity, asking questions, taking pictures and wondering what kind of article should I write. I finished by sending a dispatch, calling for American money to be used to provide decent housing that would eliminate the need for the City of God. But what would be the answer from some American readers who keep observing urban ghettos in their own backyard? Maybe at least the message would be understood as indicating that inhabitants of the City of God are seeing communism as the only way to escape the dread of their existence or that they are not ideological brothers of men marching under red banners in Moscow?

Maybe. But the beginning, the origin of the *Ciudad de Dios*, was not far from the origin of the Marxist revolution. Men and women who left Lima responded to a call from a powerful political party issued on Christmas Eve 1954. They trusted these callers, in a way that Russian masses originally trusted Lenin and his followers. Human nature - easily manipulated - does not recognize frontiers. Within days, a crowd estimated at ten thousand people, left the capital city in search of a better life. They were convinced that in the desert, away from the restrictions and control of a big city, they would be free and, one day, prosperous. Armed with bamboo sticks and equipped with homemade mats, they started a community. They built themselves shacks covered with hay and old pieces of clothing. They established strict perimeters for every family with no tolerance for trespassing. They also assumed that the tiny piece of land that the family occupied was theirs. In fact, it wasn't. The land belonged to the state. Months and years passed, and the City of God saw little improvement. The opportunity for political discontent offered itself and was immediately exploited by communists. It turned out to be fertile ground. The community, composed of the poorest of the poor, had no place to go, no one to call its representative and no one with whom to pray. The Catholic Church, a powerful voice in the predominantly Catholic nation, was only mildly involved with that desperate, forgotten community.

The inhabitants of the City of God had only Him to rely upon.

Preoccupied with my journalistic mission, I jumped from one extreme to another: from the dust and dirt of the City of God to the luxury of private clubs, from the misery of people condemned to poverty to the endless possibilities offered to energetic and sometimes not very ethical entrepreneurs, and from men and women whose only means of transportation were their own legs to youngsters driving the latest model cars. One of the inhabitants of the City of God casually remarked that it was cheaper to kill a person than to injure one. It cost less to pay a fine for killing than to be responsible for hospital bills.

I kept listening. I kept wondering who, under the circumstances, could be strong enough to resist calls for radical change. Would I? Would anyone? Are the grounds for a revolution - left or right - ripe and ready to be harvested?

My radar moved swiftly to another place, another group of people waiting for a change. Brazil, the largest of the South American countries and into Santos, the world's largest coffee port, located outside of Sau Paulo, the busiest and the most polluted part of that vast sub-continent. It is there that roughly six thousand longshoremen made their living loading and unloading coffee. They were poorly educated men but by the time I visited them, there were already the beginning rumblings of discontent. They were talking, thinking and wondering what to do about better wages, more rights and more job security. Antonio Barbosa, a 37-year-old man looking older but dreaming of retiring at forty-five, shared with me some of his dreams.

Antonio was known among his friends and colleagues as a very hard-working man. He was working on average twelve nights a month in addition to his regular daily shifts. There were times when he stayed on the docks for three days and two nights in a row. He needed the money. He had a farm that had to be paid off. He sent money to help his mother who lived in Northern Brazil, his native land. In a good month, Antonio could make as much as $140. When I met him, he confessed that times were not so good any more. In the last five months his services were needed for eighteen days and nights only.

"Was there a shortage of ships?" I inquired.

"Not at all," Antonio replied. But he did not want to work on Brazilian ships. The government, in order to keep domestic prices down, has set up different wage scales for domestic and foreign loads. A longshoreman who got a Brazilian assignment was paid about 33 cents a ton; a foreign job jumped to 50 cents. It took Antonio, working in a team of 12 men, about eight hours to load 5,000 bags or 300 tons of coffee.

"Hard work?" I inquired.

"Coffee was the easiest cargo to work with," he replied. "But altogether we need a change. Our earnings are not adequate. Our retirement pay forces men who are over sixty to continue working. So most of the men are figuring out how to make our lives a little more bearable. Various political parties come along with suggestions."

"Is the Communist Party among them?"

"Of course, but few of us take it seriously. The problem is that the management calls anyone who complains a communist. That is really not very helpful."

"But...But..." and two other men joined the conversation. "The Communist Party is a well-organized entity. They are good speakers. They attend all the meetings. They vote while others don't bother to. And they tell us that the party looks after our welfare and fights for better wages. So we follow."

Antonio kept nodding but, probably for my benefit, added a few words of explanation. "We are not sure," he said, "what kind of philosophy is behind the party. What does it really stand for? We also know that Americans are against it and Americans are also very human. When men are working on American vessels and have to carry coffee bags a distance of more than twelve feet, Americans provide additional help. Few other foreigners ever think of doing the same. So," continued Antonio, "we are caught between our desire for change and of improving our quality of life. What the communists promise and working with Americans."

At the time that I was around, the Party was definitely on the upswing. But this was not the party of Lenin and Stalin. It was a party of hope within the reality of Brazilian life.

I also left the southern continent with a set of impressions that were not exactly what I was anticipating.

Spread of communism in the American minds, and even more so in the minds of the Eastern European exiled community, meant the spread of Soviet ideology. Returning home, after writing a series of articles and a slew of memos, I penned my final paper suggesting that communism in Latin America was making steady progress, but it was not the type of movement that was taking place in Western Europe or in the United States. It was true that leaders thought along Marxist-Leninist lines. "Others," I wrote, "are communists either through poverty, lack of intellectual stimulation, need of some kind of an idea worth fighting for, or through their extreme anti-U.S. feelings. Their communism was born out of negation. Often they called themselves communists simply because they heard others calling them as such in response to their grievances and complaints."

This was the case in Washington during the McCarthy's witch-hunt. Anyone criticizing the Wisconsin Senator, or his activities, was branded a communist.

In the Southern continent, the issue was much more complicated. The Party and its faithful followers secured a hold on a much more powerful issue: nationalism. It identified itself with the inbred urge to be sovereign and independent, to fight over the very nature of the Monroe Doctrine and to capitalize on anti-American sentiments rooted deeply within the sense of unwanted dependence. The Party, in many countries, was willing to tolerate private ownership compared to unselfish and generous economic assistance from the Soviet Union with American aid often linked with security considerations. Lack of a forceful rebuttal from the Northern neighbor helped some Latinos to conveniently overlook the political strings attached to Soviet involvements.

I got a capsule of my hosts' thinking from one of the friendly, pro-American souls.

"Communism," he said, "is presented to our people as a challenge. It is a new religion with high-sounding principles and full of mysticism. So we grab it and build it up in our minds into something for which is worth fighting for." Then he looked at me with the fervor of a man looking for answers. "What are you giving us to offset that new and challenging ideology? Capitalism? But capitalism is only a way of improving one's living standards. Who would be willing to fight for it? Nobody in Latin America, anyway." It was high time for me to head home. On my itinerary was post-Peron Argentina, and economically troubled Uruguay.

I was bringing back home a justification for communist successes, demolishing the prevailing dogma of Soviet attractiveness as an ideology, in spite of my Chilean friend's vocal description of the lack of appeal of capitalism as a system. I was also bringing back, for myself, a sense that in assessing foreign and often hostile trends abroad, one should beware of applying our own Eastern European norms to different cultural and economic situations.

I was going home a little wiser.

14

Moments of Reflection

Somewhere along the long road, toward the ultimate goal of finding all of us a new nest, a new country and a new association to create an atmosphere of a family home, it was necessary to stop and reflect. That moment came when a firm offer arrived to join the United States Government.

It came cold. A piece of paper advising me that a background check was about to begin and that it was going to take time, considering the fact that I had been living abroad for some time. Some time? How about the first twenty-six years of my life? How about seven years spent in uniform under foreign commands? But it was to begin. Maybe it won't take forever. Maybe one of these days I will be allowed to report to work in one of the imposing buildings belonging to the federal government.

Behind the impersonal piece of paper, there was a human being. The mailman looked at me with a quizzical eye. "What's so exciting, young man? Do they want you to enlist?"

"Almost," I said. And I kept him standing in front of our house for a quarter of an hour, listening to the highlights of our journey. He was patient and curious. Perhaps, he was also a little jealous. I was a newly arrived immigrant. He was a native born American. I was offered a chance to have a meaningful job. He was fifty-seven years old, most of his life spent delivering letters written by strangers. He never met anyone whose letters he carried. He never knew of the joy or sadness that they brought. My case was one of the rare occasions for him. He saw joy in my eyes. He saw expectations and fear at the same time. So, he stood patiently while I talked.

My little piece of paper with official letterhead came just in time.

A small army of federal agents descended upon my friends, casual acquaintances and even family members. They asked questions, they probed and they cajoled.

"Has he ever been a member of the communist party? Have you ever noticed his tendencies to be attracted by people of the same sex? What kind of books and magazines does he read? Would you describe him as leftist in his political leanings?"

Somehow, I passed the muster. Marysia and the kids escorted me to the door on my way to my first day of work. Slowly, deliberately, I entered the building housing the United States Information Agency on New York Avenue. Someone directed me to my office; someone else gave me a badge. It was now official. I was in. I had become a federal employee.

The room was medium size with a window facing north. Close to it, a female figure sat and greeted me. "I'm Eleanor," she said flatly, "and I will be your secretary." There was neither curiosity nor even a slight indication of a welcome. She remained seated, her back to my desk located at another corner of the room. I tried to say something to the effect that this was my first day ever in this new capacity and that I was really pleased to have been appointed as a new head of the International Branch. There was no reaction. Eleanor appeared to be totally absorbed in her work. She sat behind a typewriter busily typing away.

I was not prepared for the totally unexpected situation. Eleanor was black. I had never worked with black people before. I observed them in Chattanooga and I watched them when they would come to our house to perform all kinds of chores. But here I was to be a boss, a white man whom she probably resented. Later, during our rather turbulent working relationship, I was able to understand more and learn a lot.

Eleanor was from Mississippi. Her parents were sharecroppers and she was the fifth of their eleven children. She was the only one who went to high school and later, to a secretarial school. Her dream was to go college to one day. In the meantime, she was offered a job at USIA at entry level. Most of her peers were also black. Most of her superiors were white. Some of them were from the South, harboring a traditional attitude toward the other race. Eleanor became bitter. And when she was told that her new boss was a newly minted citizen, someone who immigrated to America a few years earlier, her bitterness increased. "Don't we have enough of our own people?" she grumbled to her friends.

Unaware of the mood of the person who not only was to share my room but also be a vital part of the job I was assuming, I tried cheerfulness, plus a touch of humor, as a way of breaking the ice. Nothing worked. Eleanor avoided eye contact. She entered our common office with her sight focused on her desk. She took instructions with obvious reluctance. She would not take dictation. "How am I supposed to write letters, memoranda, notes?" she muttered. "You type them yourself," she answered in a barely audible voice, "and I will retype them clearly."

It took me a few weeks before I realized that she was unsure of her spelling and that her grammar left a lot to be desired. She was also afraid of misunderstanding my accent. But I learned all of that much later. There was suppressed anger, disappointment and an unfriendly climate on that first day.

My colleagues - heads of other branches organized geographically - were not much help. But my immediate boss understood the situation at once. He sat me down in his office and I looked in almost disbelief at the agility of the man. He was crippled. Of the FDR generation, he was felled by polio at the age of ten and his world circled around a wheelchair ever since.

Irving Wechsler was a man with a philosophical approach to life. I was the new kid on the block and he was determined to do his utmost to make me feel at home.

"Yes," he said, "she does resent you. Do you really blame her? Her entire family lived in a segregated America. She was exposed to white people who, in more instances than one, viewed her as an inferior species. She was hired a year ago and you are her third boss. She doesn't know what to expect. You know what?" Wechsler smiled with a touch of satisfaction. "Why don't you smother her with kindness? Why don't you permit her to sin, to make mistakes, to relax even if she makes a mess out of your first memoranda? How about it?"

It was a tall order for someone who entered that fragile china shop with the firm intention of doing the best he could, and for someone whose rigor of work was always a priority. How could I achieve my objectives without breaking any china and without making major mistakes if my own secretary, my right hand, had to be nursed and allowed to err? But I sensed that Wechsler was on the right track.

He was to become my guide and my father confessor. Wechsler loved to talk. He loved to discuss other people's problems and I had plenty of these. Why did I join the government so late in life, he kept asking. I know that forty-four is not exactly old age, but when he was my age, he had already fifteen years of Federal service under his belt. I had to remind him, meekly, that it has been only a few years since I got my citizenship and that it was barely eight years since we came to the United States. Was he listening? I was not sure. Slightly enamored by the sound of his own voice, Wechsler kept talking.

He was the product of an Ivy League school (Yale) and a WASP family. One of his brothers was a federal judge. The other brother was a high official at the Pentagon.

Wechsler was the only one in the family who caught polio, but not once, not ever, had I heard him complain. His attitude was that of a man who was perfectly content with the way he lived. He also had an almost unlimited ability to absorb other people's gripes and to understand other people's inability to face the normal difficulties of life.

He was obviously intrigued by my joining USIA. Of the five branches that his division comprised, mine was the least defined. The others dealt with Africa, Latin America, Soviet Union and Western Europe. The International Branch was a conglomerate. Our job was to look at international organizations sponsored by the Soviet Union, to monitor radio outputs of various communist states and to provide the Agency with statistical data on a monthly basis of the number of newspapers, magazines and periodicals that the other side produced. In short, the branch was to be a watchdog, providing solid information on the activities of the Soviet blocs. My team of six analysts assisted me with the job.

There was a statistician, a middle age Armenian with whom I at once struck a solid bond of friendship. Another was a film buff, whose assignment was related to the Communist output in the film industry. The third, a rather pedestrian fellow who spent his days compiling excerpts from Soviet, Polish, Hungarian and other communist dailies. We were all direct products of the Cold War, and I was hired on the basis of the articles I had published during my Latin American trip. But Wechsler knew, and I felt it shortly after my first day in office, that I was a painted bird.

Henry Loomis, the head of the office of Research and Intelligence, who offered me the job, was probably looking for diversity. Did he get it? I wasn't sure. Without fully realizing it, I was entering the vast world of federal bureaucracy totally unprepared. I was almost drunk with joy. Here I was, barely accustomed to the American way of life, suddenly becoming a member of the Federal work force, with a job description fitting so much into everything we stood for.

But now, as of October 1956, I was to have a new powerful partner. The United States Information Agency became my principal base. Wechsler observed my own attempts to get integrated into his tiny family with a smile and a large dose of tolerance. He was fully aware of my enthusiasm and almost missionary zeal. I was a perfect example of an anti-communist Pole. And yet, I was supposed to work and act as an American, not an Eastern European. That distinction was blurred in my mind. In the same way that I attempted to transplant the way I kept writing in Scotland to a daily newspaper in Tennessee, I kept committing the same error in my first months within the Agency. My internal memoranda were all geared towards a different audience that I, alone, was writing for. I was no longer a lonely voice representing the Polish Government in Exile. I was just one of a multi-voice organization writing for the upper strata of the American bureaucracy.

The dramatic example of my lack of proper focus came very shortly after I started working. The Hungarian Uprising brought all of us to the state of urgent alert. The White House, as well as the State Department, was calling for comprehensive analysis and I was assigned the task of writing it. Instead of producing a detached, policy-oriented paper, I wrote a lengthy attack on the Soviet Union and its intervention that was squashing the uprising. I naturally included facts and figures justifying Hungarian defiance. But it was a propaganda tract, and not something that policy makers could use for their purpose.

My bosses read it as soon as I produced it. There was a strict deadline. They were disappointed but never said so in as many words. "This is not exactly what we had in mind," remarked Henry Loomis, softly.

Wechsler rapidly assembled a team of seasoned writers and a proper policy paper was dispatched to the White House. I was left to suffer to no end. Weschler nursed me through that crisis the same way as he had when Eleanor drove me to the wall.

In the meantime, Eleanor was almost always late. She kept leaving classified documents on her desk. Wechsler knew all that. He was familiar with the phenomenon that for me bordered on insubordination.

"Remember," he kept repeating during his long-winded perorations, "you will be judged not only on the solidity of your work but also on the way you work with other people. Relationships with the men and women who work for you are a very important element. Especially," he winked, "when someone is of a different color."

I listened, barely comprehending. Do I really have to change my way of looking, judging, responding in order to be a team player? Do I really have to change or radically curb my natural instincts in order to fit into the general mold?

I should have, but I did not. The results were predictable, but I was not ready or willing to face reality. I spent almost ten years in the Federal government. I was never promoted. I remained in my grade for the entire period. At one point, I was functionally demoted. All this was in the future. In the meantime, I was still in a semi-euphoric state of mind with a new vision on my ambitious horizon. Foreign service loomed in front of me as something that would fulfill all kinds of dreams.

I wasn't sure what really made me move in that direction. We were so new in America. Marysia and the children barely started to feel at home. Our newly acquired home in Washington and our new addition to the family - Terry was born just about the same time I was accepted by the USIA - all pointed to stability. Marysia was longing for a place to call home. It had been so long since we lost our own home and so many years that we had been moving from one place to another, from one circle of friends to another.

The Washington move offered potential permanency. The older children started school. The little one required the normal dose of attention. Shortly after settling down, we restarted a discussion group on foreign policy, a continuation of what we called "Curious People" that for several years was a gathering of friends in New York. Marysia joined a tennis club, her favorite sport, and through our membership at the Edgemore Club, we met people who later became friends for life.

Why was I so restless? What was the reason for being selfish enough to disturb the process of slow, gradual integration of the family into the American life?

It took me a number of years to answer these questions. At that time, in 1958, I must have sensed the possibility of stagnation. The job at the International Branch sounded a little dull, a little pedestrian, lacking glamour or even satisfaction. But in essence I was unable, or unwilling, to look at all the members of the family. I simply forgot the larger picture. I focused entirely on my professional existence and career. Marysia, always supportive, always willing to deal with the volatility of my moods and decisions, managed somehow to see the bright side of whatever was coming our way. Unlike myself, she saw the larger picture and was deeply worried about the wisdom of my new direction.

On August 30, 1958 the preparations for these new directions went into full swing. The office was empty. Everyone went home. My little corner of an office, equipped with an old-fashioned typewriter and yellow pads, was to serve me for weeks and months to become a workshop to prepare myself for the Foreign Service examination.

The first book that I decided to devour was, *Literary History of the United States,* by Spiller, Thorp, Johnson and Candy. I knew so little about the country of our adoption. I had so much to learn. After-office hours were to be used for that purpose. Marysia, intrigued and supportive, in spite of her reservations, was willing to accept the reality of her husband returning home at ungodly hours.

My notes were voluminous. My memory tested to its limits. My commitment to plowing through literature, paintings, architecture and the history of American foreign policy was strong.

Suddenly, I began discovering America in a way that I had never anticipated. I found joy in learning about the Puritan fathers who set up Harvard College in 1636. The New York Public Library was established in 1700 by a chaplain in the Governor's office, named John Sharpe. Half a century later, a group of New Yorkers concerned about the future of the library, bought about seven hundred volumes of books and rejuvenated the institution. Just about the same time, Benjamin Franklin was instrumental in founding the Library Company in Philadelphia and Robert Keane did the same in Boston. What a great discovery it was for an Eastern European journalist searching for the roots of his adopted land. Destroying stereotypes of America being a land of cowboys and Indians. And this was only the beginning. Long evening hours of continued research and getting into the light were wonderful rewards for all the efforts and all that I had to miss by not being home with our youngsters.

The discovery continued. Benjamin Franklin, a legendary name, someone known to every school child in pre-war Poland, reentered my learning horizon. I grabbed one of his maxims, *"If you would not be forgotten as soon as you are dead and rotten, either write things worth reading, or do things worth writing."*

What am I doing right now? Writing things that some boy years from now will be interested in reading?

Ben Franklin grew to become a phenomenon. His philosophy was deeply religious. The divine government, he wrote and spoke, was a vast order to be studied. It was not a mystery. "It is God who governs the affairs of men. It is He who directs all of mankind and directed me to go into the profession of writing."

At twelve, Ben Franklin started as an apprentice in his brother's printing shop. Barely a decade later, he acquired the Pennsylvania Gazette and shortly thereafter, started Poor Richard's Almanac. Other accomplishments followed, establishment of the Academy (University of Pennsylvania) and then the American Philosophical Society, the first of American learned societies. I kept reading attempting to compare him with known European figures like, for instance, Copernicus. But Copernicus with his opening the door to modern science and understanding the movement of celestial bodies, seemed to me confined to his narrow vision by comparison. Franklin also dwelled in pure science when in 1752 he flew an electric kite, invented the lightning rod in the same year and the Franklin stove. Still, his energy and his creativity, far from being exhausted, he continued writing about such diverse topics as the danger of population growth, electricity, politics, philosophy, and diplomacy as well as causes of discontent in America.

"What is America, Daddy?" the question rang in my years. Here it is. I almost wanted to shout. Here it is and when I tried to answer my little girl, I knew very little of what I was talking about. Now, Ben Franklin led me to others like Thomas Paine and his passionate cry for liberty, and to Thomas Jefferson and his notion that all men were created equal, and to John Adams and Alexander Hamilton and later even to such less known writers of the ardently nationalistic school, like Joel Barlow, John Thumbull, Samuel Hopkins and David Humphrey. At one point, I connected the Century Club of New York, known for its exquisite rum drinks, with Fenimore Cooper. He started it as a chess club and it transformed into a rather exclusive but fascinating meeting place for men and women from literary and political worlds.

Reading, learning, spending long, lonely hours in the privacy of my office, I thanked Providence for allowing me to absorb the reality of our adopted country. One day, however, all that I had learned would be required to surface. The Foreign Service examination had a reputation of being tough and calling for precision in addition to knowledge and of keeping cool under a steady barrage of fire.

As the day approached, sleepless nights and dreams about history, literature, art and architecture recurred with painful regularity Somehow, there was not a doubt in my mind that I would make it and that I was going to be one of the first of our wave of immigrants to represent America abroad. But there were so many facts to remember, so many subtleties of American history to interpret. Let me just live through tomorrow.

The morning was hectic. I had to be sure that I would be on time, that my tie matched my shirt and that my shoes would be as shiny as possible. In short, I had to look respectable. Marysia examined me from top to bottom with her critical eye. "Ok," she said, "you are ready to go."

A panel of three Foreign Service officers awaited my arrival. They stood up when I entered. There were big smiles on their faces, strong handshakes and an invitation to sit down and to be relaxed. Easier said than done. I looked up to examine my future judges. The senior man - he sat in the middle so I figured that he must have been in charge - introduced himself as a former ambassador. He did not mention the country he served in. He just said that he was shortly to retire, that he was so pleased and honored to be able to assist in selecting future ambassadors. We all smiled politely. There was something that made me like him instantly. His strikingly blue, dancing eyes projected a human being who did not take life too seriously, someone who was eager to have a good time and who was also ready to judge people with a fair amount of tolerance.

The other two appeared to look much more conventional. Both were USIA officers dressed in dark suits, with regimental ties and rather serious expressions on their faces. Let me concentrate on the top fellow, the thought flashed through my mind. It took the panel a good ten minutes to equip themselves with coffee and cookies before anything serious started. The opening salvo came from one of the grey fellows. "Tell us briefly," he asked, "how, and why did you come to the United States?"

The unexpected question threw me off. "Well," I started, "wasn't it rather obvious that a person like me would not want to go back to communist controlled Poland?"

One of the grays appeared to be slightly irritated. "Maybe it was obvious to you, but not to us. That is why we asked the question."

I sensed the danger. A fairly lengthy description followed. It included the family visit to the American consulate in Glasgow and the young consul's surprise about our decision to emigrate. I referred to the Yalta Agreement. Then I stopped.

"After you came here, how did you manage to feed your family and survive?" the head examiner continued.

My personal history continued unfolding. But where were the questions about American history? Literature? About Walt Whitman, Emerson and Thoreau? About the Civil War? About Mark Twain's writing? I was anxious to show my knowledge and to convince my tormentors that all of us wanted desperately to be accepted, to become full Americans, but to no avail.

Moments of Reflection 185

"You went to Chattanooga? You sold pots and pans? You kept banging the walls of the United Nations?"

All three sat on the edges of their chairs, their eyes riveted on their applicant. And all three forgot that this was to have been a test of my knowledge. Somehow, in those early days of the post-World War II period, there were very few people from the immigrant ranks attempting to enter the ranks of the American Foreign Service. So I was a novelty, a rare opportunity for American-born Foreign Service officers to interact with newcomers.

I was dismissed after a couple of hours. There was not a single question with which I could prove my American expertise in the fields I had studied for months. They shook hands with me a little more warmly than at the beginning, expressed congratulations on my perseverance and even asked me to give their best wishes to my wife.

I went back to my office slightly perplexed and delighted at the same time. The remaining part of the testing, a written part, looked much less daunting after the first experience. I passed both, the oral one by a fluke and the written one on merit.

It took three more months before word came from personnel. My first foreign post was to be Cairo. My position: Information Officer. Departure date: as soon as possible. Being a rookie, a novice, I was rather ignorant on two key points: the job, which was to be the highest rank I would ever achieve, and the demand for immediate departure. This was a standard request, unrelated to the actual needs of the post. But I took it seriously, pulling Andrew and Maria out of their schools a few weeks before the end of the school year. There were tears and pain but in my total desire to achieve an unbelievable goal, I was ready to make all kinds of sacrifices.

I bragged to my brother about being the first Pole ever to enter the American Foreign Service. I was drunk with pride. Being intoxicated usually translates into irrational decisions. I instantly decided to obey. Marysia was concerned, probably slightly devastated, but said nothing. As usual, she felt that my wishes, my career, had to be our first priority. As usual, she never made me feel guilty and never suggested a selfish act on my part.

We left our newly acquired house in Bethesda and embarked on a journey to the unknown. It took me a short week to discover that

I could have delayed my arrival without any damage done to the post. The children could have finished their school year, Marysia would have had time to organize our family better and under less stressful conditions. I learned all that too late and my lesson was of short duration. I never managed, during my decade in the Foreign Service, to slow down, to think before acting and to reflect before following instructions. I guess I was trying to be a good soldier. I was also - and remain to this day – an impulsive and impatient man.

15

Egypt

There was something else that I should have learned upon my arrival in Cairo: the hierarchy within the Foreign Service. The Public Affairs Officer, the man in charge of USIS, was meeting another plane. His deputy met us. The other plane brought to Cairo a high-ranking State Department person. While the Deputy apologized profusely, I could not have cared less. The intricacies of the diplomatic protocol remained *terra incognita* for both of us.

Our quarters were simple but adequate for temporary housing. The apartment, located in Garden City, the heart of Cairo, appeared relatively clean after you passed a rather filthy and dark staircase. Before Marysia could verbalize her concern about keeping our place in a reasonably acceptable condition, a young man appeared from nowhere. "I am Osman," he announced, "and I will be glad to help. I don't need any money. I just want to help."

Here was another practical lesson. Osman stayed with us for the entire two years of our assignment. He brought his family, a wife and two children, to live with us. And he was properly paid. He entered dressed in his traditional white gallabeya, barefoot and with a couple of Egyptian pounds as his net worth. Two years later, he would call for a taxi to take him and his family to his next American home. The taxi was full of their belongings.

He was a wonderful servant and became a family friend. Nevertheless, his initial appearance confused both of us. Free help? A volunteer wanting to assist newly arrived Americans? Osman looked at me (he was not accustomed to deal with women) with his wide, innocent, black eyes, saying nothing. Just telling me, in his own way, that he had arrived and that he was ready to work.

Then he muttered in broken English that he also has a friend ready to work with him. Osman then took a broom that he brought with him and silently began to work. Marysia looked at me, I looked at her, and there was nothing else to do except to smile and to accept the inevitable. Osman entered our family.

Cairo, at that time capital of the United Arab Republic (Egypt and Libya), was an excellent starting point in our overseas assignments. The city was a mixture of culture, political alignments (leader, Abdul Nasser, was not a friend of America) and a growing nest of men conspiring to decolonize Africa.

The newcomer, a freshman, arrived full of enthusiasm, some degree of understanding and his heart wide open, ready to plunge into the maze of Middle East mentalities. Cairo awaited him calmly. The city accumulated a fair amount of experience with green Americans, optimistic and often unable to switch cultural gears. It awaited this particular American calmly, overtly pleased to see him, secretly rejoicing in his future frustrations.

The tropical climate engulfed our family, dulling our senses. Noise from a typical oriental street killed any chance of having peaceful and restful nights. An army of mosquitoes descended upon the faces of the sleeping children. No such thing as screens in the windows. New types of food caused our tummies to rebel. But we disregarded personal discomforts, forgot the noise, the griping tummy and dove into more important problems of the day.

Frustrated at home, I knew that I would find comfort, satisfaction and fulfillment on the job. My hosts offered me broad smiles and assured me that I was the very man that Washington should have sent a long time ago, and that no problem would remain unsolved.

Drunk with ambitions and desires, I flew directly to my boss's office to report. A detached and thoughtful face looked at me with a mixture of understanding and forgiveness. Polite congratulations followed and a brief reminder that outside Cairo, there was also Washington. I was willing to listen only half way, though I brought to the job a fresh mind and a fresh approach. I knew better. Being a good soldier, a newly minted diplomat, I pretended to understand the system. Weeks and months passed by, and a series of reflections filled my mind.

Here I am in Cairo, capital city of the relatively new national entity called the United Arab Republic, a marriage of two nations that would not last long. Here I am observing, looking, smelling, sensing and writing. For whom? Prosperity? Children? Washington? I really don't care. I just write.

I wrote on August 4, 1959 under the overall umbrella of *"Cairo: Three Months Later"* a note which I sent to family and friends back home.

> The U.A.R. as a first post is indeed a challenge, an opportunity, a place where a timid soul, sensitive minds and a too sophisticated social specimen may find it difficult to exist. It offers a number of excitements. It baffles by its contradictions. It is ready to mislead without meaning to. It offers the newcomer a strong dose of oriental philosophy. It calls for an almost overnight re-examination of basic values and of his natural, Western oriented psychological reflexes. It also calls for discovering ways and means to find a key to oriental minds. Such keys are often buried under tons of medieval debris, hidden among the dusty pages of the Koran and locked behind seven golden doors of a spiritual Sesame. There is no way to decide how to start or where to make an approach, and unless the new arrival doesn't feel lost and slightly unbalanced, he is either a genius, or a man who should have stayed home.
>
> The political situation is a bizarre mixture of progress and feudalism, a climate that encourages laziness and a continuous difficult fight for survival, some of the puzzling every day observations. At first, it appears that every person one meets understands, for instance, the basic affinity of American and Egyptian interests (outside of the ever present question of Israel). Yet, no implementation of that understanding follows. Egyptians are friendly, in some cases boldly critical, in other cases meekly submissive. All in all, a certain thought pattern emerges, a pattern which at first seems difficult to grasp. It goes more or less like this: we are a young, sensitive and very exposed country. After centuries of colonial domination, we have finally

emerged as a free nation. We have organized our own system of government, the one that suits best the mentality of the Egyptian people.

They like to be told what to do. They want to be led. They hate to make decisions, and in many instances they do not realize what is good for them. Therefore the Revolutionary Council, which emerged after the 1952 uprising, assumed supreme command. The President became the center of power. He provides the philosophy of the government. He is the one on whom we all lean because we want to.

Do not apply your own frame of reference to our political life. Look at our country. We have 23 million people, the lowest standard of living in the world, one of the highest rates of illiteracy, one of the highest concentrations of epidemic diseases, and a thin strip of arable land along the valley. We have established our own set of priorities: first industrialization, second education, third health, fourth cleanliness and fifth good citizenship. Only after all of this is accomplished might we be ready to throw the door open to an unlimited flow of ideas. A hungry man, an uneducated man and a destitute man are almost always unable to distinguish between good and bad ideas. A distinction has to be made for him.

We, the Egyptians who matter, those who make that choice, have always felt that we have a lot in common with the United States. Both nations were born through anti-colonial, political revolutions. Both rejected imperialism. Men who were revolutionaries, reformers and missionaries at heart have led both countries. It would not perhaps be appropriate, from the American point of view, to put George Washington and Gamel Abdel Nasser on the same level. But for us, it makes a lot of sense. Both men carved the principles of constitutional rights. Both gave their people concepts of foreign policies. Both were neutral and isolationists. But were, first nationalists, and only later citizens of the world.

This was the theory which some of our leading people cherished and discussed during the Palestinian war. As you know, that war reminds us of the American war of

> Independence. It was different in time, space and weapons, but we cannot help feeling that as much as the battle of Yorktown sealed the fate of England in the New World, so the Palestinian war sealed our fate and our future. Historically, we have been marching along the same path, but instead of recognizing affinity of destiny, the American people have rejected our outstretched hand. Our offer of friendship was disregarded. Our national existence has been minimized. Our new leadership has been consistently ridiculed.

How do you respond? How do you begin your work as someone sent over to the Egyptian desert to communicate, to persuade and to get across a notion that America cares, that America understands and that America, a far away country, often idealized but far more often demonized, is deeply interested in creating a common denominator of people's aspiration? Shall I talk to Osman about it? Shall I give him copies of SADAKA, our Arabic weekly to read? Nope, I cannot. He doesn't know how to read.

Osman came from a village deep in the Delta. His family, mother, father and seven siblings, are still there. They are the true people of Egypt. They should be reached but are they reachable? I go back to my writings a generation ago.

> They inhabit mud houses, sleep on the floor covered with rugs and conduct their daily existence from dusk to dawn by hard work in order to eat. Their minds are set, so are their moral and spiritual values. A mosque dominates their village, as much as the Koran dominates their spiritual need. Time and technology failed to catch up with them. A donkey is as much their chief means of transportation as it was during the days of Christ. The barrier that divides them from their own upper classes, touched by the luxuries of the West and enjoying living in an atomic age, is enormous. A fellah glances at a new model of an American car driven by a wealthy Egyptian, in the same way a suburban housewife in Washington looks at a tiara worn by Queen Elizabeth. There is no envy in his glance since he knows that this car is outside his dreams.

I kept reading the ancient script, recalling vividly the days and nights that made all of us, family and colleagues, bewildered and on many occasions ready to give up, and made us blame everyone except ourselves for the lack of understanding and distance that continued to separate us from them. Then I came up to the last paragraph of that script.

> But the fellahin lived through many centuries of dynasties, oppression, domination, sparks of better times and dark clouds of near famine. He is interested to see the American coming into his midst. He is flattered. He knows that the American spells wealth. He despises anyone who tells him otherwise. He sees with his own eyes the clothes Americans wear, the cars they drive and the gifts they bring. When the newly acquired American friend talks about equality, the brown face of the Egyptian farmer cracks in a multitude of smiles. 'Sure we are equal. God says so. You are equal among the wealthy, and I am equal among the poor. I can offer you what I have, a cup of tea brewed in my home. You will drink it with me if you are my friend. And you will offer me money, and tractors, and land and a new house and I will accept your offer because I am your friend. So we are equal. We share alike. We feel alike. We only live differently. *La illaha ha wa Muhammad Rasula 'Illah.*

What a wonderful way to be introduced to the mysteries of the Middle East and what a great way to make anyone arriving from the Western world feel confused, sometimes even totally lost.

Is this the way that under-developed countries treat the American AID program? That this is something proving our friendship? A friendship reciprocated by an Indian untouchable, or an Egyptian camel driver with whatever they have? On the other hand, there was some logic in what my Egyptian friend conveyed to me, the logic of someone who feels strongly that sharing is a virtue, that whatever one has, whatever one is lucky to acquire, must be shared with others. Americans have a lot, we have little but we share equally, therefore we are equal. Sounds right? Of course, it does.

Soon enough, life in this spectacular, and at the same time frustrating, capital on the Nile offered a new array of questions, surprises and confirmations of their different logic. Our gardener, Abdul Assis, who was provided, was the human dimension. The political system, attempting to eliminate unwelcome news, was another. The gardener - who proved to be indispensable - came to us from nowhere, little like Osman, but perhaps with a slightly more dignified manner. Osman just assumed that the job would be his; Abdul Assis learned through the usual grapevine that a new American family rented a house in Maadi and that the house was big and had a small garden.

There was a large palm tree overlooking the house and around the tree were flowerbeds, forgotten and totally neglected. Abdul Assis, a tall straight looking man and older than Osman, applied for the job. His English was limited so he brought an interpreter with him. The latter knew about a hundred English words, enough to negotiate on his friend's behalf. Both of them were far from asking for a favor. They came as professionals. They knew their worth. But on the other side of the negotiating table the newly arrived American was just a little too green to understand all the ramifications.

I agreed to the terms of employment, to the amount of wages and even to the suggestion - made in a very casual manner - that our new employee would be offered lodging in our basement apartment. What I was not fully aware of was that strong family values would not permit Abdul Assis to leave his family behind. Within hours, we witnessed, slightly bewildered, the arrival of his wife and four children.

"They will help in gardening," the interpreter mentioned cheerfully.

"Great," I answered with a rather artificial smile of understanding. Little did I know that grandparents were to arrive a couple of weeks later.

Two of Abdul Assis' children caught our attention. Nadia, barely three-years-old, became the inseparable companion of our daughter Terry, who was getting ready for her third birthday. Nadia naturally spoke only Arabic, an Arabic of Egyptian fellahin rather different from its classical version. Within weeks, Terry was jabbering in Nadia's language to the obvious delight of her entire family. On occasion, we tried to understand our daughter's injection of unfamiliar phrases into her English, but to no avail.

Ahmed, the oldest of our gardener's offspring, was about thirteen and was a delightful youngster with a permanent smile and never-ending eagerness to learn. He wanted to learn English. He wanted to learn how to read and write. His entire family was illiterate, but Ahmed, sensing an opportunity, clung to both of us, silently asking for help. English instructions followed. Ahmed absorbed everything and started to understand a fair amount. His time was limited since he was expected to help his father in his gardening chores. He was also going to school, but there was little evidence that the institution provided a climate allowing youngsters to learn. The daily routine that Ahmed established for himself called for an hour or so working with his father in the garden, and the remaining time of the day, spent with us. Andrew, just about the same age, taught him the rudiments of baseball. Marysia and I kept patiently going over his English vocabulary. Ahmed's smiles and the obvious delight that illuminated his face, were the best rewards that we received.

One day, something unexpected occurred, and we were faced with the possibility of losing our pupil. Straight as an arrow, his brown face adorned with the usual smile, Abdul Assis approached me indicating that he wanted to give me an important message. How did I know? Usually he was busy, digging, replanting, weeding and feeding our lonely palm tree with little inclination to interrupt his chores for an idle chat. This time, there was something that caught my attention, something that indicated to me the nature of his message. Was he quitting? Did he find a better offer from another American family? Or was he asking for a raise?

None of the above. Abdul Assis wanted to talk to me about Ahmed. "About Ahmed? Where is he? I haven't seen him for a couple of days."

The broad smile disappeared from the gardener's face. "Ahmed is sick, very sick. He was seen by a doctor who told me that Ahmed will die soon."

Our search for the doctor who made this gloomy prediction was in vain. Would he mind if we asked for another doctor? To make sure that the boy gets proper medical attention?

It was at that moment of our difficult conversation, linguistically and in terms of substance, that the mother joined Abdul Assis. They both began to talk in rapid Arabic. They forgot our limited ability to understand. We only heard, "God willing," repeated a number of times. In sheer desperation, we called Osman to be the interpreter. And finally we understood. The parents were very sad, but if this is what God wanted, they were sure that God will give them a chance to have another child and that it will be a boy. No one can interfere with divine decision. Nobody. Not even Americans. Let us see what will happen to Ahmed. There is no need for another doctor. And the two of them, the proudly erect man and his rather corpulent wife, walked back to their basement quarters.

We knew instantly what we had to do. Ahmed was whisked to the nearest hospital where he was diagnosed as suffering from a severe case of pneumonia. His chances were linked to the possibility of securing adequate quantities of penicillin. The Egyptian hospital had none.

The Embassy doctor knew what to do. Within hours, the required dose of penicillin was delivered to the hospital where Ahmed was admitted. Within days, the boy regained his appetite. Within two weeks he was ready to be released and allowed to go home. There was no way that one could describe Abdul Assis' gratitude to us. But there was also never any doubt in his mind that it was God's will and that we were simply His instruments. Were we? I often had my doubts. The Egyptian God somehow failed to cure the multitude of humanity that suffered through hunger, misery, poverty and ignorance. How about our own God? I stopped for a minute, reflecting on the sights of urban decay visible all over the large American cities. Same things? Different geography? Different beliefs? Digging deeper and deeper into religious faith on one side and the fate of humanity on the other side, I doubted, doubting even about the existence of divinity. Maybe God is just an invention of us humans, to be able to escape our own responsibility for our own lives? Maybe He is just there, a ghost of lost illusions, an ephemeral being that we invoke every time there appears a void in our own thinking? God willing. *Il Sha Allah.*

In the meantime, the United Arab Republic continued to present us with challenges, surprises, and on special occasions, one of the most dangerous moments of our Egyptian saga. It would be of my own making.

The challenges, outside of professional existence affecting my work, popped up also in our personal and family life. We named our dog, "Malish," a wonderful Arabic word indicating total inability to cope with a problem. Egyptians would say *malish* after breaking a precious piece of antiquity or when faced with a victim of a traffic accident lying half-dead in the middle of a busy street or when, never compassionate, nature brings an army of mosquitoes, eating you alive. In short, *malish* was an indication of human acceptance of the unavoidable. Once uttered, it almost had the power of religious confession. It provided absolution to the person that was using it as a tool and as a way of saying, "I am helpless. I continue living the best I can."

We loved our Malish. He was the breed of Egyptian street dog. He had a long tail, an expression of his eyes projecting loyalty and his own version of love. He was a mixture of several canine cultures, none of which left a distinct mark on his undistinguished body. He came from nowhere, attached himself to our family and was determined to be one of its members. It is possible that this was his biggest mistake.

One day he disappeared. We looked for him everywhere, searched adjoining streets and asked our neighbors if they had seen him. Malish was nowhere to be seen. It was a couple of weeks later that our gardener discovered his battered body hidden under a garbage can. It was obvious that he did not die a natural death. He was killed. We never knew by whom; we never knew why. But Osman had his own theory. Men were surprised and jealous, observing a dog that was treated better than some of the people living outside of the American household.

The dog's crisis was followed, shortly after, by a nanny crisis.

The nanny, Assisa, was hired upon a recommendation by one of our other servants. We had seven of them at one point. She looked efficient, capable, strong and willing to take care of our Terry who at that time was two and half years old. It turned out that she was very strong willed and rather inflexible with the ways that she considered beneficial to our child.

Bath time was to be kept daily around 6 p.m., and that precipitated the crisis. At first, we did not react to Terry's cries. We attributed them to the normal behavior of a child dealing with a stranger. But when her cries kept occurring every night, we decided to investigate. It was a delicate task. Assisa indicating, in as many words, that with her long experience and knowledge she was fully capable to do her work without any parental interference. So Marysia tiptoed to the bathroom to investigate. She found the little girl crying her lungs out. Her skin was a dark, reddish color. Marysia put her hands in the water. It was almost boiling! Assisa, eager to make sure that her pupil be properly washed, was putting Terry in water that would make any human being crying for help. No way was she persuaded to change her ways. No way was she willing to admit her error. So we lost our nanny, unable to find a compromise, unable to negotiate, and unable to save Terry from past evening tortures.

16

The Lumumba Saga

A major professional challenge occurred shortly thereafter. It was caused by a combination of poor judgment, naiveté and my lack of fully understanding what the nature and power of a police state was.

The background of the incident, which I was directly involved in, transcended our natural, professional boundaries. It was purely political. It was also intertwined with Egyptian-Soviet and Egyptian-African relations. In his book, *Innocents Abroad*, published shortly after his death, John Esterline, my direct boss, holding the position of the Country Public Affairs Officer, succinctly described the situation:

> Gamal Abdul Nasser's bid to extend his regime influence beyond the Egyptian borders was not confined to Syria. Throughout our years in Cairo and Damascus, the Egyptians were aggressively engaged in activities to achieve "the liberation of black Africa." In conformance with the second among his three circles thesis, Nasser had proclaimed: 'We cannot, under any circumstances, however much we may desire it, remain aloof from the terrible and sanguinary conflict going on there between 5 million whites and 200 million Africans. We cannot do so for an important and obvious reason: we are in Africa. The peoples of Africa will continue to look to us, who guard their northern gate and who constitute their link with the outside world.' The clearest expression of this thesis was his intervention in the affairs of the Congo in early 1961.

Patrice Lumumba was the first prime minister of the Congo - formerly the Belgian Congo and subsequently the Republic of Zaire. A post office employee and labor leader, Lumumba in 1958 founded the Movement National Congolese, the first Congolese political party, and became prime minister of the new state when Belgium abruptly granted the territory independence June 30, 1960.

To Nasser, the avidly anti-Western, pro-USSR, Lumumba appeared to be the best hope for advancing Egyptian objectives, namely, the eradication of all influence in Africa. At the same time he hoped to substitute Egyptian influence for the fairly successful Israeli influence in several of the newly independent African states.

The Egyptian president, however, miscalculated. Situations in the newly emerging African states have never been free of complications. Internal strife produces chaotic conditions. Nasser's equivalent in the Congo, President Kasavubu, dismissed Lumumba. Army Chief of Staff, Joseph Mobutu, who subsequently ruined his country through greed and terror, arrested Lumumba. But that was not enough of the local complications. Lumumba escaped from detention only to be apprehended by another player in this political game, Moise Tshombe, who declared himself president. In early February, Lumumba was executed - according to various academic sources - by Tshombe mercenaries.

How did we get involved in that bizarre charade?

On February 11, the Cairo press announced Lumumba's death and the following day it began, according to Esterline, "a vitriolic and emotional attack on the West." It was the West that killed him, screamed front-page headlines. "Belgium, France, Britain and the United States are the murderers."

That was enough to incite an Egyptian mob. The first victim was the Belgian embassy, burned to the ground. The next one on the target list was the USIS Library. It was attacked with rocks and sticks. Fires were started, but not too successfully. However, most of the library's windows were broken with sizable rocks, one of which found its way to my own desk, a rock that I retained as a significant reminder of our difficult days.

The Lumumba Saga

There was no way for us to sit still and allow the official news media to present the United States as responsible for Lumumba's demise. John Esterline and I designed a plan to counteract in print.

The USIS print shop sprang into action. We started early, just about 7 a.m. The crew was ready. Machines activated, men running around feeding paper, John and I ready to compose what was needed. We hit on a simple solution: the text of three speeches delivered by President Kennedy, Adlai Stevenson, U.S. Ambassador to the United Nations, and the Secretary General of that august body, Dag Hammerskoeld. What could have been more neutral, we reasoned? They all addressed the burning issue of the Congo. All three directly and indirectly denied any American involvement.

We knew, however, that we had to cut a couple of corners in order to get our product to the general public. The text had to be in Arabic. According to the prevailing Egyptian rule, everything published in Arabic by any diplomatic missions, had to be submitted to the Ministry of Information for approval. That takes considerable amount of time. Furthermore, there was a fair amount of doubt in our minds as to whether we would secure an approval.

We skipped that step. The brochure was translated, printed and ready for distribution. How was that to be accomplished? We omitted the attribution. It should have been "USIS Cairo." We left it blank. We thus entered into the area of gray propaganda, almost subversive, as we learned later.

Several thousand copies awaited John and me when we returned to the Embassy several hours later. Distribution? Once again, our bravado ran ahead of our minds. We concluded that each of us would personally, or through our Egyptian contacts, deposit multiple copies of the pamphlet at locations where Cairo's political and social elite were known to gather during the mid-evening hours. Movie theaters were assigned to me.

Blissfully and never giving it a thought, I drove in my white Ford convertible with diplomatic license plates, to downtown Cairo. Then, seemingly proceeding to see a film, I placed a bundle of our pamphlets on a bench inside the first movie house that I encountered.

I then visited about four more theaters and did the same. At the last stop, a young boy observed me and asked me in broken English what I was doing. I responded that I am simply leaving some "interesting material" for people to read. Then I went home pleased, proud and delighted, with a feeling of accomplishment. The hour was too late to call John. A restful, undisturbed sleep grabbed me almost instantly. A good number of "Lumumba pamphlets" were left on the front seat of my car.

The usual drive along Cornish, with my top down, proceeded rather smoothly. Nothing special, nothing unusual. 'How about these pamphlets?' a thought crossed my mind. 'How about tossing a few of them along the way?' After all, there are quite a few pedestrians walking around, and within seconds, prevailing wind helped by my non-driving hand carry our products into the Egyptian air.

And all hell broke loose.

Police sirens pierced the quiet, sunny morning. A car, without any visible markings, passed me at high speed, waving hands sticking out of its windows, warned other vehicles to give way. The car screeched to a halt and four men ran at full speed in my direction. Two of them placed themselves on both sides of my car and ordered me to get out. I just sat there. "Don't you see my diplomatic licenses plates?" I responded in English.

"Get out!" they shouted in Arabic only. No English. And one of them reached for my arms. I got out peacefully.

Squeezed between two husky Egyptian policemen, in the back seat of their car, I attempted to start a conversation. There was no point. Evidently, responding to rather strict orders, the men were asked to deliver me to the ultimate destination, the Ministry of Security. Later, I learned that they posted themselves in front of our house several hours earlier. The action was well coordinated and I became a prime suspect. Was this the boy who observed me in front of the movie houses?

He was indeed. Before long, I was lined up and surrounded by seven or eight husky Egyptians. The boy was asked to identify the "foreigner," and the full play of my detention began to unfold.

At first, after a rather hectic ride in the speeding police car, I was led through the corridors of the Ministry of Security, to a large room of the boss. The corridors were crowded with law enforcement officers and their victims. I looked around, fascinated by a sight, which I would not have been able to observe under normal circumstances. The Ministry was off-limits to foreign diplomats. Without a word exchanged between us, my captors opened large, impressive, mahogany doors, saluted and left.

The man, slightly built, with a graying moustache, stood up and extended his hand. I at once took the initiative.

"May I ask, sir, the reason for my arrest? Why am I here? Could you please explain?"

A slight smile danced on Hassan Talaat's lips. "I am sure that we will be able to explain everything shortly," he responded, motioning me to take a seat. I was told that subversive material was found along the route that I have traveled. "Some of my men even thought that it came directly from your car. So we will have to investigate the matter. It will not take too long. Just make yourself at home. In the meantime, I will do my best to clarify this unfortunate incident. You see, Mr. Nagorski, I am in charge of the Ministry's division dealing with material that is viewed as being hostile to our government. So I have no choice but to look very seriously into the matter. And by the way, I am so sorry that we cannot offer you anything to drink. This is our first day of Ramadan. We all have to fast. Maybe later we might be able to share coffee and cake."

How long do they intend to keep me here?

A daring thought crossed my mind. "May I use your phone and call the Embassy? I am sure there are people wondering what happened to me."

There was a sign of puzzlement on the face of my host. But it lasted only a second or two. "Of course, here it is." And with expansive gesture of both hands, he invited me to sit in his seat, behind the desk. The telephone was placed in front of me. I dialed the Embassy.

It was John Esterline who picked up the phone. In his book, *Innocents Abroad*, he wrote:

> The next morning, I awaited Zyg's arrival with anticipation. When he had not appeared at 8:30 I began to worry. Within minutes, I was called to the phone. Zyg was on the line, "John," he said. "I am at the Ministry of the Interior and I cannot come in to the office."

"Why not, Zyg?" I asked, my heart sinking.

"They are holding me here, John. There has been a slight misunderstanding. Remember the Arabic language pamphlet we intended to submit to the Information Department for clearance?" he asked.

"Yes, of course," I responded, "but why are you being detained?"

"Well, I was driving along the Cornish this morning with my car windows open to enjoy the fresh breezes. Some of the pamphlets we were going to submit to the censor blew out of the window, quite by accident, of course."

"Why are you being detained?" I persisted.

"The authorities harbor the view that I was distributing unauthorized pamphlets. Shortly after the pamphlets fluttered out of my car, I was forced to the curb by members of the national security police who seem to have been following me. Two of the security agents put me in a government sedan and brought me here."

"Are you being mistreated?" I demanded.

"No," said Zyg. "On the contrary, my hosts are most polite and in spite of Ramadan, brought me a roll and coffee. They are simply detaining me without further explanation."

"Give me your number and I'll call you every half hour while I'll try to figure out what we should do," I said and hung up.

Stunned as I was by the news and the dilemma of having to decide what to do next, I admired Zyg for his canniness. His tale of flattering pamphlets was a masterpiece, given the circumstances. Zyg knew, of course, that I would be extremely reluctant to inform the ambassador, which could escalate the problem to that of an international incident, and Zyg (and I) could end up being declared *persona non grata*. We might lose our jobs as well.

So he kept hoping that our Egyptian hosts would simply decide to "teach Zyg a lesson" and release me. He also kept calling me every half hour or so until about 11:30 a.m. Then "Zyg's hosts" informed John that no more calls were to be accepted on my behalf. At this point John, with his heart on his sleeve, decided to inform the ambassador. While we, in Cairo, were engaged in the waiting game, on the other side of the Atlantic, a small drama was playing itself out.

A sharp telephone ring woke up my opposite number, press attaché of the Egyptian Embassy, in Washington. Well-known in diplomatic as well as social circles of the capital, the young and successful Egyptian envoy, who had married into a prominent American family, picked up the phone reluctantly. "What now?" he muttered to himself. "Another Egyptian sailor arrested for drunkenness?"

What he heard made him wide-awake within seconds. "The American press attaché was arrested in Cairo. Unless he is released within the next twenty-four hours, you will have to pack your bags. So you better move fast." The caller from the Department of State hung up.

International telephone lines in the early sixties were not as easily accessible as they are today. After numerous attempts, a connection was made with the Ministry of the Interior. Rapid Arabic conversation followed. The man in Washington was a favorite of the foreign minister. He was shortly on the line and matters began moving rather fast on the Egyptian side.

Not so on the side of the Americans in Cairo. Here is another account written by John Esterline:

> "Mr. Ambassador," I began quaking within, "the Ministry of the Interior is holding Zyg Nagorski incommunicado at the ministry headquarters. The Egyptians are polite and he is physically comfortable, but they have told him he may no longer have access to the telephone." Coward that I was, I described in the most general terms our plot to distribute the offending pamphlet, noting only that Zyg was apprehended on the way to the embassy and that unattributed pamphlet had been found in his car.
>
> The DCM and the Ambassador, Norbert Anschuetz and John Reinhardt, traded glances and to my utter surprise, their faces showed little concern. They hesitated a moment, then with a slightly sardonic smile, Anschuetz suggested

they do nothing for the moment. He may have reasoned that Egyptian security agents had not realized that they were detaining a member of the diplomatic corps and that Zyg would be freed as soon as higher-level authorities learned of the incident. But I got the definite impression that Anschuetz was implying that super-patriotism has its limits and we had clearly breached them by our clandestine operation.

Reinhardt agreed with Norb and instructed me to keep him informed. The meeting ended without my being lectured to, for which I was grateful, but my angst increased because I remained in exactly the same, helpless situation. I had reported the dilemma to my superiors and they turned the problem back to me.

In the meantime, I was still inside my makeshift prison. From my vantage point, it looked as if my Embassy's superiors were slow to grasp the significance of my fate. I knew, of course, nothing about the developments in Washington and in Cairo. By the end of the day, when darkness descended on all the neighboring streets, I suddenly noticed that the parking lot of the ministry went completely dark. Usually it was lit most of the night.

Soon, the mystery was resolved. An official embassy car, flying American flags, pulled up with the DCM and John Esterline. But it was dark and uninviting. The only soldier guarding the place informed the DCM that I was gone and that no one was there to receive me. Norbert Anschuetz stepped out of the car to peak inside. He saw nothing of consequence. His companion, however, John Esterline pointed at my white Ford parked inside. "He's gone?" John asked the soldier. "How about his car? Did he walk out?" The slightly confused guard just shrugged his shoulders. He was obviously an innocent bystander. The American flag had very few options left, except retreating back to the Embassy.

In the meantime, the mood inside the room where I was kept changed drastically. There were no more offers of coffee. The telephone was now off limits. My formerly gentle host, with whom I discussed the nature of civil disobedience, was replaced by a couple of grim faced individuals in uniforms who formed an investigating team.

Where did I receive the subversive material aimed at overthrowing the Egyptian government? Who gave it to me? Who are the other plotters? Give names, functions and addresses. My answers did not satisfy the pair. The pamphlet could not have been produced without permission and directives from Washington. It was an obvious attempt by the American authorities to destabilize Egypt. The consequences could have been most serious. It was fortunate that Egyptian security forces were vigilant enough to sound an alert early and were able to apprehend the would-be diplomat.

I listened to all of that with growing anxiety. It was no longer a minor issue (later, I was told that Nasser himself ordered my arrest). It sounded to me that, for whatever reasons, the Egyptians wanted to blow the whole thing out of proportion. I was unable to communicate with the outside world. A vision of months spent in an Egyptian jail danced in my mind. There was not much that I could do and the Embassy must have been equally cut off from any contacts.

I was apprehended around 9 a.m. During the day, out of sheer boredom, I opened my briefcase and started working on my Arabic vocabulary.

"What a splendid idea," blurted Hassan Talaat. "You must be planning to be with us in Egypt for a long time. You never know, of course, with the Foreign Service, but a solid investment in language makes the government reluctant to shift people. But it is so good to see people like yourself seriously applying yourself to learn about us." Hassan was all smiles. "Arabs are so little known to Americans. We are sure you will be our great ambassador."

A couple of phone calls interrupted his monologue. He responded in rapid Arabic, somewhat more rapid than before I opened my book. A sudden severity changed his facial expression. "Why do you want to learn Arabic? Tell me the real story, will you please?"

Slightly taken aback by the dramatic change of his mood, I hit, spontaneously, on what I thought was a brilliant retort. "Supposing I would like to be able to read President Nasser's speeches in the original, rather than translation?"

Hassan's look mirrored his inner turmoil. First, there was a dancing smile at the corner of his lips. Then, it turned into the worried expression of a man fearing that someone was making fun of him. Then, gradually, into the reflective mood of a man who found his answer. "This would be a total waste of time, my dear friend. Gamal Abdul Nasser is our George Washington. He delivered us from the oppressive regime of King Farouk. He is the one who straightened the backbone of every Arab in the face of Western imperialism. And he speaks like George Washington. If you, mister press counselor, would be willing to re-read your American history instead of trying to learn our language, you would be better able to understand our historical development."

I could not help but to admire my captor's intellectual flexibility.

Ramadan worked only during the day, and close to midnight I decided that it was time for a little nap. I was still in the same room. The only difference was that I was alone. Maybe they are all enjoying a feast after the daylong fast?

My sleep wasn't allowed to last long. Heavy steps of two different individuals interrupted whatever dreams I was ready to have. One of the new arrivals spoke some English. "Please follow us. The Embassy car is waiting for you outside."

I fell into the arms of John Esterline, as sleepy and as tired as I was. "How come? How did you arrange it?" John did not know. Neither did I.

The middle-of-the-night telephone call to my Egyptian counterpart worked. He was free to stay in Washington. I was free to go home.

The world press picked up the story to the great discomfort of my family and friends scattered around various capitals. There were, however, a couple of unexpected fringe benefits. One was of a substantive nature, the other, of an amusing one.

The Egyptian press, who used the incident to depict American perfidy and anti-Egyptian bias, used their front pages to write the story and feature it prominently, pictures of my car, could not restrain itself from giving their readers the full treatment. Al Ahram and Al Gamourihia the two most popular dailies reproduced in full our pamphlet. We could not have hoped for a better publicity.

The amusing facet had to wait a while. A few months later, I received a new assignment. We were to go to South Korea. Although the location was a surprise, Korea was a totally unknown region both professionally and intellectually. We were glad to leave Egypt. The family was not happy. My work - as in turned out later - was probably the most satisfying assignment I had in the Foreign Service and was grinding to a halt. In spite of my father's desperate letters urging me to refuse the Korean position, we both decided to go. In the normal, traditional manner in which the Foreign Service operated, the Embassy wanted to host a farewell party for us. But it was not to be. It was the Egyptian Ministry of Information that called the Ambassador's office and requested permission to do the farewell party for us. I was stunned and all kinds of reflections came to mind. Are they so pleased that we were leaving? Or is this a gesture saying in as many words that they made a mistake and are making up for it? No matter, the party was a great success.

A lot of our friends accepted the formal invitation. The two Amin brothers, Mustafa and Ali, the icons of Egyptian journalistic profession, proudly entered carrying at least 250 pounds of flesh each. So did Hussanen Heckel, the mouthpiece of the President, known for his penchant for impressing foreign visitors by asking them to leave the room for a few minutes. "The President is on the line," he would mention sheepishly.

There were numerous others. Quite a few of whom wrote editorials depicting my actions as inspired by some dark forces of American intelligence. It was not me who wrote what I wrote - went the convoluted way of Egyptian logic - it was the Big Brother who dictated this to me. But that was yesterday. Today, we were once again best friends, brothers, totally immune to some of the past excesses of journalistic rhetoric. So we drank together, we promised ourselves eternal friendship. The farewell reception was declared a total success.

But the biggest surprise occurred towards the very end of the occasion. From the corner of my eye, I noticed two soldier-like figures entering the house. Both wore immaculate suits, matching ties and white shirts. One of them looked around, noticed me standing at the end of the reception area and moved briskly in my direction.

"What a pleasure to see you under different circumstances," and an extended hand grabbed mine in a warm gesture. I looked up. Was this really him? Yes, it was. Hassan Talaat, my host at the Ministry of Interior, who greeted me at first with understanding and outstretched arms, only to abandon me later to a team of interrogators, was standing in front of me. In the spirit of newly emerging Egyptian-American cooperation we laughed heartily and embraced each other with the traditional Egyptian greetings: you are my brother.

The Lumumba saga appeared to be over.

As any Foreign Service officer would testify, each assignment develops its own profile. Or rather profiles. There is a natural one reflecting professional duties. Linked to it, inevitably, are numerous personal branches. For married men, their wives' attitudes, positions and interests are of key importance. For couples with children, there are additional profiles affecting the youngsters' lives. In our case, the multi-faceted profiles developed early in the game.

For Marysia, an essentially shy and introverted person, diplomatic existence offered few attractions. Official dinners, luncheons and receptions were viewed as chores. It took us a good few months to connect with people across the diplomatic spectrum. With some, it was easier. The Indian Ambassador and his wife offered their embassy premises for meetings of African dissidents whom we had invited on a number of occasions to meet in our large basement. There were a few Germans with whom we found common interests. But every time we would enter a large reception room, either at another embassy or in one of the official Egyptian government locations, I would observe a slightly artificial, almost frozen smile on Marysia's face. She is ready, I would whisper to myself, ready to greet, to make small talk and to dream about going home.

Attempting to make the most out of each function, I would abandon my poor spouse in an effort to meet new contacts. Marysia, unless approached by another female guest, would move gently around the room observing artwork, Egyptian artifacts or oriental rugs. Then, dutifully, when asked about her family and her husband's work, she would recite the virtues of our youngest, who at the age of three and a fraction, was already speaking fluent kitchen Arabic, and of the journalistic interests of our son, Andrew.

Little did we know at our early Egyptian days, that Marysia would be much more the center of attention that I would ever be. Daily papers occasionally mentioned the activities of the American press attaché, but they would never solicit his picture to be prominently displayed on the front page of a Sunday magazine. It was Marysia who earned that distinction.

An avid tennis player, she promptly joined others interested in the white sport. At that time, early '60s, few Egyptian women played. Marysia enrolled in the Gezira Club, where the diplomatic community enjoyed special privileges, but also ventured outside encouraging her Egyptian female friends to learn the game. She also discovered that quite a few younger Egyptian girls were busy on the courts, and offered to give them instructions. Gradually, she became a fixture on various tennis activities. Her involvement offered both of us a different and much more genuine access to the Egyptian community.

A day arrived when the Egyptian Lawn Tennis Association decided to organize a national tournament. Everybody was encouraged to participate, including foreigners. The rest was history.

Marysia was declared champion of the United Arab Republic in women's singles. Her picture, with her runner-up, was featured on the cover of a prominent Sunday magazine. She was forever freed from talking about her offspring at diplomatic functions. The new topic was tennis. On rare occasions, people would ask what was her husband doing and she gracefully obliged with a short answer.

Preoccupied with youngsters, Terry, Andrew and Marysia Jr., and five servants who drifted one-by-one into our household, Marysia had little time to develop her other talents and interests. They would have to wait until our second foreign assignment in South Korea. It would be in Korea where Marysia unleashed her full energy in assisting Korean women in their efforts to find an equal, or at least semi-equal, status in their society. It was also there that she mobilized major efforts to find homes for mixed blood Korean children in the United States. In Korea, pure blood guaranteed both acceptance and opportunities, but mixed blood individuals, whether black or white, had very limited chances of living normal, happy lives.

Long before Korea, a major challenge within the family structure occurred, provided by our oldest daughter, the same daughter who had inquired about America in Scotland, and who was by then a strong willed, determined eighteen year old person.

Maria had decided to marry an Egyptian boy.

The boy was nice and slightly non-descript. He had artistic talents, drew nice sketches including a light profile of this 'chosen girl.' His father was a well-known businessman and the family, in spite of being Jewish in a predominantly Muslim country, was well off. The problem was of a much more serious nature. An American woman, or any foreign woman, marrying an Egyptian citizen, would automatically lose all her independence. She would not be allowed to leave the country without her husband's permission; he would be in total control of her life and in control of her economic status.

In short, it was still a slightly medieval relationship that Maria would be entering into. But how could you explain these intricacies of this future life to a girl deeply in love?

There was no way to accomplish our objectives, no way to reason when youthful emotions prevailed. I had to take the matter into my hands. With full support of her mother, we made a rather drastic decision. The girl had to return to America.

After these many years, I can still feel the pain and see the tears of my devastated daughter. The airport scene remains vivid in my mind. Our eldest youngster sobbing uncontrollably inside the Pan American plane, the plane taxing out and both of us waving to the unseen silhouette of our departing child.

At the other end of our daughter Maria's voyage home, a couple of our faithful friends awaited her, offering home, hospitality and a substitute of parental love.

17

South Korea

Another profile of the Foreign Service existence entered our lives with the force of thunder. The South Korean assignment arrived in a short, calm and bureaucratically wooden telegram from Washington. The new job: information officer assigned to the AID Mission. At that time – the early 60's - South Korea was on the top of the list of the American assistance program. The country was poor with a per capita income around $160 per annum, the export volume negligible and the agricultural production inadequate to feed the country's population. On the streets of Seoul, there were very few cars. Buses, made of corrugated tin, procured from discarded American machines, polluted the countryside with passion.

But all of that was still in the future. I read about it, tried to study the country of my next assignment and imagined the continent that was to be a discovery land for all of us. But we were still in Cairo. We were still deeply immersed in analyzing the drastic change that the next stop was apt to mean for our lifestyle. The time to think about it was probably the best when the Embassy required me to be the duty officer. It was shortly before that night spent at the front desk at the entrance of our compound, that I learned how the little pamphlet changed our destination. I was to have been nominated to a position in Beirut. After the detention, there was no way that the Agency would send me to another Arab country.

At one point, during my rather boring evening, I decided to take a stroll outside of the Embassy building. Reflections crowded my mind. I was leaving behind a period of almost missionary enthusiasm, unfulfilled and unrealistic ambitions and many lost opportunities. I was also leaving Egypt as a veteran of two years' service representing the country of my adoption. I felt that I had been accepted almost entirely by my peers. I also learned how much my European background proved to be an asset to my work.

An elderly American tourist interrupted my deep thoughts. He was slightly lost and wanted some guidance and help. So he walked towards the Embassy and, seeing me standing there, asked me whether I was the duty officer.

"Yes, sir," I responded. "I am."

"How great," the man exploded with genuine joy, "to meet a fellow American. May I have your name?"

"Zygmunt Nagorski."

A slightly puzzled look crossed the tourist's face. "How about the Ambassador? What is his name?"

"John Rheinhard, sir," I responded, "but he is not in town."

"Who, then, is his deputy?"

"Norbert Anschuetz. He is around."

The bewildered tourist scratched his head, looked closely at the marine guard standing next to me. "Are you sure that this is the American Embassy?" he mumbled and shaking his head slowly. He walked away. What is America, Daddy?

Maybe the purely American tourist was unable to recognize this America.

Movers, a small army of Egyptian workers that swarmed into our house grabbing everything, including half full ashtrays, kept reminding everyone that the departure date was close by. To make sure that we did not miss anything of special interest, we decided to take a last trip along the Mediterranean coast. El Alamein was our first stop, the place of bloody battles between the Allies and Germany armies in World War II, my war. It was not easy to explain it to a five-year-old, not even to a fourteen-year-old.

We walked in silence. Three separate, distinctly different cemeteries entered into our vision. The Allied one, principally British with an occasional Polish name under the insignia of Polish Second Corps, lies under a simple forest of white crosses. Everyone was equal. Everyone had earned his cross. Italians buried their dead inside a crypt located in a large mausoleum. Their soldiers rest under two wings of an imposing building. Upon entering, a visitor loses the normal solemnity found in a cemetery. The inside looked more like a bank. Italians, who perished there, were each given a place that looked like a safe deposit box or set drawers.

Little Terry kept looking at me. "Why are they mistreated? Why were they given so much less space than was given to the others, British, Poles and Australians?"

Next were the remnants of the great German army. We entered into a heavy, Baroque, almost Wagnerian building, crowded with black marble and gold lettering. Everything looked as if it was taken directly from the book of Nibelungi. Men were resting inside large, overly decorated and rather pretentious sarcophagi. This time it was Andrew who was hungry for an explanation. Was there an explanation? How could I tell both of these young people, still entering life, that humanity, even in death, retains its differences? That even in an attempt to pay ultimate tribute to men and, at that time, also a few women, national characteristics were scrupulously preserved?

We returned to Cairo full of reflections. It was Andrew who broke the silence. "Will I be drafted one day? Will I have to be a soldier?"

His mother provided an immediate answer. "I hope not, Adi. I pray that you will not."

It would not have been my instant reaction. I observed the two of them, mother and son, hugging each other to underline their common abhorrence of a possible war. Unable to shake off my own military experience when, at the age of 21, I had to enlist and spend a year as a private, I always felt that the experience, painful and often distasteful, helped me to move from being an adolescent to being a man. It also moved me from the sheltered existence of a boy spoiled by his father's affluent lifestyle, to a situation that forced me to share days and nights with men with whom I would have never met otherwise. A non-commissioned officer, who drilled and cursed us in rather unprintable language, was a simple peasant. My next-door neighbor - by "next door," I mean, in next sleeping bunker - was a truck driver. In short, it was a great lesson of democracy, a great lesson to come out of my comfortable cave, and a great lesson to feel the pain of being out of my normal habitat.

Did I really share my wife's desire to protect my only son from being a soldier?

The question haunted me a decade later when the country was in the middle of the Vietnam debate, a debate that polarized my son's and my views.

Cairo's mosques disappeared from our vision. We were on our way to the next unknown. But in the meantime, there would be home leave in an almost two month interval. Two months revisiting friends and re-establishing our shallow American roots. The family could not wait. It was the New York skyline that replaced the outline of Cairo's mosques.

Upon returning home, this time, we proudly flashed our American diplomatic passports. "Welcome home," the man behind the window examined our passports, smiled at Terry and with an expansive gesture, waved us in. We were coming home, weren't we?

New York greeted us with familiar noise, dirt, traffic jams and masses of humanity. Not much changed from the day - about thirteen years earlier - when we landed for the first time on American soil. This time, however, we knew what to expect; this time we were going to stay with friends, American friends and this time, we were returning not as refugees, but as proud owners of American diplomatic passports, almost as if our wildest dreams were about to come true.

It was the peaceful, affluent and friendly suburban Westchester village of Bronxville that offered us a roof over our head. The host and hostess, both belonging to old American families, greeted our family with open arms. The house was spacious and our quarters perfectly adequate. The initial dinner brought out numerous layers of curiosity. They inquired about our Egyptian experience. We inquired about the way things had changed during our absence. The dinner lasted long hours. They learned as much as they cared to about our first foreign assignment. We learned as much as we wanted to about their daily lives in suburban America.

The Bronxville home, an affluent New York suburb, gave us a wonderful base. Admiring the generosity of our friends who opened their home for our gang of four, we settled in. We were all in a hurry, there was so much to accomplish and see, so many people to visit, so many items to buy, so many things to discuss with my government superiors. There was also the unfinished business of

Maria, our eldest daughter, expelled by her parents from Cairo and waitressing at one of the local Schrafts, and who anxiously awaited our arrival. In short, our agenda appeared very full.

In addition, we were both full of anticipation about sharing our Egyptian experience with whoever wanted to listen. After all, is not the Middle East one of the key areas of American foreign policy? How much longer is Jerusalem going to be divided? We were there and saw the impenetrable wall that prevented Arabs and Jews to live together. We traveled to Syria and Beirut. We experienced a rather strange act of Syrian border guards erasing Israel from our road maps, which we secured from a local automobile club. We also listened to long, cumbersome speeches by numerous Arab officials, including Abdul Nasser. The colorful story of my brief detention by the Egyptian security people was naturally on top of my list. We were ready to explode with the endless number of anecdotes, politically significant developments and serious reflections how they were to affect American foreign policy during the years to come.

Two after-dinner occasions, within the confines of our friends' home, offered a great opportunity to speak, to share and even to pontificate. A handful of people, about twenty in all, gathered for our perorations. They listened, asked thoughtful, penetrating questions, dove for the dessert and left, full of compliments and expressions of gratitude, leaving us hungry for more. But there were not to be any more. Daily life took over. Children had to be driven to school, baseball games had to be watched, dinners cooked and an occasional luncheon for visiting firemen prepared. Days were too short to accommodate normal, not too exciting, but nevertheless necessary, chores. The role of Egypt in the formulation of the American foreign policy was not on top of people's agenda.

The re-entry process, that was just about to start, brought us back to reality. We were, after all, strange birds, relatively recent Americans, this was 1961 and our citizenship was granted in 1953. Marysia kept describing Egyptian poverty, Andrew kept begging to secure tickets for the next New York Giants baseball game and little Terry, at the mature age of five, was a nonplussed witness. She was full of nostalgic thoughts about her friend Nadia. Did she like New York? "Sure, why not," she mumbled under her breath. "But what will happen to Nadia?" Her father, mother and other siblings were asked to move from our house in Maadi. "Will Nadia be able to have a little garden to play in, the way she did with us?"

There was a big world of rediscovery. The question, 'What is America, Daddy?' kept recurring in our minds. Little did we know how difficult it was to re-enter. Foreign service took us, mostly myself, out of reality.

For a couple of years, there was little to remind us of our Polish roots. Daily work, daily play, daily contacts were all conducted on the basis of our official position. We were American diplomats. The diplomatic community accepted us as such. I, for one, was almost intoxicated with a sense of belonging and a feeling of having been accepted.

Every morning, surrounded by top officers of the Embassy, I was the first one to speak. My assignment was both simple and utilitarian: to sum up the morning editions of the Cairo press. A staff of readers and interpreters were ready by seven a.m. with the highlights of key articles. It was they, not me, who did the work. I was just the front man, usually unable, due to lack of linguistic skills, to verify the accuracy of what was put on my desk. A couple of Arabic-speaking officers would occasionally question my reports. As a rule, however, my little speech was accepted and often acted upon.

In New York, where we were spending our leave, our mornings were different. The house in which we stayed was far from being tidy. Most of the beds were undone all day, piles of dirty dishes stood up in the sink as a painful reminder of the hasty departure of our hosts. How wonderful it would have been to have our *suffragi* around.

"What did you say?" Marysia looked at me with horror. "Two years ago, leaving for Egypt, we never had, nor could afford, any help. Have you really been spoiled rotten? Spoiled?"

I wasn't sure.

Once again, arriving on the American shores with our Polish accent faithfully retained, we were not automatically taken as natives. On a few occasions in Egypt we were asked of our country of origin. Seldom because few of our local friends could have even imagined that someone born outside of the States could have been sent to represent the country abroad. Only on special occasions, when it served official purpose, my past was invoked. The case in point was my short detention. No native American, a couple of newspapers suggested, would have been so stupid to distribute illegal material on the streets of Cairo. Maybe they had a point? Maybe they read better than anyone else the super patriotic urges of a newly minted citizen?

A new avalanche of issues, not fully observed before our Egyptian experience, entered our visions. Racial inequalities, observed but not fully absorbed by us while in Tennessee, were one of the issues. Homelessness on the streets of affluent New York City was another. Aggressiveness of the multitude of sales people turned out to be difficult to resist. Walking along the garment district and observing from a distance an army of women bent over Singer sowing machines, I kept wondering about the difference, if any, of labor conditions in poor Cairo and rich New York. And we both kept comparing the huge difference of income, way of life and chances of improving one's lot, between the two metropolises. Maybe there were none?

There was another aspect of American life that came back to us forcefully: the multitude of choices. It came back, because we experienced it before, arriving from war ravaged England. This time our perspectives were enriched by the Egyptian experience. A visit to a medium-sized supermarket threw Andrew and Terry into shock and then later into an appetite to buy everything in sight. A famous toy store on Fifth Avenue almost tore our family apart. Bergdorf Goodman, a place where a decade or so earlier I ventured in innocently and walked out with a gold choker for Marysia, this time featured simple dresses with price tags starting in the hundreds of dollars. In front of this symbol of affluence, a black man played electric guitar, waiting for charitable gestures from busy, self-absorbed pedestrians.

We joined the crowd, looking slightly bewildered but appearing as if we belonged, as if we were members of the same self-absorbed humanity. Were we? We probably were not. There was, however, one member of the family who definitely was. Maria, our college-bound, Cairo-expelled daughter, had a job. She was a waitress.

Her workplace was a semi-fashionable restaurant in a very

fashionable suburb of Westchester. At the mature age of nineteen, she was earning her keep by collecting tips. Members of the self-absorbed humanity were the providers. She watched them come and go. She suffered with some, played with others and had fun with many. It was a young mother with three youngsters, including one toddler, who entered the place with the whirl of her full skirt accompanied by the noise of her kids. The booth that was offered was not good enough. A round table in the middle of the floor was a preferred location. It was our daughter's area. Marysia scrutinized her waitress with a penetrating and almost frightening eye. The two younger children amused themselves by throwing salt and pepper on each other. A rather complicated order followed. The mother changed her mind a couple of times while other customers signaled their impatience.

"Shall I give you a couple of minutes?" Maria asked, in her most soothing, polite voice.

"Well, young lady, I am just about ready to order. That white sauce that is described with the fish. What kind is it?"

"It is with white wine, Madam. I am told it is good."

"I did not ask your opinion," Marysia told her daughter. "Just answer my questions, okay?"

"Mommy, mommy, I want ice cream," Terry pleaded.

"Just a minute, sweetie," Marysia calmed her youngest. She then turned to her daughter/waitress, "Do you have ice cream?"

"Yes, we do. But if you will excuse me…"

"What did you say? Don't you know that the customer is your boss? That you're supposed to serve first and think of yourself later?"

Maria's anger started boiling in her chest. "I know that, Madam. But you are not the only customer here. I must serve others as well."

Marysia gathered her wide skirt as if ready to leave. But she was not entirely in charge. The two youngsters were not about to give up. They wanted to eat and they were ready to wait for their ice cream.

Maria won the encounter and the matron did not leave any tip.

An elderly gentleman, with a fading flower in his lapel, greeted his waitress with a broad smile and suggested that she should select for him the best meal of the day. A middle-aged, single woman wanted to share with Maria her views of the world and her distaste with men. She was recently divorced.

"Don't you ever get married. Just play around. Get them attached to you for a week or so, and move on." She offered more advice, "Women must learn how to be shrewd. Otherwise, they will just take advantage of you and drop you mercilessly."

There were other patrons at Maria's restaurant, young men who wanted a date, old women who drank their only cup of coffee for an hour or so, searching for someone with whom they could converse, even businessmen with their bulging attaché cases, too absorbed in their deals to even notice someone who was bringing their meals. Maria was observing the microcosm of humanity while earning a few dollars each tiring and exhausting day.

My marching orders read Seoul, South Korea. My father, still deeply disturbed by what we all heard about that distant, unknown and at one time, hermetically sealed peninsula, sent me a desperate call.

"Don't go. Save your family."

But we went. There were curiosity and challenges, and both turned out to be fully justified.

To make the most out of our home leave, we decided to go by train across the continent. At that time, the government was generous enough to provide first class airfare and sleeping car accommodations for Foreign Service people. We boarded a Pullman in Chicago. What a great adventure.

It is always a unique sensation looking from the window of a fast moving train. Nothing appears permanent. Flat fields ready to be plowed, houses embraced by picturesque fields and tiny little figures of humans rushing towards unknown destinations. Even powerful chains of snow-covered mountains pass through the passenger's field of vision rapidly. Is there anything else, any better experience to demonstrate the temporary, rapidly changing and seldom predictable, nature of human existence?

We left the swarming humanity of Chicago behind. Boarding our train, we met the man who was to be our guardian and our guide for the long transcontinental journey. He wore the slightly tired uniform of a conductor; his cap was formal but not his eyes. They were dancing with expectations. 'Who are those people entering my domain?' his eyes were asking. 'Where do they go? After all,' he probably thought to himself, 'I have been on that train for twenty-six years. I should know the type. But these four speak a funny language. The boy was more quiet than most boys his age.'

Randolph Washington did not have to wait too long to satisfy his curiosity. But he planned his strategy ahead of time. First, he would tell them about his life in Nashville, Tennessee, then about his experiences of being a black man looking for a job.

On our side, we watched the graying, slightly stooped man in uniform, unsure of what to expect. We knew that for the next three days we would have to endure each other. He could make our journey miserable or he could become a fast friend. Terry, a grown-up lady approaching her fifth birthday, was not a bit inhibited. "Are you going to use your whistle every time that the train stops?"

"Sure I will, sweetie. Tell me your name first," Randolph responded.

"Terry Nagorski."

"That is a pretty name, mighty pretty. Mine is Randolph. People call me Ralph sometimes. It's easier. And I heard all of you speaking another language. Where are you from?"

Terry looked, slightly alarmed, at her brother. "Poland," Andrew chipped in. "We speak Polish."

The black man kept smiling. "From Poland? But you don't speak the way you dad does. Are you coming from Poland now?"

"Well, no," Marysia joined the conversation. "We are really coming from Egypt."

"Well Madam, that mighty fine, mighty fine. From Egypt? So you aren't Poles? Egyptians?"

"No, we are not," I smiled in amusement. "We are Americans. You see..."

"Americans, real Americans? Just traveling across the country for fun?"

Terry came back. "No, we are going to Korea. Do you know if they have ice cream there?"

Randolph looked at his passengers for second or so. He was not amused. They were making fun of him, an old and a respectable fellow. "Goodnight, Madam," he said solemnly and firmly closed the door to our compartment.

The train kept speeding forward.

"Don't go. Save your family. Ask for another assignment." Father was worried. He knew nothing about Korea, except that a war was fought there and that it was a forbidden land where, in the past, the natives put Christian missionaries to death.

We read his letters, we pondered the assignment, but somehow neither of us took such a dramatic view of our next station in life.

Kimpo airport, serving Seoul and the rest of the peninsula, looked small, provincial and not particularly inviting. Greeted by an official of the United States Information Service, we were ushered through the passport and luggage control points, got into the embassy car and entered the Korean capital.

Little did we realize that we were about to observe a country that was not only emerging from a major armed conflict, from the end of one dictatorship (Sigman Lee) and entering into another one (Pang Chong He), but was also being led into one of the most spectacular economic revivals. Our vehicle passed a parade of busses. Andrew looked with dismay. "What are they, Daddy?"

Their engines were encompassed by a body made of discarded army tin plates. They rattled, apparently ready to fall apart. Somehow, they kept together in spite of a surge of humanity clinging to every available space. Passenger cars were few and far between. Horses and human power were much more in evidence. Rickshas, pulled by men whose bodies did not indicate special strength, prevailed. On one or two occasions, we spotted men with bells attached to their garments. Behind them were strange looking contraptions covered with a sort of a blanket. Our embassy driver was eager to explain. "Koreans," he volunteered his comments, "are strange people. They collect human waste and use it as fertilizer. This is the reason our people hate to drive into the countryside. The smell is rather unpleasant."

The children's faces displayed a depth of disgust. "Is this true, Mother?" Andrew asked.

It was true, of course. It was also true that Korea's favorite meal, *Kimchi*, produced a different type of consequence equally offensive to Western's taste. Made of cabbage and kept in sealed barrels for months to ferment, *Kimchi* entered human bodies with a vengeance. It made it convey not only the strength of individual meals, but also an odor that permeated for a long time. Nowhere was this more evident than in concert halls and movie houses. Koreans en masse provided an uninitiated foreigner with a sense of olfactory dismay, often leading to a rapid escape.

There was, however, no escape from other realities of Korean life, realities that proved exciting and almost exhilarating while observing the budding energy, the unlimited curiosity and high degree of work ethics of the population.

The two young women who joined our household as domestic servants provided the family with the first exposure to many of those characteristics. Mrs. Lee and Mrs. Kim were both in their twenties. Mrs. Lee was the very first of the applicants. Small in stature, like most Korean women, she did not beg or appear anxious. She just mentioned that she would like to work for us, that she had done work for an American family before and that there were many things she had learned. Her little daughter was the same age as our Terry.

It was Mrs. Lee who brought her companion along. They moved soundlessly around the house and there was seldom a day when we would see them grumpy or unhappy. But unlike some of our Egyptian helpers, they never attempted to please us.

Mrs. Lee, whose first name we never learned, shared with all of us her sunny composure. She also shared with us her family story. The war, a decade earlier, shattered her existence. Her father and older brother were both killed. Now, she lived with her mother and two sisters. All of them worked. All of them, one way or another, were linked to the American presence. Her mother cared for Mrs. Lee's daughter, but in rare moments of showing her emotions, she would talk about her little one with tears in her eyes. Her husband was a driver for a large trucking company. They saw each other on days when he was home, once or twice a month.

The sunny disposition, the silent way the two women moved around, the entire surroundings of a house assigned to us, an old Japanese-built adobe, were some of the key elements that kept reminding our family of the nature of our move. The Egyptian desert was replaced with rice paddies, hills and water. We left behind a multitude of humanity, depleted by sickness and perpetually searching for space, and entered into a peninsula that was free of debilitating diseases. We left behind men and women whose work ethic was heavily eroded by climate and tradition, and arrived among people whose lives were hardened by the harshness of the climate, and winters that called for special efforts to keep warm, people for whom hard work was a normal, daily staple. The two cultures could not have been more different.

The Korean chapter kept writing itself in sporadic incidents. It kept offering challenges and deep anguish. Challenges were within our relationship with the Koreans themselves. Anguish was caused, more often than not, by my colleagues within the Embassy. I discovered quickly that I was able to communicate better with a group of Korean students that I met every Saturday, than with my own Embassy superiors. How come? I would question myself.

South Korea has just undergone a dramatic transformation. One dictatorship was replaced by another. Civilians were thrown out and the military came in. On the surface, not much changed. People went to work with a similar approach as before, the economy looked better and employment remained steady. But the press - the key information source - remained muzzled. Nothing had changed. Instead of praising Sigman Lee, the prior leader, the front pages of daily papers now featured Park Chong Hee, the newest strong man. Park Chong Hee's speeches, boring, long and predictable, were reproduced verbatim.

But in spite of the superimposed uniformity, men and women moving around the busy streets of Seoul had not altered their daily habits. There seemed to be a purpose in their gait. There appeared to be a goal in their endeavors. Maybe the "national goal," announced proudly and loudly by the generals in power, caught the people's imagination? The goal to eradicate corruption, waste and the ever-present black market may have really penetrated popular minds. I wasn't sure, being too new and inexperienced in oriental society. The generals had also announced the need of austerity to keep the economy looking constantly stronger, but at the same time to satisfy Americans who continued to be the main source of capital. Once the need was announced, a decree followed: austerity will be enforced.

No imports allowed, no luxury items, no foreign fabrics and no foreign vehicles. Koreans were asked to buy only what they could produce themselves in local shops, usually housed in open wooden shacks. Drabness of clothing gave most streets a gray look. The quality of bicycles, which was the primary transportation tool, as well as other products of utilitarian nature were crude and rough. But from time to time colors and smiles cut across the grayness. Korean women wore blouses and skirts made of gorgeous local silk full of striking colors.

For the family, every single member of it, Korea opened a new and exciting vista. One member, however, fighting for her sanity and survival, was left out. Maria, the oldest and the most difficult at that time of her youth, twenty, kept writing long and often convoluted letters from her station in life, working as a waitress in Schraft, the suburban restaurant in Scarsdale, N.Y. Little Maria, the child forcibly deported from Egypt to America, spent her time living with friends of ours, dreaming about her Egyptian boyfriend and attempting to please her difficult customers.

Thus, there were parallel tracks within our relatively small clan. Our tracks were full of excitement, from helicopter's flights with local American dignitaries to Marysia's involvement with a newly organized Association of Korean University Women, to Andrew's accomplishments inside the military school.

There was still another branch of the family back in America that we were very conscious about. My parents, now in their sixties and seventies, arrived in New York harbor in 1951 and were still attempting to create for themselves some kind of semblance of a meaningful existence. While Marysia and I were fully immersed in what, at that time, looked like a rewarding occupation, rather proud of having been accepted as full-fledged Americans, the other generations - younger and older - were struggling.

The question that the "little girl," who was currently struggling in New York, asked at the very beginning of our American saga, "what is America, Daddy?" had been answered in many different ways for different people. Father, educated and deeply rooted in European tradition, culture and customs, continued to adhere to them. The only way to do so was for him to immerse himself in the group of Polish exiles. He was often alienated by, what he considered, crude and primitive American culture. He was easily put off by seemingly polite expressions of interest, friendship and other formulas used by most Americans, more often than not conveying anything of substance.

But even within the Polish circles, he had many frustrations. Accustomed to his own workshop as a prominent lawyer in pre-war Warsaw, he did not have much patience to wait for the cumbersome process leading eventually to collective decisions. The Polish Institute of Arts and Science offered him partial employment but was not the most efficient or rewarding place to work. Thus, his answer to little Maria's question was dramatically different from ours. We were on the front line of a purely American struggle for recognition outside of America's borders. He was, or tried to be, on the front line of his native country's struggle for a place within the framework of the great power's foreign policies. Our mutual goals overlapped as long as we were in Great Britain. The moment that the decision was made to emigrate further west, the very need to survive, made it difficult to continue our Polish crusade. At the same time, there was very little doubt in our minds that leaving the parents in London would be condemning them to a limited and economically deprived existence. They responded to our calls and left their beloved continent behind.

And now we were in South Korea, in Asia, a place that had never been on our mental horizon. We were in a country that had been, not unlike Poland, occupied and controlled by many others: first the Chinese, then the Mongols, later the Japanese and finally the Americans. And also, not unlike our native land, the Korean peninsula was struggling with all its force to be able to stand on its own, economically, politically and militarily.

Our Polish origin served us well in that land of perpetual fighters. Yet, without fully realizing it, we were drifting away from the key goal of our original decision, a goal to spend time outside of our native land to work on behalf of that land.

American Foreign Service was great. It was fun and it was recognition of one's personal worth. A short moment of reflection could not help but bring to realization that the road that brought me to that new station of life was paved with stones labeled "pragmatism." The two principal needs have been met, a need to make a living and a need to be recognized.

The glamour of diplomacy shined high on my mental horizon. I dove into it with delight. I bragged about it to family and friends alike. The only sane voice was that of Marysia's. She saw it the way it was, more surface than substance. She wasn't swayed by the official functions and she hated small talk around dinner tables in ambassadorial residences. She was able to see through the declarations of eternal friendship. She was also burdened with the role of a spouse. Intellectually and emotionally, fully equipped to be a person of her own, the tyranny of custom weighed heavily on Marysia's psychological wellbeing.

The Korean assignment offered various possibilities for both of us to find segments of satisfaction. For Marysia, the outlets were the Korean women's group and involvement in the Korean University Women's Association, and of course, tennis. The day of special glory came when she prevailed in the finals of the national matches, becoming the Korean champion in singles. Her Korean opponent dissolved in sobs and a flood of tears.

But that was not all, Marysia acted as a gracious hostess at numerous luncheons and dinners that we hosted. And whenever an occasion presented itself, she was able to fully partake in discussions with the moguls of Korean media and political and economic activists. A member of the Korean Ministry of Information became a personal friend along with his wife who, usually relegated within the Korean society to a subordinated role, flourished in Marysia's company.

The assignment permitted me to immerse myself in the role of an American envoy conveying the message of a distant power, controlling many levers of the local society. The most potent level was the military presence, followed by the economy. In both fields, the job that I was given, information officer within the office of Public Affairs, allowed me considerable freedom of action. It also provided a thrill, excitement and quite often, an illusion of importance.

There was a helicopter flight to a remote part of the country. Our purpose was to deliver a lecture on the potential threat of the Soviet-backed army of North Korea. A jeep awaited me at the other end, a jeep with a two-star general flag flying off its fenders. Men and officers saluted as we passed by. Some stopped in order to stiffen their backs in a formally required position.

Having been elected president of that important organization, it was up to me to preside when a meeting at the local military school featured the U.S. Commander-in-Chief as speaker. The general, in full uniform and decorations, paid lavish tribute to the institutions of the military schools and to civilians involved. I beamed with pride.

Every Saturday afternoon, a group of Korean students gathered at the building belonging to the Embassy for a session. Its overt purpose was to improve their linguistic skills. Its covert desire was to bring together young men and women, and let them speak on any topic of their choice: birth control, the educational reforms, Korean foreign policy or relations with two of their most important partners, the United States and Japan.

The students loved each occasion. They grabbed at the opportunity to lambaste America and they fully unloaded their contempt and hatred for Japan. In their mischievous way, they kept comparing Korean-Japanese relations to Russian-Polish relations. Debates, discussions and even passionate and heated arguments, rare in typical Asian environments, dominated the encounters. My role was to be the "orchestra conductor," to introduce each topic and to occasionally bring calm and order. I was looking forward to every coming Saturday. On one occasion, I managed to bring one of my embassy's colleagues as a special attraction.

Saturdays, however, were rather sacrosanct within the American family culture. To bypass a sense of neglect of my own children, I kept bringing them, one-by-one, to the KASA meeting - Korean American Students Association. These meetings existed and were fully functional during the entire three years of our Korean assignment.

Another type of assignment led me to the countryside.

A couple of hours drive from Seoul, a huge fertilizer plant polluted that countryside. The biggest plant of its kind in Korea, contributing considerably to the fertility of the land and to the well being of Korean farmers, had been a showpiece of American contributions for a long time. Built by a team of American engineers, operated at first by imported experts, and financed entirely by Americans, the plant was viewed as a prime example of intelligent use of our AID funds. The place figured prominently on every itinerary of visiting congressmen.

It immediately entered into my plans for Korean journalists. It had been some time since they wrote anything about it. A military bus was easily secured and a skilled American guide mobilized. Lunch was prepared by the plant's management and a trip organized for fifteen happy scribes and as many photographers. Most of the daily press dutifully published long articles about the wonders of American technology. For a couple of days, I walked, bathed in the glory of a job well done.

On occasion, however, the glory was replaced by a sense of painful reality. Shortly after our arrival, I went to visit one of the two most powerful men in Korea. The director of USOM, Jim Killan, was an imposing man, towering over most of us with his 6'2" frame and looking sharply into a newcomer's eyes. "Are you another petitioner?" he seemed to convey a hidden question. "A fellow in need of a contract? A favor? A letter of introduction?"

I needed neither. Appointed initially as a liaison man with the AID agency, I assumed, in my naiveté, that my arrival would be known at USOM. I marched confidently into the director's office, only to be met by a friendly smile and total lack of recognition. "Ah," he said. "Great. Nice to meet you. Good luck in your new job."

That wasn't good enough for me. I wanted more. I expected involvement and understanding of the inner-workings of the office, of conceptual thinking of the director and his staff. Could I be included in the weekly meetings of the senior staff, meetings known within the agency as Vespers?

I could not help noticing a rapid exchange of glances between Jim Killan and his secretary. This fellow must be pretty smart if he discovered our Vespers so soon after arrival. It was to be a fairly confidential name for what otherwise should have been known in bureaucratic terms as a weekly staff gathering. The name derived from the notion, widely discussed within USOM, that Vesper attendees were assured of total confidence and non-attributions. Now, this newcomer, totally green about our work, wants to be included?

The Director wanted to secure wider opinion. "We will let you know in a couple of weeks."

Then I was accepted, but not for long. There were two meetings. Each of them was full of details, yet few touched on matters of policy. My silence must have been weighing heavily on the minds of men - because there were only men - accustomed to lively exchanges within the perimeter of known individuals. At one point, thinking of a rather minor issue of public perception, I dared to suggest darkening of USOM's building after office hours. Electricity was scarce in the Korean capital at that time. Shouldn't we set an example within the American official compounds?

A week later, I arrived at the usual time. Jim spotted me, got up from his chair and, wrapping his powerful arm around my back, walked me towards an exit. "It probably will be better if you don't come anymore. The men did not feel comfortable with a stranger around. Sorry about that." And he was gone with one member of the Vespers community passing me by with his eyes glued to the floor.

They had to rethink their vision and focus at a much higher elevation when a series of dramatic events challenged their complacency.

Koreans were neither able nor willing to forget and to forgive. The Japanese occupation lasted thirty-five long years, from 1910 to 1945. Japan had to lose the war to be forced out of Korea. And now, their new friends and strong allies were trying to force a free Korea to normalize relations with their most hated enemy. No way.

The streets of Seoul were suddenly filled with a sea of humanity. Led by students, many of them barely born by the time the occupation ended, Koreans marched in front of the American official buildings, protesting.

"No normalization!"

"No fraternization!"

"No forgiveness for torture, humiliation and for using Korean women as prostitutes for Japanese soldiers. America, wake up!" they shouted on the top of their lungs. "Put yourself in our position!"

I stood at the window of my office watching. Their march was orderly and their slogans, printed neatly in Hanguk (Korean alphabet) and English, were clear and belligerent. They were also anti-American, something not viewed with tolerance by the government of General Park Chong Hee.

It was as if all of a sudden, sunshine disappeared and the dark clouds of a storm descended upon the marchers. From side streets, hidden behind buildings, hundreds of policemen armed with rubber sticks attacked. The marching crowd stood mute momentarily and then counter-attacked. Students and soldiers tackled each other with a ferocity that I had never witnessed. However, the marchers were no match for the trained policemen. The melee lasted less than ten minutes. Scores of demonstrators were carted away into police vans. The rest dispersed in a hurry. The demonstration was over.

Was this a familiar sight? Was it similar to Poland and Hungary in 1956 or East Germany in 1953? Or was I unfair to our Korean allies by making this comparison? How would I handle the events in our official press releases? How would it appear in our weekly newsreel, that my film section was producing and distributing to movie houses all over the country?

"What is America, Daddy?" flashed across my mental screen and there was only one answer. We played it straight, with a full report on the marchers, police brutality and jail sentences. My embassy bosses never reprimanded me. The post never heard a word of criticism from Washington. Only a few of Korean officials stopped returning my telephone calls.

And then there was my big birthday party.

It started modestly. The two of us decided to go to the officers' club to celebrate. After all, making it to the half-century mark was a rather important event. A couple of friends spotting us sitting alone at a table came over. Marysia mumbled something to the effect that the bottle of champagne was not our daily fare. "So, why today?" the guests inquired. The secret was out. Within minutes, no less than twenty people surrounded us. Tables were put together and the singing of "happy birthday" lasted well past midnight.

The birthday drinking was a rather benign affair. There was another one that lasted even longer and did not have a happy ending. One of the traditional Korean institutions was the Kiseng House. It had Japanese roots. In Japan, the geisha houses established a couple of centuries earlier served in contemporary days as a place of relaxation for tired businessmen not particularly attracted to their home lives. It was there that especially selected young and attractive women were ready to serve their visitors. Services were varied. Outside of serving drinks and food, Japanese geishas were known for their singing and music. Sex was not excluded, but not something that was automatically expected. Introduced to Korea during the Japanese occupation, it turned out to be a cruder version of the original.

One of my favorite colleagues at the Embassy was Philip Habib, the political counselor. Of Lebanese origin, witty and shrewd, Phil loved to have fun. Invited to the Kiseng House by one of his numerous Korean friends, he suggested that I go along. Curious and not yet exposed to anything as typically local as the Kiseng House, I grabbed the opportunity. Little did I know that Phil would one day reach the highest rank of the foreign service, that of career ambassador, and that it would be up to him to negotiate with a delegation of North Vietnamese, along with Avarel Harriman, a way to end the American involvement.

At the moment, we were both being driven to an elegant house in downtown Seoul, other matters on our minds.

A long table, beautifully arranged, awaited our arrival. Two other Americans, unknown to us, joined the group. About ten Korean businessmen and a couple of journalists were already on hand. We were seated in the local style, on cushions with our legs stretched under the table. Behind each of us a young woman, dressed in traditional Korean attire, made sure that our cushions were properly placed and that our glasses filled. Every guest faced one of the Korean hosts. The ritual demanded a number of toasts, initiated first by the hosts and later by the guests. The first toast revealed the content of our glasses. I expected sake, a rather mild local drink. It turned out that we were treated royally by Korean standards. Our glasses contained nothing but scotch, no ice, no soda, just pure undiluted whisky.

I remembered about a dozen toasts. My memory went blank on the rest of the night, only that the young angel was refilling my glass with tremendous efficiency. I wasn't sure how I got home. The only recollection that remained was the great amusement of the Korean guard at the entrance to our embassy compound. He smiled, looking at me with a mix of compassion and joy as my unsteady legs attempted to find my way home. Marysia greeted me at the door expecting a normal, although a bit late, return. Within minutes, I was in bed with an icepack on my forehead.

I was told that Phil went home without any visible effects. And he probably gulped more toasts than I did.

18

France

We had begun preparations for yet another transition. First, there was Egypt and then Korea. The next station on our Foreign Service itinerary was to be Paris. A dream assignment? It would be an assignment that plunged me into the depths of depression.

Human institutions have a life of their own. Initiated, originally, in order to provide a framework, to facilitate interactions and to make sure that individuals, inclined to step outside of accepted norms, learned the limits of their freedom. Institutions have the tendency of outgrowing their mandate. Human beings, the creators of these new "monsters," soon discovered their almost total dependency. Young men entering religious orders knew in advance that the church is bound to control their lives, as were men and women entering the military career. Within the private sector, corporate communities are less rigid but armed with powerful weapons of economic welfare; sooner or later they assume the role of a controlling factor. It would be, therefore, logical and natural for anyone becoming a government bureaucrat to expect the same. Not me.

Drunk with a sense of tremendous accomplishment, repeating to myself and to anyone who wanted to listen how lucky I was to enter the ranks of civil and, later, foreign service, I relegated all other thoughts to the back of my mind. The most important facts were simple. Barely three years after obtaining citizenship, I was a GS 14 civil servant. Barely six years after this monumental event, I was given an American diplomatic passport. Should I have worried about my freedom or about the institution I was about to enter? I did not have the faintest idea about its structure, hierarchy or the chain of command within the small official unit, the Embassy of the United States.

I was to learn fast, probably faster than an average person finding himself in a similar position. Because I nursed unrealistic dreams and because I had ambitions that had been awakened by an initial series of successes, ambitions that surpassed reality.

Barely six months into the new career in Egypt, I eagerly scanned the semi-annual promotion list, disappointed that my name was not there. Spoiled by early laudatory performance reports written by my immediate supervisor, the public affairs officer, I expected the Washington counterparts to notice, to act and to promote. I totally overlooked other factors that any personnel officer was apt to notice, the family dissatisfaction with the location (Egypt), my frequent criticism of various aspects of USIS activities and my tendency to act and move alone. In short, I was not a perfect example of an officer who could be easily assessed and moved from place to place.

In my second post, Korea, I was in the limelight more than the man who was my boss. His philosophy was different, even the conclusions we reached after any kind of judgment were diametrically opposed. His attitude towards the "natives" was full of contempt, reinforced by his wife's even more negative opinion of Koreans at large. The results were easily predictable. My performance ratings went down from a five in Egypt to a two in some categories like "loyalty" and "dependability." My boss, easy-going, a strong believer in the hierarchical structure of Foreign Service and not a particularly hard worker, hated my guts.

Almost a decade after our service there, during a dinner with a former KASA student in a New York restaurant, who was now a successful business entrepreneur, I received a job offer. Would we be willing to return to Korea in a different capacity, as a partner in his venture? He had started a toy factory and had grown beyond expectations. He needed an American to be one of his senior executives. There will be a house in Seoul, an attractive salary and plenty of bonuses. Would I come?

Flattered, amused and touched by his friendship, I looked at Marysia. She raised her glass and proposed a toast to our friend. "We belong here," she said. "We've pulled our roots once before. We cannot do it again."

I remembered, vividly, at that moment how a large group of

Korean students danced a farewell dance at the Kimpo airport while saying goodbye to our little family.

Bureaucracy worked on its own, totally detached from human potential. I was leaving Korea with the glory of solid accomplishments. There was another man who left Korea a couple of months earlier. Samuel Berger, our ambassador there, wrote to Carl Rowan, Director of USIA about the work that Marysia and I had left behind. We knew nothing about his letter. We learned about it long after the Foreign Service.

> As I leave Korea, I want especially to call to your attention the outstanding work which has been done here by one of your USIS officers, Mr. Zygmunt Nagorski, Jr. and by his wife, Marysia. During the whole of my tour, they have worked hard and long with success to serve the United States Information Service, the Embassy, and the United States Operation Mission in Korea. I have nothing but praise for their work with Korean youth, Korean women, with intellectuals and the press, and with the U.S. military.
>
> It is always refreshing, encouraging and stimulating to have a unique couple like this on one's staff. If I have come to know them better than most USIS officers it is precisely because they stood out from most of the others, and because they have gone about their work with zest, imagination, intelligence, energy and quietness - qualities which I value greatly.
>
> In my twenty-two years of overseas work, I long ago came to the conclusion that success in the conduct of our foreign relations rests as much on persons as on policy. Everywhere I have served I have searched for talented officers among my associates who have the combination of qualities needed for dealing with difficult problems in complicated countries. I regard Mr. Nagorski as one of these.
>
> If you are searching for an exceptional officer to handle difficult problems either in Washington or abroad, I recommend Mr. Nagorski to you.
>
> Mr. Nagorski is not aware that I am writing this letter.

The letter was written on July 7, 1964, a month before I had received news of my new post. The Paris assignment, announced in a friendly letter from the personnel director of the Agency, looked great until the job designation arrived. After spending five years as the country information officer in two locations, I was assigned as assistant information man in the French capital. A normal career pattern would indicate an upward move. But my direction was the opposite; it was a step down in my career development.

The institution, known as the foreign service of the United States, took over. The past, punctuated by solid inroads made into local societies, was not even mentioned. What mattered were efficiency reports and opinions of men higher on the totem pole. But there was no way to hide the very fact that I was crushed.

Enter human resilience; enter the human ability to adjust. A series of talks ensued in Washington where various alternatives were touched upon. Unbeknownst to me, I was nominated to be the information officer in Saigon. I learned about it long after I left the Agency. The bottom line of the entire turbulent and psychologically devastating appointment was acquiescence.

Paris under General Charles DeGaulle proved to be everything that we had expected, a low level job, but a great location with life in the suburbs, allowing immersion in the French community. And for a change, a boss who was cultured, highly educated and was an Ambassador who would become a legend in the Foreign Service. His name was Charles Bohlen. He was a veteran of tough assignments, including the ambassadorship in the Soviet Union and one of the top advisers of President Roosevelt. Now, Bohlen had to carry the cross of Lorraine. Charles DeGaulle, with his well-known contempt for Americans, was not an easy Chief Executive Officer to please.

Vaucresson, a small village, offered a good school, an idyllic setting, which in the past had inspired impressionist painters, and was an easy commute by train to Paris. Around our new location lived French families. Most of them were old and well established. Most of them were traditional and strongly patriotic. The only exception was our landlord and his wife. Relatively new in the village, probably no more than a couple of decades, Monsieur Bercal was viewed with a degree of detachment and slim tolerance by the rest of the community. He was not only a newcomer; he was also a man from the lower class. As soon as the war ended, we were duly informed, Monsieur Bercal established himself as a merchant collecting and selling scrap metals. Somehow, he must have done well. By the time we rented his house, he was able to acquire a substantial piece of property known as a "palace" in the main square of Vaucresson.

It was there that Madame Bercal reigned. She was a small woman, with distinguished features, giving the impression of permanent anger. Her sharp nose, curved lips and rather unkempt hair did not invite intimacy or even a conversation. It took us a fair amount of time to break through her exterior and establish some kind of relationship. This was necessary in view of the fact that she was the family treasurer. Our rents had to be paid promptly and delivered to her. We could only imagine the potential storm caused by anyone being a day or a few hours late in paying her dues.

Her husband, on the other hand, was a jovial, typical French bourgeois, middle class, who would never turn down a glass of wine. A few months after we got acquainted, we received a semi-formal invitation to celebrate the New Year with them. All four of us walked to the "palace" for the occasion. The children, Terry, 8, and Andrew, 17, gawked with disbelief at the rather gaudy interior, and the two of us wondered what to expect. But Monsieur Bercal, who on many occasions proclaimed that he liked big things and big displays, *J'aime les choses grande*, lived up to his principles. We were all served champagne in tall glasses, nothing unusual. The special touch was provided by our host who placed twenty-dollar gold coins at the bottom of each glass. We admired his creativity, we joked about his wealth and we were almost ready to thank him for his generosity. Fortunately, other guests arrived, interrupting our stream of social politeness.

By the end of the reception, Monsieur Bercal carefully collected all the coins. Our kids, openly disappointed, swore never to set foot in the "palace" again.

Vaucresson proved to be a blessing. It was quiet, unassuming and gave me the chance to commute to Paris by a train. It was a blessing simply to participate in the daily ritual of Frenchmen and women totally detached from the usual crowd of diplomats and their French peers that we were exposed to. Sitting between a solid matron and her husband, chatting with a young lawyer starting his career, discussing politics with a blue-collar worker, normally immersed in his study of Paris Soir or other not too complicated newspapers, provided me a different window of opportunity. Most of the people working for the government were crooks I was informed. All of them steal money earned by men who spend their lives working hard and honestly. They levy taxes. Isn't that the best way to rob people of their earnings, earnings that should belong to individuals, not to the bloated bureaucracy?

The thirty-five minute commute, from Vaucresson to Paris, provided me with the best intelligence on the mood of the people of France, governed at that time by the historical figure of Monsieur le General.

At the end of the train line was the job: assistant information officer.

The offices of the United States Information Services were located at the ancient palace at Faubourg St. Honore. Later, transformed into the official residence of the Ambassador, it fully regained its splendor. But at the time of my arrival, it looked rather gray and unkempt, with poorly painted rooms and long corridors, bare walls and fairly unappealing exterior. Compared to the large, airy office that I occupied in Korea, my new location had the dimensions of a closet. Its lone window, probably unwashed for weeks, faced a parking lot. My duties were spelled out, rather casually, by the man who had the title of Information Officer and was thus my immediate boss: films, TV, radio and special projects, as well as publications, and occasional visitors. The rest was left unspoken. I figured out that whatever would be considered cumbersome or uninteresting was bound to be thrown in my direction.

Fortunately, some of these "uninteresting items" turned out to be my saving grace.

The Annual Air Show was one of them and the Television Festival in Monte Carlo, another. And, naturally, the Cannes Film Festival, an annual circus of parades, social entertainment and a gathering of the world biggest egos, fell into my lap.

The Paris assignment, in spite of a series of deep disappointments, offered a couple of golden nuggets. I clung to them with every ounce of my body and soul. The disappointments were centered on career developments. Not only was I demoted, but when the list of conversion arrived at the post, my name was also omitted. The conversion was to formally appoint people to the rank of Foreign Service Officers, equal to the positions held at the State department. It was to be Presidential appointment. My semi-official explanation, received from a friendly official in Washington, was that the Director could not recommend me in clear conscience due to my past efficiency reports. Two negative aspects were cited: harshness in treating subordinates and lack of sound judgment. My Korean past, which I considered our best foreign assignment, was catching up with me.

There was also another rather ominous sentence in a letter that I received from an old friend, who happened to be in charge of personnel. "The Director has asked some of the Agency's key executives to review the records of all those officers not nominated and advise him regarding their future." The sentence started the process, a long one, and the one that eventually led our little family back to the States, then eventually led me to Vietnam and ultimately, to one of the most satisfying jobs that I ever held. But this was all way out into the future, the future that no one could have predicted or anticipated.

In the meantime, there was a job to be done. In the very first efficiency report that I received from Paris I sensed the recognition and began to feel that maybe there was a light at the end of the tunnel. "It was something of a blow to Mr. Nagorski's pride to be assigned as Assistant Information Officer when he has been IO at his previous posts. However, he did not sulk over this, but rolled up his sleeves and went to work with energy and enthusiasm." The reviewing officer did not realize that I had no choice and that it would have been against my personality, my own self-worth to sit idly contemplating the past injustice. There was a need, a dramatic need to act, to dive into whatever new possibilities presented themselves.

The 26th semi-annual Air and Space Show in Paris was the first one to tackle. How did it land at my doorstep? I wasn't sure. It did not matter. Here it was, a wonderful event, full of implications for the American image on French soil.

The first word about the nature of the American delegation coming from Washington arrived at 2:30 a.m. at the residence of the public affairs officer. The message was brief and somewhat startling: "The Vice-President of the United States, the NASA Administrator and three astronauts James McDivitt, Edward White and John Glenn, would land at Le Bourget that very afternoon."

The entire team of USIS workers went into orbit. By the time the Presidential jet touched down at the airport, we were ready to swing into action.

The Air Show was full of anticipated glitter. Luxuriously furnished tents stood side-by-side like mushrooms that spring out after an early drizzle. Each tent represented a manufacturer, a supplier or a "friend" of the aerospace industry. Champagne flew in abundance. The most elaborate menus were offered to the special guests. The entire atmosphere was full of anticipation, somewhat artificial joy assisted by an army of experienced hustlers. Deals were made, promises exchanged and the show lived up to its reputation as being the top open-air market.

That was the only way to get involved, to dive into every aspect of the occasion. I did it with gusto and all of the past sufferings disappeared. I was swimming and having a great time.

A great opportunity presented itself when on a Sunday morning, John Glenn and his wife decided to go to church. Notre Dame was their obvious choice. A couple of minutes after they left the embassy, I was asked to follow them, to help and maybe to guide. Paris, after all, was for them more of a *terra incognita* than outer space.

A fast car was immediately produced, our indispensable local man, Monsieur LaFontaine, mobilized and off we went.

Notre Dame was crowded to capacity. I walked slowly examining every pew, stared at by irritated churchgoers, trying to find the American astronaut. It took me a good five minutes before I spotted the tall figure of the future senator. From that moment on, I took charge of the events.

First, one of the Notre Dame's curators was alerted to the fact that one of the American astronauts was in attendance. Immediately, word went out to the priest celebrating the mass. There was enough time for him to stop before the final blessing of the faithful to make the announcement. Necks starting craning, eyes desperately searching for the famous man. I led the curator to Glenn and the crowd, instead of leaving the church, moved in wave after wave to John. Pieces of papers were thrust into his hands for autographs. When finally we reached a corridor leading to the interior, press photographers, obviously alerted by some publicity-oriented priest, started clicking their cameras.

A grand tour of the cathedral followed. We climbed steep stairs usually off limits to every day tourists, walked on the roof which offered a spectacular view of Paris, admired old frescos hidden from down below, touched some of the gargoyles and left the church with full satisfaction of a job well done. The next day's newspapers duly reported the lucky day for good Catholics who went to church on Sunday: "They were able to see, to touch and even to talk to a genuine American astronaut."

The Vice President, who at the same time was given an audience with the General, was impressed as was the Ambassador and my boss and all of our USIS team. But I was simply lucky. I found my target and he played my game. Along the way, the entire cast of actors performed, the crowd, the curators, newspaper photographers and all the rest of the auxiliaries.

The grayness of the job was interrupted again by a different kind of event. Since within my portfolio were films, radio and television, I was asked to attend, assess and report back on the event of rather peculiar significance: the Cannes Film Festival.

The Festival, described by one of my fellow officers, was a "runaway circus of politics, intrigues and some almost incidental, film showing." Film stars of all description elbowed past each other toward the first rows of performances, gala dinners, short cruises on yachts belonging to other celebrities and other similar events.

May was a good month for the family. Schools were on spring break and children were excited beyond description at the prospects of going to the French Riviera. And we were going first class, with the Festival organizers picking up the tab. The Carlton hotel, with its splendor, opened up its doors to our family. Our rooms were spacious and the view of the sea superb. Food, prepared by a team of French chefs, could not have been better. In the hallways and in the lobby, we encountered celebrities of all kinds, Charles Boyer here, Gina Lolabrigida there.

Film critics from all over the world crowded the bar. Idle aristocrats descended on Cannes from the five corners of the world. Local millionaires were outbidding each other in offering super elegant dinners and fancy cocktails. The circus was in full swing. But in spite of all the distractions, there was a job to be done, a job to make sure that American films were shown, admired and bought. I was under the careful watch of producers, sponsors and by the head of the U.S. Motion Picture Export Association. The task wasn't easy.

The place was teeming with gossip and such easily bruised egos of intrigues aiming at the fiercely competitive market, so it was necessary to maneuver gently, to manipulate people without them perceiving the manipulation, and to be on good terms with as many players in that strange game as possible. Prior to the Festival, the U.S. Information Agency produced a film about life and death of President Kennedy. "Years of Lightning, Day of Drum" was a dramatic presentation, full of passion and devotion to the various tasks that the young President outlined for himself. After endless negotiations, we were able not only to produce a French version of the documentary, but also able to assure its national distribution. My next job was to make sure that it would be screened at the Festival.

The glittering audience attended the showing. The tragic loss of the most popular American president ever, the poignancy of the film, its ability to project a vibrant, young worrier determined to move America into a new direction, captured the usually cynical crowd. There were tears, loud applause and enthusiastic revues. Our little team, which labored behind the scenes, was elated. Days of tribulations, almost despair were behind us.

Memories of endless luncheons and dinners with producers, organizers and other moguls that dominated the decision-making apparatus of the festival, were erased from our tired minds. The feat of having the film featured at Cannes was hailed by Ambassador Bohlen as an outstanding achievement. The insignificant job that I landed in Paris had its exciting moments.

Excitement was not limited to professional accomplishments. Sitting at some important table at an equally "important" event,

Marysia and I were able to observe an illustrious parade of beautiful people. Jewelry, furs (yes, furs in the month of May, on the French Riviera), women's heads fresh from local and very expensive coiffeurs, men's latest fashions in blue, white and black tuxedos, all formed a panorama to be discovered, contemplated and even some times, admired. Yet we both realized that we have moved into an artificial world. Like the movies that the men and women attending the Festival created, so was the atmosphere at Cannes: beautiful, in living colors but totally detached from real life. The more illusion films created, the more successful they became. Most of the theater-going crowd was, it seemed to us, seeking illusions. Once discovered and experienced, it was almost immediately moved into a notion of reality. It was no longer illusion. It was real. Actors and actresses, producers and even people who were used as props, easily confused their acting with real life. Ronald Reagan was a prime example of that transformation.

The Cannes Festival can easily be classified as a perk. It was a perk within the scope of a rather gray and dull description of my other duties. It combined involvement in this annual circus, making an input through the Embassy's film production and at the same time, bringing the family into the luxury of French Riviera.

Our hotel was one of the best. It featured a private beach reachable by equally private tunnel under the busy Corniche. For Andrew and Terry, our two youngest offspring, this was a type of vacation that nothing else would top. For the two of us, it was another type of reality. We knew that we could not have possibly afforded anything comparable on our own.

Before returning to the daily chores at our Paris location, another perk came our way, the International Television Festival in Monte Carlo. The only drawback was viewing three or four TV productions every day. The benefits were another week or so in the luxurious environment of the Grand Hotel in Monte Carlo and moving around with a different entertainment crowd, young men and women dedicated to the idea of making this relatively new art relevant, serious and at the same time, entertaining. There was much less phoniness, much less playing for cameras and much less artificiality. In short, it was a relief.

There was little relief upon return to Paris. The man who was the writer of my efficiency report best captured the situation. Richard Monsen, at that time Deputy Public Relations officer, could not have been more sympathetic and more complimentary, and yet he was unwilling to take another step to make my professional life restored to its earlier satisfaction. Here is, in part, what he wrote.

> As a result of his outstanding performance during the Air Show and the visit of the Vice President (Humphrey), I am submitting a recommendation that he be given a special citation.
>
> He has had two heavy blows since coming here. The first one was not being appointed Information Officer when the IO was assigned to Saigon. I did not recommend the appointment and I told him quite frankly why, that the past record gave him a reputation of limited judgment and of rigid treatment of subordinates. The second blow was his elimination from the list of those recommended by the Director for Foreign Service Officer status. This was a hard one, and his first reaction was to resign, then to request transfer to domestic government service.
>
> Characteristically he got busy instead, and he told me the other day he had no time to worry about the matter further. Such attitude is exemplary, and we shall be seeing ways for getting him on the FSO list, when the machinery for such a move is established.

Establishing machinery within the government structure is usually a long, dragging, and endless process. I had neither the time nor the patience. Within months of the "two blows," in reality not fully related to them, I decided to end my Foreign Service career. It was a painful, difficult decision. But I was helped dramatically in making it by a team of close friends, who on the other side of the ocean, plotted to find a niche for me. A cable from Sam Hayes, President of the Foreign Policy Association, clinched the deal. I was offered a job: the location was New York and the salary comparable to what I was earning in Paris. My duties would be to develop and strengthen the network of World Affairs Councils in the United States.

There was the usual cocktail party bidding us farewell. Ironically, it was combined with a welcome reception for the incoming new Information Officer. The four of us, the newcomer and his wife and Marysia and I, stood dutifully in the reception line. A parade of well-wishers shook our hands and smiled diplomatically.

The Paris departure occurred in 1966. I was at that time fifty-four years old. At that time, neither myself nor Marysia nor anyone else in our family was able to predict that this would be the beginning of a new, professional career. Looking back, the answer should have been easy. We were leaving behind the life of a nomadic family, which, through luck, determination and a fair amount of hard work, managed to do well. We were leaving behind the memories of ancient Egypt and we could not help recalling the day that I had spent under arrest in an elegant office of one of my tormentors, punctuated by personal failures and successes. We reflected on a mob's attack on the building of the Embassy. We were leaving behind South Korea, its exuberance and its ability to climb the ladder of economic recovery. It was also in Seoul that on October 30, 1963 one of the local newspapers (*Kyunghyan Shinmun*) published an article with a rather unusual headline: "Mrs. Nagorski, sports queen, holds Korean tennis in her hands." It went on.

> Mrs. Nagorski won the championship of the 18th National Tennis Tournament. Thus, she boasts of the championship for three years in a row. Although a mother of one son and two daughters, including a coed, she won the title by contesting with young rivals. Mrs. Nagorski was humble to say, 'I am not much of a champion but my victory was only possible because Korean tennis has a short history.' The American lady, of Polish descent, was overflowing with energy and youthfulness, which can hardly be found in Korean women of similar ages. Since she first came to Korea in 1961 with her husband, who is now information officer at the American Embassy in Seoul, she monopolized the cup each succeeding year. She said Korean women tennis champions are too passive in their enthusiasm for tennis because they continue to play with the few players they know, instead of making progress by playing with many

people. She regrets that there are no Korean tennis players who call on her for games.

Mrs. Nagorski started playing tennis when she was in high school in Warsaw. Her husband is also a good tennis player (wrong!) and her son Andrew, holds the championship of the American school at Yongsan.

When asked to comment on the Korean press since her husband is the information officer, she replied that she enjoys reading newspapers but not talking about them. Looking at her not only as a tennis champion, but as an energetic middle-aged lady who can contest with girls as young as her daughter, I cannot help envying her when I think of Korean women who get old so quickly.

And there was Paris, with frustrations, beauty, professional disappointments and personal, family attachments and delights. In short, the years spent in the foreign service of the United States never anticipated even in our boldest dreams, and only enriched our lives. Little did we know that our return to America would be greeted with a multitude of surprises.

19

The Return

The jump from Vaucresson to Scarsdale, NY was also from a small, quaint, distant suburb in Paris to a large, modern, affluent suburb in New York. We landed back in America during the painful days of the Vietnam engagement. Our only son was about to approach draft age. My strongly myopic vision saw the Asian adventure as the only way to arrest further Communist encroachments. In my new position, I was ready to preach that gospel to the audiences, the uninformed, but easily moved by patriotic slogans, Americans.

I was blessed by having few doubts about the righteousness of our position. The only voice of sanity coming to my closed mind was that of other family members. Marysia, my wife and steady companion, had doubts. My son, Andrew, went even further. He sensed the fatality of the American engagement, himself a veteran of the civil rights movement. He was not at all convinced that our role in South Vietnam was to include heavy military involvement. He was far from being a pacifist but instinctively, he feared Vietnam.

Within a brief period of two years, full of activities, family conflicts, ultimate inner conversions and unpredictable fate brought me face to face with the Vietnam reality.

I landed in Saigon shortly after the Tet Offensive, the first major American defeat of the war. The journey from Paris to Saigon, via New York City, Salt Lake City, Omaha and a multitude of other localities where World Affairs Council were either in existence or in formation, was a remarkable way to learn, to meditate and to change. It was an unpredictable journey, as were most others during our turbulent lives.

This journey started thanks to short deliberations of three men who huddled together in a New York joint. Bob MacDonald, John Richardson and Harry Boardman, old and faithful friends, received a distress call. Would you please figure out how to prepare a soft landing pad for a returning family? How to make sure that the Nagorski clan will have enough to eat after returning from a series of Foreign Service adventures?

It was Bob who hit the lucky number. The Foreign Policy Association, an outfit where he worked after spending nearly a lifetime in a successful business venture, had just received a grant. The Ford Foundation decided in its ultimate wisdom that the barbarians living outside of the New York-Washington region should be educated about foreign policy. A network of World Affairs Councils scattered around the country were to be used as vehicles. In places where Councils did not exist, the Foundation wanted them to be created.

A staff meeting was held at the FPA headquarters. Do we know anyone who could be brought in to head the project?

Bob MacDonald knew someone.

The FPA office in New York City was rather drab and austere, so was my initial reception. Sam Hayes, a rather detached and cold personality, was nevertheless gracious in welcoming a new member of his staff. The money was there. The position was secured with good possibility for an extension. But, of course, it all depends on how successful we are going to be.

Success? How will that be measured? By the number of new entities created around the country? By a higher level of people's involvement and interest in foreign policy?

No one had an answer. The field was new. The position I was to occupy was equally untested. How about looking at first at one of the Councils, which was considered almost a model for everyone else?

I took a train to Philadelphia. Ruth Miller, president of the Philadelphia Council, awaited my arrival. A strong friendship developed almost instantly. Who was she? A past middle-aged woman, gray hair, a little wrinkled face that lit up with a broad, natural smile. She was also a dynamo at work. Her job was to bring blue-blooded Philadelphians - and anybody else who cared - toward a better understanding of America's role in the world and to communicate a simple message that the main-line inhabitants are important, but not predominant. That they cannot live in isolation, enjoying their affluence, their fame and their influence on local politics. She created a Board composed of some key luminaries of the city. From time to time she would slip an unknown name into that illustrious crowd. It might be a woman who made herself a name as provider of assistance to hungry and to homeless, or it could be a black or a Hispanic. Her chairman of the Board, a man with as wide a vision as her own, knew about her subversive work and always looked the other way.

Ruth obviously did not need any help, yet she received me with an expression of gratitude. Anyone arriving from FPA Headquarters was to be welcomed. What can that arrival do?

"Well," Ruth answered, "with your connections ('my connections?' I almost burst laughing), you can secure a parade of first-rate speakers for our functions."

"Like who?" I asked.

"Well, Secretary of State, some key ambassadors, maybe one or two members of the National Security Council, visiting heads of states. Whoever. We need our message to be communicated to our members as forcefully as possible. The war in Vietnam keeps eroding our influence. Philadelphia, a patriotic but highly critical city, requires a sophisticated and subtle approach."

I was immediately struck by her Vietnam reference. It touched upon a painful subject. The war was eroding people's influence in foreign policy? It should have been just the opposite. Firmly believing in the domino theory, schooled and deeply influenced by anti-communist views, I was a strong supporter of American involvement. I wrote editorials to the New York Times to that effect. I made speeches defending President Johnson's decisions that kept escalating the conflict.

It was my son, Andrew, who threw cold water on my uncritical approach. Of draft age, but exempt on account of being a student at Amherst College, Andrew, after a long period of reflection and after talking to his mother and me, made up his mind that Vietnam was an unjust war. Never doubting the communist threat and its dominant role in his family's native country of Poland, he was unable to see any similarity with the situation in that distant Asian country.

Solid in his own value system, deeply attached to his church, mostly through the influence of his mother, Andrew joined numerous protesters marching up and down various avenues, streets, and highways denouncing America's role. During the time that I was readjusting to the United States and when I was embarking on a new, unpredictable and unknown professional road, he was rather firmly rooted in his beliefs. And when the time came for me to start doubting and an opportunity offered itself for me to look Vietnam directly in the eyes, Andrew silently observed and waited.

In the meantime, immersed in the new job, sparked by a passion for injecting fervor into the gray masses of America in the field of foreign affairs, I kept moving around. It was Cincinnati one day and Phoenix the next. There was a Kentucky Rotary Club speech in the morning and an after-dinner pronouncement in Southern California. There were radio shows and television interviews, press conferences in public and endless hours standing at obscure bars surrounded by hungry journalists looking for a story.

"Who is that guy?" many of them asked. "Who comes to Cody, California with a message that we should care about Belgium? What's behind it? Who pays him? CIA? FBI? Maybe he is just a fanatic?"

As usual, the simple explanations describing FPA and the Ford Foundation were dismissed. They were too simple and not juicy enough, too boring to listen to and write about it. During question and answer periods, the customary entertainment of every evening performance, most audiences easily revealed themselves.

"Why should we pay taxes to finance inept Europeans? What's the use of having American troops risking their lives in remote corners of the world? Let others do it. It is great that we are teaching those dirty commies in Vietnam a lesson. They should know better next time."

Sometimes, there was comic relief. After a long dissertation, describing the concept of foreign aid to a mixed group of farmers, miners and a sprinkle of lawyers and dentists, an old woman stood patiently in line of well wishers congratulating me on whatever I said. When her turn finally came, she took my hand in both of hers and with a genuine expression she said, "It is so good to welcome you to our little community, Mr. Nagasaki. After all, we fought a war against your people and now we are friends. Thank you, thank you very much." I embraced her warmly.

Was Middle America really interested in foreign affairs? I kept asking myself that question looking at the multitude of faces, the multitude of every day problems that many people encountered during those unsteady days of the 1960's. We won the big war and were now entangled in a relatively small one.

Officially, and within the law, we were no longer a nation of segregated races, and yet de facto segregation was all around us. The economy was in good shape, yet poverty, hunger and homelessness were still very much on the surface of big cities. Tolerance and peaceful resolutions of disputes were on the lips of every political figure, and yet a series of assassinations shook the very moral backbone of the nation. Was there any room left for men and women to turn their faces outward and reflect on the state of the world? Were we asking too much?

I had to believe that we were not. I had to believe that America, our adopted land of promise and opportunities would never turn her back on the rest of the planet. If America retreated into its shell, who else would take over the baton of leadership? The Soviet Union? Defeated Germany? Tired, old England? There was no one else. It had to be America's destiny. That belief, that almost fanatical faith, made my new job easy, fulfilling and providing a dose of great satisfaction. Every time my listeners, new friends or casual acquaintances betrayed their ignorance, I was getting another boost. There were plenty of empty spaces to be filled with tidbits of knowledge. I plowed through them with the zeal of a missionary. One of the most unlikely places that made me feel more useful than ever was Detroit. This is where a coalition of business and trade unions created, through painstaking efforts to convince, persuade and put into action, a brand new World Affairs Council of Great Detroit.

Its council's birth was delivered by an army of Detroit's citizens. There was the usual cluster of well-meaning old women ready to spring into action in order to save the world. But there were also others. Walter Cisler was one of them.

Still functioning as the top man at Detroit Edison, with a wide range of people who worked with him, depended on him or simply were his friends, Walter put a great deal of energy behind the project. It was he who mobilized key labor leaders to support the idea. It was he who invested some of Edison's money in order to start the Council. And it was Walter who extended to me not only his personal friendship but also his full support.

A series of meetings featuring prominent foreign policy experts followed. A modest, but perfectly adequate office space was secured, staffed by a young woman I brought over from New York. Ida Avis was personable and ready to assume the job of a key person in that new enterprise. It turned out that she gained more than just a job. Within a few months, she landed a husband, a successful and well-connected federal judge.

While I was attempting to spread the word of interdependence, a word about the inevitability of the American destiny, Marysia and the kids kept adjusting themselves to a very different reality. Looking at a place that we could afford, but even more importantly, at a locality with a good public school, we stumbled shortly after returning from Paris, into Scarsdale, an affluent New York suburb.

On the wrong side of the tracks (we did not know that it was wrong), we found a house. We got the required mortgage and the house was ours. It had four bedrooms, was walking distance from the train station and was listed at thirty-seven thousand dollars. The year was 1966. The backyard offered flowerbeds and in front, there was a huge tree that both supported and threatened to destroy the stone terrace. The street was quiet and modest. But for the first time since Cairo, Seoul and Paris, we were on our own. What a treat. It was up to her, the mother, wife, teacher, provider and altogether adhesive of the family, to build a bridge between our past of wandering pilgrims to the new present of well-established, solid citizens. It meant developing contacts with teachers and neighbors, and responding to the cries of anguish from the children, who were unaccustomed to the new educational environments. It meant making sure that the local church would accept us as the new parishioners, and it meant being on call for all the logistical requirements of teenagers, a nine-year-old and a traveling husband.

The full impact of this wonderful dream, which some people have about a suburban existence, landed with the force of a

The Return

hurricane on Marysia's shoulders. She took it in stride. The mere return home was enough to unleash energy, enthusiasm and a sense of belonging. Observing her radiant facial expressions, when nothing was more exciting than shopping, escorting Terry to school or attending a PTA meeting, I had a strange feeling. The foreign service days were full of activity, and gave us a sense of importance, but they were a little like being on the margin of every day life. Warsaw, our only permanent home that we ever had, was history. It was Marysia who always wanted to go to America. It was Marysia who taught me English. It was Marysia who accepted our overseas assignments as necessary for my professional career. But in the back of her mind, and in the depths of her desires, was always a vision of a home in the States. And now we were here, not as recently arrived immigrants, but as former American diplomats. A job waited for me. A house waited for the family. Schools and colleges waited for our next generation. Her smile seemed to be eternal.

A day came about, an inevitable day, when our dreams were suddenly shattered. Marysia, by that time, was very much at home in the Scarsdale community. Terry had by now developed a cluster of good friends. Andrew, enrolled at Amherst, called our new place his home. So did his older sister, Maria. My job, calling for a fair amount of travel, was modest but exciting. The framework of our new existence gave the family a great dose of satisfaction. Then the telephone call to my hotel room in Salt Lake City brought home the fragility of that framework.

I was informed calmly by the president of the Foreign Policy Association, under whose auspices my work was conducted, that the Ford Foundation grant, which financed the development of the World Affairs Councils nationwide, would not be renewed. My job was to evaporate within the next couple of months.

At first, I was stunned. It was Sam Hayes himself on the line. I always knew that he was a pragmatic man, seldom influenced by emotions. I always knew that conversations with him were rather cold and detached. But this incident just threw me off. Here I was, in the field, working on one of the key projects that was built into the entire web of assignments and Sam had to call me to give me the bad news. Couldn't he wait upon my return?

It took all of my available self-control to continue on my mission.

It also took a lot of restraint not to call home. Our fate, however, turned into the most unexpected direction as a consequence of that phone call. A direction that was both dramatic as well as memorable. But no one would have predicted that type of a sudden turn in our American saga.

Marysia, with her usual positive outlook, was not too disturbed. There were two kids to look after. There was a fair amount of charitable work that she was engaged in. There was her eternal love for tennis and she had enough optimism to make anybody feel upbeat. It would be me who was not relaxed about the new situation. It was barely two years since we came back from Paris. It had been barely a year since we settled in our new house. Do we have to start all over? Do we have to go through similar experiences as we did twenty years earlier upon our arrival from Scotland?

Marysia's optimistic approach, her deep faith that someone much higher than us is watching over our little family, prevailed. Then, Ruth Miller called.

The World Affairs Council of Philadelphia will soon need a new leader. She has been there long enough. It was time to look for a worthy replacement. Would I be interested?

Inside our rather small kitchen, the family performed a tribal dance. Maps of Philadelphia and its environments appeared from nowhere and covered the dining room table. Did you hear about the Main Line? Someone told me that this is where one should live. A voice of cold reality entered the euphoric group. Could we afford a $100,000 house?

The meeting with a team of the directors assigned to the task of finding Ruth's successors followed. We all knew each other. We all liked each other and I sensed that we were engaged in a ritual with the conclusion being highly predictable. I was offered the job. The salary would be $20,000 a year. I accepted in the flash of a second. At home, serious preparations for a major move began.

The telephone kept ringing. There were congratulations from the team of men who concocted our initial return from overseas. There were parents, delighted to learn that we will not be far away. And there was a stranger calling from nowhere. "My name is Bob Panero and I am working for the Hudson Institute," he announced. "Your name was given to us by a friend of yours. We are in the process of forming a team that would go to Vietnam. Our task would be to assess Vietnam's economic potential in war conditions. Would you be interested in joining us?"

Would I?

I bought the official line that the fall of Vietnam would start the Communist avalanche in South East Asia. I was a good soldier but torn internally by doubts, doubts installed in my soul by the men and women whom I trusted, by Andrew and his friends, and by appeals printed in daily papers bearing the signatures of people whose judgments I always valued.

But wasn't it true that Vietnamese communists are apt to be as much on the orthodox side of the party as their Polish counterparts, that they will form another satellite state subservient to Moscow?

Bob Panero was willing to wait for my answer. My instinct kept telling me to go. How would I be able to assess the value of the war, to ascertain protesters' claims and to judge my own commitments to the notion of belligerency? How would I be able to live with myself after rejecting an opportunity of that kind?

A family caucus was held. Marysia, always a cool head on similar occasions, was not entirely opposed. Andrew was intrigued, perhaps hoping that his father would finally see the wisdom of his own approach. Terry, the youngest, smelled an adventure.

There were two calls to be made: one to Philadelphia expressing profound apologies, and the other to the Hudson Institute, accepting the assignment. How much did I know about the Hudson Institute? How much did I know about its creator, Herman Khan, whose philosophy prevailed? Who was Panero? What was to be my role? Should it be prudent to ask first a number of questions before saying yes? Naturally it would have been.

But one of my problems during the entire span of my life was my inability to wait and my inability to reject, what I considered an opportunity whether it was or not. The next thing I knew was a trip to Croton-on-the-Hudson to meet my future colleagues.

The group was colorful to say the least. Panero, my future boss, was a short, plump Latino with a wonderful flair of dreaming and fantasizing. His right-hand person was a Latino woman, whose beauty, intelligence and warmth were ready to seduce any doubters. Three additional males, every one from different backgrounds, comprised the team. All three had flowery pasts and were not fitting exactly into the normal social environs. Hunger for adventure was written all over their faces. And the entire team worshiped Herman Khan. He was the guru, the prophet, and the Rodin's thinker. Even the little Panero, whose self-confidence was his overwhelming characteristic, felt humble in Khan's presence.

It wasn't long before I was brought before Herman.

The informality of the encounter, the simple room, Herman's open shirt collar and Panero cracking jokes, were not enough to put me at ease. I was facing a mountain of a man; his face was round, his body weighed at least three hundred pounds and his eyes were barely visible between layers of fat. Herman did not bother to get up to greet a stranger. The effort was obviously too big. He extended his hand, mumbled a few words of welcome, thanked Bob for bringing me around and immediately launched into long-winded, detailed plans for solving the problem of Vietnam. "It is so simple," he proclaimed, "all the manpower that we have put over there to defeat the Vietcong will not be enough unless other measures are taken. We have to isolate the enemy. There is only one way to do so, to erect an electrified fence along the dividing line between North and South. Once this is accomplished, the Vietcong operating on our side of the fence will be deprived of food, ammunition and supplies of any kind.

"Within months or even weeks, they will have no other choice but to surrender. Our job, this time, will be to do the feasibility study. Once it is done we will come back and present our finding to the top echelon at the Pentagon. They obviously consider our project interesting enough since they gave us a grant to work on it. Once on the ground, our team will have a hell of a challenge. I am convinced that we can do it. We have first class engineers among us, technicians who know how to operate a complicated electrical system and you." Herman opened his eyes widely and looked straight at me. "Who, I am told, can do a first class job in selling our plans to the South Vietnamese. We need a 'public relations' man."

So this is what my role was going to be?

There was not a flicker of recognition on his part of my puzzlement. Besides, he wasn't through yet. "While we will be preoccupied in doing the blueprinting of that big project, which will stop the war sooner than anyone could predict today, we have other plans up our sleeves. Let me give you one example." There was a long pause. Herman's eyes were closed, his breathing heavy, his entire body immobile. I glanced at Panero, but there was no visible sign of concern. Later, I was to learn that this was normal, anticipated behavior. But the first-time encounter was slightly disconcerting.

"Medical facilities in that part of the world are not great in comparison to what we have at home. And yet our casualties are heavy. In addition, we have relatively few American doctors. How can we make their expertise available to a larger number of men and women wounded in combat? Modern technology is going to help us. There is a scheme afoot that will accomplish our objective: a television hook-up that will be available all over Vietnam, from large cities to the smallest localities in the Delta, a hook-up that will allow two way visual communications. A doctor in Saigon will be able to see and to converse with a doctor or patient in any part of the country. He will be able to view x-rays, to examine people and to prescribe the necessary cure."

Herman stopped again as if overwhelmed by the enormity of the idea itself. Then he briefly looked at Panero. "It will be up to you guys to figure out how to wire the country in the most efficient and affordable way."

I left Herman's room slightly dazzled. Was he dreaming? Or were his two plans within the spheres of being "technically possible?" Were they realistic enough for the U.S. military to take them seriously?

I was determined to check them myself. Philadelphia, the World Affairs Council, meetings and discussions paled by comparison. Whatever was to await me in that new and unexpected adventure, I was not only ready to plunge in, I was excited and impatient. Going to Vietnam is apt to give me a definite answer. Is this a just or unjust war? Was Andrew correct in protesting? Or was I, with all my ambivalence, on the right track?

The answer came to me much sooner than I anticipated. I entered unknown territory. I was there to check my own theories. I was there also due to the circumstances of our lives, refugees from a Soviet imposed system. I was committed to stop that very system from spreading. Were there any doubts? If there were, I refused to acknowledge their existence.

But I should have listened to them. It was Marysia, as always a cool and reasonable head, that willingly opened the dining room table discussion. "What do we know about the outfit that all of a sudden discovered you? The team does not inspire immediate confidence. Herman Khan's name is well known, but he is not a political scientist. He does not strike me as a deep thinker, in spite of his books predicting the future." As to the others, she stopped mid-sentence. "Besides, we are all torn about that conflict in far away Asia. We are torn and there are probably many other ways to find out more about it than traveling thousands of miles. With you gone, Andrew in college, it will be up to me to keep not only the family together, but also have to keep wondering about your whereabouts. After all, you will be entering a war zone. Do we all think that in order to satisfy your curiosity, you should drop an opportunity offered to you to run an interesting, dynamic organization in Philadelphia? To leave all of us behind with serious uncertainty about the usefulness of your escapade?"

Marysia looked at me, expecting an answer or a husband who could reason and reflect. She also knew that her husband's stubbornness and his constant urge to move, discover and meet a challenge were elements difficult to budge.

At the end, she kissed me goodbye and probably prayed for my safe return.

20

Vietnam

The octopus' tentacles await a traveler from the outside, peaceful world of the Saigon International Airport. He leaves the air-conditioned haven, his last link with this type of environment. He gets immersed in hot, humid air that penetrates his pores. His wide-open eyes, searching and awaiting, meet a sea of unsmiling, serious-minded faces of an army of clerks. Not that they are unfriendly, they just have a job to do, to stamp, to seal, to examine and to verify whatever documents that an arriving stranger presents and to make sure that the stranger is not an enemy.

The clerks' cages are tiny and their official equipment impressive. A single-file line forms composed of tired, worn out passengers. The clerks wait until the first face, anxious, uncertain, attempting to smile, appears in front of them. Then the clerks settle to work. Every man - there were no women clerks at that time in Saigon - has his place in the hierarchy of things. Each must perform his function and maintain the dignity of the office and the trust placed in him by the government. Each, therefore, must take time. Fast dismissal, fast action would imply that the job was unimportant, the task trivial, his own personal contribution rather meager. The line waits. It does not move slowly, it crawls. It breaks down from time to time when a tired figure folds, attempting to rest. A row of clerical heads turns toward the figure with oriental expressions indicating nothing. But the mere fact that they turned and looked and stopped their work for a precious few seconds sends tremors down the waiting line. The offending figure straightens his back, stands still and resumes the crawl. The line relaxes. Clerks resume their work. Saigon airport reasserts its personality.

At the top of the line, winners emerge. Their papers are stamped and the time arrives to try to regain possession of their bags. Another family of clerks await their turn to perform a ritual. The bags are opened and duly examined. When an unaccustomed traveler questions the validity of incoming control, he is dismissed with another stare, silent but vocal.

The routine continues through a minor fight between two or three porters eager to serve, taxi drivers arguing a price and finally, departure to the city. The city, like an octopus whose meat graces most affluent Vietnamese tables, extends its long arms and grabs the visitor with all its tropical passion. He enters into its inner sanctum bewildered and lost. Streets densely lined with trading centers, shops hiding living quarters, hammocks for soldiers to sleep on off-duty hours, and the regal gracefulness of Vietnamese girls, who changed their rickshaws, elephants and donkeys for Hondas and bicycles, remain the background of his first impressions. Chaotic traffic adds to his confusion. An absence of wartime atmosphere destroys the first of his preconceived notions.

Dazed, facing unreal reality, he is finally deposited into his air-conditioned hotel room, surrounded by servants ready to meet his wishes. He then collapses for the blessed hours of unconsciousness during which the Occident gradually evolves into the Orient. Senses are dulled, values are changed and the visitor begins to acquire a new skin. Softer on the outside but heavily lined to eliminate, or at least to reduce, the shock.

The team assembled in Bob Panero's room. There were six of us – five men and one woman. Lupe was warm, all smiling, and always ready to help make our lives a little more cheerful. She was also Bob's girlfriend (at least, this is what was assumed). Therefore she was untouchable. Men, as usual awaiting instructions, were being boisterous. Bob opened a bottle of Scotch, poured some into each of our glasses and the session began.

My power of concentration was not there. I was still outside breathing the air of Saigon. Instead of listening, instead of absorbing the fruits of Herman Khan's imagination, I kept my eyes focused on the window. Where are the signs of a deadly conflict? What was I doing there? Observing? Like watching an adventure on a television screen? Am I a member of that team, or just an imposter?

I came to Vietnam not really to be of any use to Herman, to Bob or to the others, but for my own, rather peculiar reasons. I was searching for the truth. I was looking for answers. Was I guilty of misleading people who counted on my contribution?

Bob Panero noticed my lack of interest. I was brought back to reality. "How about you?" I heard him addressing me directly. "Starting to sense the real mood of the people? Among all of us, engineers, technicians, city planners, you are the only one with a humanistic background. We brought you here to supplement our narrow vision." A murmur of subdued laughter failed to interrupt his peroration. "And to inquire into the softer aspects of Vietnamese lives. There is one aspect of that life that no one, to the best of our knowledge, investigated scientifically."

Bob stopped, looking around. All eyes were on him. "The country is heavily populated by prostitutes. They dominate some of the markets. Their pimps have easy access to our soldiers. Why don't you go out, pick up one or two of these ladies of the night, talk to them, find out as much as you can about their worlds and report back to us? While working you can, of course, have a little fun. How about it?"

Now all eyes were on me.

Was he kidding? Was this to be one of his usually crude jokes? Then it hit me. He was quite serious. It fit into his plans. And I was the odd man on his team. It was a way to use me, a way to justify my presence.

"Bob," I heard Lupe's voice, "you are really silly."

He cut her off with a sharp gesture of hand. The team was waiting.

Then I heard my own voice as if coming out of a mouth of someone else. "I'll be glad to undertake the task. But I might need some help. Why don't you go out first, find out where the best brothel is located, inquire how many girls are going to be willing to talk to an American and how much it will cost and then come back and report to the group. And by the way, you may have some fun while you work." Then I got up and walked out. An outburst of loud laughter followed me on the staircase.

Laughter, sobs and desperate cries followed me everywhere I went.

I met John in a bar. He was in uniform like most of the other customers. He was from Portland, Oregon and he was about to go home in another week or so.

"Good riddance. A year was plenty." He saw so much.

"What did you see, Johnny? Did you see action?"

Johnny turned his slightly glazed eyes in the direction of the voice and looked hard, trying to penetrate the layer of fog in front. His hand automatically searched for another drink and the barman obliged. "I saw plenty of action. Men in battles throwing themselves against mines and grenades. One was a young lieutenant determined to find protection for his men. So he climbed a hill to look the area over and a machine gun barked and got him across his knees and one bullet struck higher and ripped open his stomach.

"I saw more. I saw fellows with their heads blown off, their faces smashed and they had to be wrapped all around so no one would see them any more. I have been seeing them come and go, one after the other, with their unseeing eyes focused on eternity and their stiff hands holding onto their rifles, or grenades or a simple stick. Then I took the rifle and put them to sleep in a peaceful way. And their faces changed from anger and pain to blissful expressions of nothingness. The fellows I saw die..."

The barman hurriedly pushed another drink into his warm hand.

"Where did you see that much action, Johnny?" I asked. He was slow, deliberate, and precise in measuring his answer. Tears clouded his vision.

"Nowhere. Just nowhere. I was a mortician. Wonderful job. I got my reward. I changed their faces. I moved them closer to God."

The Vietnamese barman stood gaping with a half-filled glass dangling from his limp hand.

Vietnam is a discovery. It is a discovery of a culture that defies stereotypes. It is a discovery of a place that neither my father nor any of our ancestors had even heard of. It is also a discovery of human minds that react, think and assess differently, like a shoe shine boy, who looks at the big American GI imagining that man's world, or a beggar with a leg lost in the American-made war, or an old woman whose only possession is a bundle of firewood that she managed to collect, and all of whom must instinctively hate the big men.

What does a shoeshine boy think? Fast on his feet, proud of his accomplishments, he has no home outside of the Saigon streets. Born into war-torn society, the little Vietnamese boy must have some thoughts of his own. Who are the big white men who can afford such expensive shoes? Who are they to come up from time to time with a tip higher than his father's daily take-in? Why do they tip the way they do? Why are some good, and others cruel? Why do they resist shoe shining when it is offered and yet come to him without being asked? Why do some have such funny pictures painted on their arms, and a steady movement of jaws chewing something? How does their country look? Why have they come to Vietnam? Are they so bent on making war that they travel all over the world finding a suitable place? Or maybe they are just soldiers looking for battles. Why don't they fight in their own country?

What does a GI think? He towers over the boy kneeling at his feet, watching the fast movements of a brush, steady and strong movements of a polishing rag. He looks at the dark, childish head bent down and pats it gently. The boy looks up and responds with a warm smile. The tip should be large since the man is nice. The boy knows. The soldier would like to talk, to ask, to inquire, but how? He does not know the language. Or maybe he wouldn't know what to ask or how to climb over a barrier between a Western man and an Oriental child?

The GI is perplexed.

He came directly from Vermont. On his 21st birthday, he was drafted. He heard of Vietnam, a country that was somewhere in Asia and was threatening American security. That was what his local papers reported. But he read a little more by getting books from the school's library. Yet the place repulsed him. Its smell offended his senses. Its reality was difficult to comprehend. What was he doing in the middle of their society, a society clearly satisfied, well established, with morals and values having been formed centuries ago? He read that they were derived from a multitude of races: Melanesians, Indonesians, Negroids, Mongolians, and that in pre-historic days, they traversed Indonesian central massif and marched South along the China Sea. What else has he heard about Vietnam? Darn little. Once he arrived, he learned more. His platoon commander at one point gathered his troops and talked about it.

He told the men that Vietnamese had their own, ancient culture and - to everyone's surprise - linked it with music. Their folk songs of the Tonkiness central region and of the North Annam coastal strip, affirm that the upper part of the Tonkin Delta is the native land of Vietnamese people. The commander, who taught Asian history at one of the American colleges, kept telling these men more than some of them wanted to know. He kept referring to music. The most ancient musical traditions discovered were those of the ancient citadel of Co Lauom, which was discovered inside the tomb of King An Duong, dating from 3rd century B.C. It was in that citadel, which was fiercely defended against the invading Chinese troops led by General Trieu Da, that many historians and archaeologists see the mother cell of the Vietnamese people.

So he kept listening, kept learning, but all that was not enough to establish contact with his little shoe shining friend. What could he do? What should he learn to reach out and to comprehend?

The boy and the soldier symbolized the dilemma for me, the newcomer, the stranger, and another white face arriving from nowhere. I kept observing, attempting to analyze, and at the same time, feeling imprisoned in my air-conditioned hotel room surrounded by my buddies from the Hudson Institute. Would I ever be able to penetrate the Orient the way it presented itself to me? Would I ever be able to comprehend our presence and our involvement? Andrew's face appeared on my mental screen, Andrew and his college friends marching in a demonstration. They were young, idealistic and a little romantic. But were they right? I still did not know.

The crowd surrounding me was middle-aged, overweight, heavy drinkers but appeared equally dedicated to their task, helping America win that war. One of them was an expert in bridge building, the other a forester who knew how to tame a forest and change it into a safe heaven for fighting troops. The head of the team, Bob Panero, was a master of all trades. An awful thought suddenly crossed my mind: is he a man for hire? A soldier of fortune who would serve any master providing he was well paid? I caught myself short. Don't even allow yourself to be so cynical. If you do, aren't you a part of the very same game?

The Vietnamese street does not allow time to be philosophical.

It continues to provide a constant stream of pictures that is impossible to overlook.

There is an old woman balancing two heavy baskets on her back, with a large straw hat hovering over her weather beaten face. A few feet from her several little boys offer their services to American car owners. They will watch over the vehicles for whatever time is necessary. Some inexperienced men refuse. The boys wait patiently before going to work. Tires are slashed and the boys disappear into the human multitude. Native soldiers sleep in hammocks tied between two trees. Merchants sip strong coffee; half-naked infants play in uncollected garbage. A fat rat smiles at them with the satisfaction of someone who knows how to live.

Then I kept watching the strangers, men and women who came to that tiny speck of a country to save it. They are all civilians and they walk along Saigon's streets with their eyes fixed into the future. They don't notice old women, young boys, beggars, garbage or whatever. They pass along, walking briskly, chirping cheerfully about the ways that their plans were progressing and how great it will be to have another hospital, an army of medics or a new team of engineers. In the meantime, the very people for whom all these projects were destined live in blissful ignorance of the great future that these strangers were planning for them, yet without them.

There is no way to avoid a little philosophizing. There is no way that a mind can be given a time to rest. Too many contradictory signals are received, registered and calling for at least some partial answers.

The team I was a member of classified itself as social engineers. Maybe social engineers must be detached. Cold. Free of sentimental attachments. Perhaps warm human beings injected into early planning would complicate matters too much. They are so unstable, so vulnerable, so unpredictable, uneasy to control, maintain and to make run the way that a well-oiled machine does. Maybe the greatest engineering feats come from human detachments. The pyramids were not built with a humanistic approach, but a theology of death. Prisoners of war constructed roman roads. Some of the greatest monuments of modern architecture came into being out of the sweat and tears of millions of workers who sacrificed themselves on the altar of human progress.

In the meantime, the war was all around us. I kept being challenged day in and day out to observe, reflect and arrive slowly and painfully into some kind of final conclusion.

But I am getting ahead of myself.

On the radar of my sub-consciousness, a parade of human silhouettes kept marching on, leaving behind strong footprints. The high-ranking American official kept quarrelling with the authorities. He resigned his military commission in order to be free. He challenged the American optimistic predictions about boys getting home for Christmas. He challenged the level of expenditures for chemicals to defoliate Vietnam ($44 million a year). Military significance of that action was marginal; psychologically, it was a tragic error. And out of his own, private outpost, he attempted to derail the U.S. faulty way of waging the war. He kept telling me all that in his subdued, soft, melodious voice. He was a missionary of his cause. I was to learn a few months later that he fell victim to one of the Vietcong's night raids. Little did they know that they had killed someone who worked hard to save them.

A Jesuit priest somehow entered my orbit. French educated, American born, he was in Vietnam for two years, including the time that the French occupied the country. He knew the place well. When the American war started, he was on the other side of the dividing line. Then he kept moving back and forth. "It is easy," he suggested. "Just do not speak English. It is safe. Would you like to take a trip with me?"

His jeep was recognized by both American and Vietcong guards. We were waved in and out. All of a sudden, I realized that I was in the enemy territory. A sense of excitement and a sense of another discovery settled in. The first medium-sized town we drove through looked quiet, no military units, no uniforms, and no soldiers. It took me little time to realize that the Vietcong components do not wear uniforms. Black pants are enough. It took me even a little more time to realize the basic difference: in the South, we were the occupiers; in the North, they were at home.

My newly acquired friend, his clerical collar prominently displayed, greeted men and women on both sides of the dividing line with equal warmth. "There was, and there is," he whispered in my ear, "no need for this war."

On our way back, we passed solid American warehouses guarded by heavily armed soldiers. The most valuable goods were kept inside: military supplies, canned food and luxury items designated for post exchanges.

"Did you know that American guards risk court-martial should anyone get access to a warehouse? And yet, there is a price for everything it costs a Vietcong agent about $2,000 for five minutes inside. At a pre-arranged time, usually in the early morning hours, the doors swing open and one or two men rush in. They grab anything within reach and disappear into the night."

"How do you know that?" I asked, hoping that he would have no answer.

The priest just smiled. "I saw the men and I saw their goods. And I also saw the actual deed. For a man of God, it is much easier to learn about human weaknesses as well as human skills."

"As well as human suffering?" I did not need him when I walked along the Street Without Joy. It leads nowhere. Instead of trees, there were bare cots; instead of traffic, there were lights and moaning people. The street was inside a provincial hospital at Can Tho, the largest city in the Delta. I started walking along. It was an orthopedic ward, women and men with limbs covered with bloody bandages and children suffering from grenade wounds. Vietnamese doctors operating under primitive conditions, windows and doors wide-open with masses of flies and mosquitoes entering unopposed. A middle-aged American nurse, a volunteer attempting to be in five places at the same time, came to Vietnam fourteen months earlier, determined to stay as long as she was needed.

People sit in their beds and stare at us. So we moved along only to be stared at with even more penetrating expressions. The next ward is designated for prisoners of war. Women, whose legs were shattered, looked at me. Mothers sitting next to their badly wounded infants looked at me. Men looked at me. They were all chained to their beds, by Saigon's request. Our doctor guide made a gesture of despair. "I tried and tried to change the rule. These men are not capable of escaping. We are just adding to their suffering."

At the end of the Street Without Joy, civilian prisoners are kept. They are political suspects. They also looked at us, but this time bolder, much less resigned. Theirs was a look of contempt, or perhaps of human recognition. You could be in my place tomorrow, one of the pairs of eyes was saying. Watch out, don't pity me, I don't want your pity, I am a man like you, although caged.

Ready to flee, to move on, I started walking briskly toward the end of the corridor when a tiny hand extended itself to me through the bars. A two year old boy wanted to play. Inside the cage sat his mother. She was caught, labeled a suspect and thrown into jail. Since no one was left to look after the child, he went with her, the youngest prisoner of the lot.

There were other encounters. One of them was a Cabinet minister, known for his unorthodox views. He was a mild man, in his early forties, a graduate of the London School of Economics, who saw his country through the Geneva Agreement in 1954 as a member of Saigon's delegation. I sustained another kind of look. This time it was a cold, detached expression. "Why don't you in America forget about the whole thing, pack up and go home? Aren't your people a little tired of Vietnam?"

"Tired?"

"Yes, tired. So are the Vietnamese. Of war, the American presence and our dependency. Every additional dollar spent here, every additional American dispatched to Vietnam increases that dependency. It's no good for either side. Dependency breeds contempt. It breeds resentment. Why don't you go home?"

Our Hudson Institute team was just about ready to do so, but not the way that the minister suggested, not with the notion that America should follow our lead.

There was a high-style farewell dinner. Full of reflections, my eyes still seeing the hospital and clinics, refugee houses and jungle villages, my ears still ringing with the minister's message. I was transformed into a smiling guest of a smiling host. He was clean-shaven, well scrubbed and in excellent health. We sat in bamboo chairs on a terrace of his splendid colonial white house, overlooking a manicured yard. Servants in white tunics brought us drinks. On the screens and just under the roof, lizards kept chasing butterflies and other insects, fat, affluent lizards, much bigger then the ones in my hotel, lizards proportionate to the splendor of the residence. The dinner was Chinese, and the dishes were of superb quality.

We talked big money, big projects and big people. When I dared to inject impressions of the Delta, of hospitals, of chained prisoners to their bed, a silence followed. Someone then asked how much do I know about other underdeveloped countries? And from then on, I was isolated, neglected, forgotten.

I got up, sank my feet into the deep carpeting and then half slept through the rest of the feast. The two worlds, the one of the minister and the other of the mogul, have never met. It was almost like looking and thinking of the imperial city of Hue, where emperors lived and reigned, where armies fought and bled, including the American army, and which survived all the calamities and is still a living, thriving community. That world, which the minister envisaged once we would depart, had little in common with his compatriots living off the war.

In 1968, I wrote:

> One day in the future, when the war is over and conveniently forgotten, when all foreigners are gone and Vietnam restored to normalcy, it will be so new that no one would recognize it again. The Westerners will do their best to rebuild it in order to relegate to the farther corners of their mind the anguish, the decisions, the political blunders and the military defeats. The Vietnamese, reflective, quiet and adaptable to life as their gods dictate it, would try to have a country in which their war heroes are venerated, victories remembered, defeats forgotten, and from which a new textbook of history emerges adding unprecedented glory to the tiny speck of a country capable of destroying huge invading armies. The two textbooks, one prepared in the West and the other in the East, will be as different in context as the characters in which they will be written.

It was soon thereafter that I returned home. Andrew, my rebellious son, was still at Amherst. My first call was to him. I was not yet ready to compare different texts dealing with the Vietnam War. I simply had the urge to tell him that he was right and I was wrong. To tell him that for the first time since we immigrated to America, I had doubts about the country's wisdom and its leaders' judgments. And also that I was hoping that his generation will never commit such monumental blunders, such monumental national disasters leading to the useless deaths of thousands of young Americans and hundreds of thousands of Vietnamese.

Andrew called back. He understood. He also blessed the day that I decided to visit the battlefields. After a moment of quiet reflection, probably while walking in the woods, or swimming in the ocean, I asked myself a question. Okay, I kept saying, you have been lucky, cunning and industrious in finding jobs that made a difference. In addition, you have been unbelievably lucky having the type of family that you have, walking into a Warsaw nightclub and finding a perfect wife, producing three children, none of them planned and the first one conceived and born in the middle of one of the worst wars known to humanity. The second one, born on the day that Poles all over the world keep celebrating the anniversary of their democratic constitution (May 3) and on the eve of our departure to America, an unknown continent and totally unpredictable future, and the third child arriving almost at the same time as I was to begin my role as a federal bureaucrat. Family and work kept providing two bookends. Was there anything in between?

It was Marysia who kept filling the gap. Her involvements with people, who were so much less privileged than we were, filled whatever free time she had. In addition, she kept being a breadwinner, taking little, insignificant jobs in order to avoid a deficit family budget. There was, however, one extremely important facet of her life that created a strong spiritual bond for all of us.

Marysia's spirituality, her strong attachment to the church - seeing at the same time that church's weaknesses and errors - touched all five of us one way or another. It was not religiosity; it was a simple code of strong ethics and morality that emanated from her. The two older children took their mother's lead and adopted it to their own life style. I have been more reluctant. In my own case, after passing through a period of strong Roman-Catholic attachments, I drifted away from the church. My attachment was due much more to the influence of a couple of strong individuals, my classroom priest at high school, and a bishop during the university years. Neither of my parents were strong religious individuals. This is why I was looking outside of the family for moral support. Confessions gave me a way out. Absolutions provided a sense of relief. And throughout my entire life, I kept looking towards God - whoever He is - for guidance and for forgiveness. I was looking for my God in a selfish manner. Whenever I felt lost, whenever I needed a spiritual push, whenever I was undertaking a difficult task, I would mumble to myself some familiar words of almost forgotten prayers. My only hope that these prayers were heard was part of my school days religious teaching. It stated clearly that God gives preference to sinners. The difference between Marysia and myself - which I sensed throughout our entire marriage - was Marysia's solidity against my own tendency to be superficial.

Our three offspring were an interesting mixture of the two of us. The oldest, Maria, kept reminding me of myself. Her teenage years were spent more on boys and on having fun than on school, reading or contemplating the beauties of art, music or other segments of cultural life. It took her a number of years to focus on her future interests, the social ills of America. She went from one college to another, earned money waitressing, and drifted from one place to another. My story was very much along the same lines. It took me two solid years in college to start working solidly. Endless bridge games filled our many hours, as well as a membership into a fraternity, where silly games and equally silly procedures excited my youthful and rather empty head.

Andrew came next. Family genes must have had a conference call and decided that the boy should be more like his mother. There was a touch of humility in most of his actions, a willingness to listen rather than to speak first, and an ironclad notion that there is nothing more important than honesty, both intellectual and spiritual. His mother's early upbringing, her inner strength derived from her faith, formed his inheritance.

Terry, the afterthought, born when Marysia was almost reaching the end of when motherhood was possible, turned out to be the most complicated person for her parents to accept, understand and eventually come close to considering the most precious. It would be difficult to pinpoint the exact time that Terry's personality started to form. In Egypt, as a three-year-old baby, she learned Arabic from her playmate, another girl her age, the daughter of our gardener. In Paris, where we spent another couple of years, she learned French and attempted to learn the violin.

Returning home, Terry was chastised by her schoolmates. The class simply rejected her, a big blow for a ten-year old. Transferred to the International School in Manhattan, she became a very rebellious young lady. Our dinner table conversations usually turned out to be confrontational. The rebellion was evident in the way she dressed, in the way she treated both of us and in the way that her mannerism and outside appearance conveyed the notion of someone who wanted to be different. Little did we know how different she was. It fell to Andrew and his wife Christina to convey the nature of that difference to us. The setting was almost idyllic; the time was rather appropriate. The four of us were facing a burning fire in a rustic Vermont house belonging to our friends. Our drinks were ready to warm our bodies; our moods were melancholic and nostalgic, talking about similar winters spent in our native land. When a moment of silence occurred, Andrew looked at Christina and she gave him an eye signal.

"We feel that the time is ripe to tell you," Andrew started, "that Terry is a lesbian."

Neither of us said a word. I felt an excruciating pain in my chest. Marysia sat there, equally stunned. From pain, my feelings jumped into suppressed anger, from anger to rejection, from rejection to condemnation. There was not a single trace at that moment of an attempt to understand. The notion of being a father of a lesbian was just too overwhelming to absorb. The notion that Terry was about to start her adult life in a manner so offensive, and so abnormal to us, made me almost ready to wash my hands of her forever.

It took time - one of the best healing tools - thinking and rediscovering my youngest child. The rediscovering led me, perhaps both of us, to peel off the layers of prejudices, assumptions and society's approach to the issue and to see the human being behind all those. A human being, who partly due to her sexual preference, needed, maybe even more than our other two, a close relationship with her parents. We were, for all practical purposes, her only immediate family outside of her siblings. Faster than any one of us could have predicted, our relationship developed into a close, warm and mutual understanding. It went even further than that; it allowed both of us not only to accept the fact that her companions were other women, but also to evolve into, at first, tolerance, and later, full acceptance of these companions.

Our three children, growing up under different circumstances, formed a family with solid roots and firm, strong inner ties. They also turned out to be our joy, satisfaction and pride once old age knocked on our doors.

The two bookends had to be kept alive at the same time. With the Vietnam experience behind me and with my Hudson Institute team concentrating on a set of new adventures, on different ways to contribute towards safety of the planet Earth, I kept feeling more and more out of place. Robert Panero, our team leader, accepted me as his "senior partner" who could be used any way he wanted to.

Others, on our trip to Mexico, where we kept interrupting our fishing trips and our royal meals with sessions on economic developments of that difficult, and yet joyous nation, tolerated my presence with a barely hidden sense of amusement. They knew perfectly well that I was not a trained economist. Neither were they. They also knew that I was unprepared to think the way they have, in that any assignment was possible as long as it was handsomely rewarded and any new skill could be easily learned. Somehow it did not sit too well with my approach of the task ahead.

A phone call from New York found me on the edge of a hotel pool in Miami Beach. A black steward in a white tuxedo brought me a portable phone. At the other end of the line was an old friend inquiring about my interest in taking a one-year job at the Council on Foreign Relations. He wanted a sabbatical and his slot will be open. Bob Panero, sitting opposite me, kept reading the newspaper, pretending not to listen. When I revealed the content of the conversation, indicating my intention to take the offer, Bob suggested for me to take some time for reflection.

"Do you really want to join that stuffy institution? To be a small clerk rather than a free wheeling entrepreneur? To sit behind a desk in New York instead of exploring new regions of the world? To be a bureaucrat instead of someone who could easily spread his wings and make a real contribution?"

Prior to our Vietnam experience, I would have been much more inclined to listen to Bob. Prior to the Mexican trip, my doubts could have been a little less strong. But sitting in luxurious surroundings and observing my professional companions, I was ready to jump on the New York inquiry. And I did almost instantly, to the visible disappointment of Hudson's team. How can anybody reject a life of adventure, luxury and money, to a pedestrian existence in New York City? They bade me goodbye over a glass of champagne. A sense of compassion hung in the air. A feeling of understanding was visibly missing.

21

Council on Foreign Relations

The memory bank bulges with data. The inner-self, critical and painfully honest, still hurts. A review of one of the most significant decades of our lives in America is a mixture of pain and joy.

The decade started on a note that still leaves open wounds. The wound closed during an evening full of friends, admirers and others expecting a powerful farewell song. Instead, they got a mediocre, insignificant and boring peroration. The middle was more than significant.

Little did I realize the true nature of the institution I was about to enter. An old friend, a member of the foursome that attempted to find us a place to earn decent money when we were coming back from Paris, decided to accept an offer from one of the major foundations, to spend a year in an academic environment. In order to do so, he needed someone to do his job at the Council. He knew I was searching. He knew that I did a decent job for the Foreign Policy Association. He knew I was fresh from Vietnam. In addition, he was aware of both my strong and weak points. You could do my job for a year and maybe later on we could both fit into the Council. His job was director of meetings, one of the key staff positions.

Harry Boardman introduced me to the two men who were to approve or disapprove of his selection. George Franklin and David MacEachron took me to lunch and the deal was clinched. I was to start the following week. My salary would be $25,000 per annum. I inherited four staff members, a mountain of files and a new program year, which was to start with the appearance of German Chancellor Schushning at the Council's black tie dinner. It was clearly defined as a one year, temporary appointment.

The family was delighted. At the rather advanced age of fifty-six, I was entering into the American job market with the prospect of work that would suit me well. Yet little did Marysia and I both realize how unsophisticated we were in approaching our entry into the very symbol of the American establishment. I knew next to nothing about the Council's Board of Directors. I only dimly remembered its history and its role after the First World War. I was not aware that it was a permanent target of the right-wing political fringe. In short we both, were beautifully ignorant.

The decision to accept the offer was to change our family's lives dramatically. It opened the door to political involvements not only at home, but also abroad. It created an atmosphere of perceived and occasionally realistic personal influence. It moved us up the Foreign Service ladder in creating connections with men and women of serious influence. It also changed the pattern of family existence, making the man of the house much less available. On the other side of the equation, it opened the possibilities for Marysia and me to meet and make friends and interact with key international players.

The Council, as we were to discover later, had been on a "hit list" of all kinds of fringe right-wing groups. Accused of having communist sympathies, of promoting world government, of being unpatriotic and altogether devoid of American values, most of us working for it were painted with the same brush. On one occasion, while being interviewed by a radio commentator in South Carolina, I was paid a final compliment at the end of our dialogue. "For a socialist, you are a pretty smart guy," and the radio interviewer laughed with self-amused satisfaction.

At the other end of the political spectrum, the Council was one of ten institutions viewed by the political left as a bastion of military industrial complex, defending status quo and being oblivious to progress. For us, the newcomers, the organization offered unprecedented access to some of the brightest people around.

One of my colleagues was Hamilton Fish Armstrong, a legendary figure in American journalism and a solid member of the Establishment. At that time, he was Editor of "Foreign Affairs," a close friend of Harry Boardman, the man I was to substitute for. Later, popularly called Ham, he was replaced by another blue chip member of the Establishment, William Bundy, whose brother, MacGeorge Bundy, President of the Ford Foundation, was a frequent visitor at the Council. The Board was equally blue chip: David Rockefeller, John J. McCloy, Douglas Dillen, Peter Peterson and a slew of other dignitaries. From now on, I was to have direct access to every one of them. Fully realizing the distance, yet not always able to stop myself, I used that access often.

At times, it was too easy. At times, I kept forgetting how insignificant I was within the framework of the newly acquired position. But, as most people know, it is very pleasant to live with one's illusions.

Ham examined me with a rather skeptical eye. Harry Boardman has done an exceptionally good job in bringing to the Council an array of foreign policy stars from all over the world. He was a strong believer in the sanctity in the institution. Only members were to be invited to functions. The selection process to acquire new members was to be rigorous and entirely confidential. In short, he represented the conservative wing. There were others, younger and more daring, who on rare occasions voiced their revolutionary ideas. They included calls for more women members, younger members and minorities. In addition, the new ideas would attempt to break the barrier between the taboos of inviting, as speakers, people not necessarily belonging to the ruling elites. Neither Ham nor Harry was enamored with these propositions.

Every time I entered Ham's office, I was intimidated. His personality permeated the entire Council. His physical appearance, bushy hair, penetrating eyes and face cut with deep lines, gave anyone who met him for the first time a sense of intellectual inferiority. In my case, it was considerably accentuated by knowing how highly he valued Harry and how doubtful he was that anyone could replace him. I tried to do my best to please him, to secure his advice, his counsel, but I never felt at ease with him. A distinct psychological barrier was there, in spite of Ham's visible efforts to put me at ease.

Within the framework of my office, I started feeling at home. A gallery of fascinating men and women entered my horizon. I kept inviting them, talking with them and often forgetting that I was just a tiny link between them and the institution I was working for. Cyrus Vance came in, long before he was named Secretary of State. Adlai Stevenson, Margaret Thatcher, Francois Mitterand, Helmut Kohl and Edward Heath received my invitations and dutifully complied. None of them had yet reached the pinnacles of their careers.

It was a wonderful feeling of accomplishment. It was also a feeling of satisfaction, but also fun in discovery. It was also an intense period of learning about foreign policy and the way that it was made, discussed, manipulated and finally adopted. In more than one way, I was a witness to the process, a silent observer in the kitchen of policy. Immersed in it, on some occasions being able to be a participant, within the confines of the Council itself, I was drunk with a sense of belonging. In fact, I was destined to be a migratory bird to be departing as soon as the time was to be up.

An event occurred that changed the nature of migration. The time was moving unbelievably fast while I was substituting for Harry. Even my title indicated the temporary nature of the assignment and the ticking clock as I was "acting" director of meetings.

It was a long day and darkness descended upon Manhattan while I was still at my desk. Only a few people were still working. One of them was a senior assistant of mine whom I inherited from Harry, like everybody else. She was a rather shy, rather withdrawn individual and our relations were strictly business. There was seldom a light moment with her, seldom any bantering. So I was quite surprised to hear a knock on my door and see her enter, long after official working hours passed. "Can I talk to you in confidence?" she asked.

"Of course," was my automatic answer.

"I am a little lost what to do with a copy of a memorandum that I found among Harry's old files. It is a memorandum addressed to the Board. It is stamped confidential. I never saw it before." She handed me two pages long document. It was from Harry to the chairman of the board. It addressed his concern about the way that the Council was run. It was extremely critical of George Franklin and David MacEachron. It also included suggestions on how to save the institution from the very inept way it has been run so far by these two individuals.

I was stunned. The last thing that I was expecting of Harry was disloyalty. In addition, I was appalled by the accusation, which sounded unjust. After almost a year with the Council, I not only grew found of George but also became impressed by his dedication to the job. He wasn't there for the money. He was independently wealthy. He was also married to a Rockefeller.

My young associate scrutinized my reactions. "What shall I do with it?" she finally asked. "Destroy? File? Or give it to George for him to take whatever action he would see fit to take?"

I was faced with a cruel dilemma. By that time Harry has already indicated to George and others that he wanted to return to his old job. In talking to me, he suggested that I could possibly stay on as his assistant. But that was both uncertain and not too attractive to me.

Now, as if from the clear, blue sky, I was handed a tool that could solve the problem. There was little doubt in my mind that the memorandum, if given to George, would end Harry's career.

My first answer was to shift the decision from myself to the finder of the document. "Do whatever you feel you should do," I told her. After a couple of days, she came back to me, still unable to make up her mind. "If I were in your place," I finally said, "I would probably tell George about Harry's thinking. But once again, it is up to you."

She translated my answer in the way that it sounded. She went to see George and handed him the memorandum.

Harry was fired and I was appointed director of meetings, permanently. I spent ten fruitful, fulfilling years at the Council, but the way that I helped to open the doors to myself left a deep scar on my conscience. Harry, who was later told about the way that my advice was interpreted, never forgave me. Our friendship was over and a sense of guilt, justified or not, remained with me for the rest of my life.

The decade was punctuated by sense of deep satisfaction. Here I was, in the heart of American establishment, rubbing elbows with the cream of the world's political elite, making close, and in some cases, permanent friendships with exciting and brilliant minds and on occasion, venturing into unchartered waters of international politics. In more than one instance, my wings were clipped. In more than one instance, my freelance initiatives landed me in rather precarious and dangerous positions.

The first occurred when during the Vietnam conflict, I invited young men who were in the forefront of the protest movement to the Council. This was not viewed as a wise decision. Some members were deeply offended, but a large number of them came to listen to Sam Brown, who at that time was an unofficial leader of the anti-war movement. The overall reaction was positive. Among the younger members of the establishment, I encountered nothing but praise. "It is high time," one of them commented, "for the Council to recognize different voices than those of appointed officials."

The Vietnam War in1971 was a deeply dividing element. My ambivalence in earlier years abruptly ended after visiting that country. Yet, in my official capacity, I had to be neutral. I had to provide CFR members with a balanced view. A meeting with Sam Brown was to accomplish that objective, in spite of the fact that I sympathized with him and his movement. The problem that I faced was the fact that the administration of the Council was well aware of my views.

Somehow, once again for reasons unknown to me, no action was taken even to reprimand me. The Council's Study Staff, a group of seriously minded scholars, decided that the entire anti-war movement would be worth a series of meetings. Needless to say, my team of advisers felt rewarded.

A different, much more politically explosive, situation occurred a couple years later. While in Italy, on a five-week sabbatical, invited by the Rockefeller Foundation, I met with a handful of leaders from the Italian Communist Party. I went to a Communist run school for young members of the Party and wrote an article, prominently published in the New York Times, suggesting that a dialogue should be initiated between Washington and Italian communists. At that time, the Communist Party was the largest party in the Italian parliament. It garnered almost 35% of the popular vote.

Happily involved in my writing at the luxurious Villa Serbelloni, I knew very little about the hell that was let loose as a result of my op-ed piece. The article was interpreted as an un-official position of the Council. Yet, it was written without consulting anyone except my wife. We both felt rather good about it, considering my well-established anti-communist credentials.

The *Times*, without checking with me, identified me with the Council. Italian press jumped on the occasion. So did some European periodicals, interpreting my lonely voice as a trial balloon initiated by semi-official circles close to State Department.

William Rusher, publisher of *National Review*, a well-known right-wing periodical, wrote a column essentially repeating the same thesis. Rusher's logic was simple: Zygmunt Nagorski works for the Council on Foreign Relations, The New York Times published his piece, these are solid proofs that the entire move was synchronized at the highest level. And the *Financial Times of London*, in an editorial, implied that the Rockefeller-financed Council on Foreign Relations was attempting to soften the American stand vis-à-vis the Italian reds.

Two difficult and none too pleasant meetings followed upon our return home. The man in charge of a good chunk of State Department policy, with the title of Counselor, invited me for a chat. Helmut Sonnenfeld had never been a friendly face. This time, his questions were sharp, his displeasure visible and my explanations viewed with a skeptical eye. The other encounter was closer to home. Joseph Reed, an assistant and a faithful follower of David Rockefeller, asked me to meet his boss and my Chairman of the Board. My attitude was both humble and explanatory. I attempted to explain my policy recommendations, an explanation that did not go very far. I also strongly underlined my innocence regarding identification. David, whose facial expressions are never easy to read, offered a number of suggestions for the future and was obviously not too happy with the entire affair. I noticed in him, as well in a number of key players within the Council's leadership strata, a built-in negative attitude toward controversial issues. It was much better to avoid conflicts than to face them boldly. I had created a policy dilemma by opening up a very controversial issue on how to deal with communist parties freely elected within the Western, non-communist part of Europe.

To begin with, it was not my job in the strictly hierarchical system. Secondly, the policy was well established and strictly observed as not having anything to do with Western European communist parties.

The Council's studies programs offered an array of national security, economic and social issues. It attracted some of the best minds of the nation and was quoted extensively in policy and scholarly publications. Among some of the key topics under scrutiny: a look at constructive engagement with China, commercial diplomacy in Asia, Russia and its neighbors, an enlarging of NATO and reforming education in Latin America.

My role at the Council was exciting but, like any newcomer, I kept stumbling; I kept overreaching through my often-misplaced concepts regarding the role of my modest position. Two more examples come to mind.

On a number of occasions, people attempted to solicit invitations to speak at the Council. At one point, I received a call from David Rockefeller's office that a prominent member of the academia would like to be invited. I knew the man well and was surprised that he chose the round about way to convey the message. Later, I understood. It would have been a major blow to his ego should I have turned him down. A request from my chairman would have automatically - in his mind - secured an invitation. It did, but the applicant's fear of my refusal was totally misplaced. He was a brilliant writer, policy maker (he later became National Security Adviser) and a fascinating speaker. His only missing link in my eyes was his lack of a sense of humor. When, at one point, I suggested that he lighten his presentation at a special meeting for sons and daughters of CFR members, he listened, yet totally disregarded my suggestion. Afterwards, he looked at me with the air of someone who clearly won his point. "You wanted me to be funny, didn't you?" he shot a parting remark.

A different kind of approach came much earlier. One of the congressmen, newly appointed to the post of U.S. Ambassador to the United Nations, asked his aide to approach CFR about an invitation to speak. A call was directed to my office. I listened with noncommittal silence and in a voice indicating both understanding and tolerance; I suggested to the caller that the newly minted ambassador should call us six months later after he learned his job. The congressman's name was George Bush.

Then, on another occasion, unable to control my native feelings as a Pole, I broke one of the Council's taboos of non-attribution.

It has been an iron rule that no member could be quoted in the press regarding the nature and the context of speeches delivered at CFR. The speaker, in this instance, was General Wojciech Jaruzelski, then Prime Minister of the People's Republic of Poland. I was sitting in the audience. The General delivered a rather insignificant peroration. As usual, members were called upon to ask questions. In the typical manner of a politician trained in "socialist" dialogues, Jaruzelski's answers were lengthy - rather short of substance but accomplishing his objective to fill the time. I just could not resist. "I congratulate you, General," I started my question, "for adopting one of the American ways. You seemed to have learned a lot from the nature of our filibusters applied by the United States Congress. But could you avoid the temptation and give us a short and concise reply to a question related to your position regarding the fate of Poles who are trying to introduce democratic principles into your system? Poles who point to the fact that Poland is no longer a sovereign state?"

There was an audible sense of discomfort among the audience. The General, after listening to the translation, moved forcefully in his anger, objections and total rejection of the premise of the question.

At the end, CFR members, a distinctly polite and tolerant group, gave him a restrained but loud ovation. I assumed that the General left the building convinced that he won the argument.

A battery of television cameras and a cluster of reporters kept watch outside of the building. One of them, a young woman whom I knew well, asked me if she could use my name in reporting the exchange on filibuster. I said, sure, why not? After all, this was a rather important moment for me in being able to challenge a communist leader of my native land.

This was not the way that the CFR establishment viewed the incident. The New York Times article used my question as one of the key points in reporting on the meeting. My name was printed accordingly. The reporter was immediately approached by the Council's spokesman, asking for an explanation. She replied truthfully, "Zyg gave me permission to use his name."

A special Board meeting was called. It was a grave and almost unprecedented case to consider a possibility of revoking my membership. The decision was tabled pending further explanation to be obtained from the accused. I wrote a long letter, acknowledging my mistake, but explaining it in both personal and political terms. The letter, addressed to the secretary of the Board, John Swing, was a mixture of factual and emotional arguments. It was circulated among the entire membership of the Board. The movement to censure me, or even to expel me was instantly dropped.

In the meantime, Marysia was approached by an organization called The International Center in New York, specializing in working with and for newly arrived foreigners, particularly students, businessmen and refugees. Founded in 1961, the work of the International Center and its mission is to provide a bridge to America for foreign newcomers through a volunteer staff of over 1000 individuals who teach English on a one-on-one basis. This led Marysia to a meaningful period of involvement with an organization that was taking care of people like us. Eventually, she became a member of the board, and I, basking in her glory, received a special award established for foreign-born individuals who have made significant contributions to American life. In addition to facilitating the life of newly arrived men and women on American soil, she also played a significant role in the transition that our family made from being refugees to full-fledged members of the American society.

The entire decade of my work at the Pratt House, the Council's beautiful headquarters on 68th Street in Manhattan, had been one of the most significant and most memorable periods of my life. I established close links with many fascinating individuals. Some of them became friends for life. And when an offer came to join the Aspen Institute of Humanistic Studies - at the time of my retirement from the Council (I was getting to the miracle age of sixty-five) - I knew that it was partly due to both Marysia's and my friendship established with Joe and Ann Slater, President of the Institute. We met them at the Council a number of years earlier, but the offer came rather unexpectedly after a meeting at another organization that we had been involved in.

The Mid-Atlantic Club of New York, initiated by another friend, Jim Huntley, and led by us for a number of years, had a luncheon meeting for the German foreign minister. I was in the chair. The

Slaters asked us to stay for a few minutes longer and the offer was made at that time. My instinctive reply was to express surprise that they were not looking for a younger man. But it took us just a day of thinking before I accepted this most attractive proposition.

22

The Aspen Institute

What was the key question that my little girl asked? What is America, Daddy? What did I answer, knowing next to nothing about that distant land that we were about to enter? The Aspen offer, that came unexpectedly, helped once again to formulate my answer to that little girl's question.

America, my dear young lady, offers both challenges and opportunities. Would we have had similar possibilities in Europe? In our native land? In England or Scotland? Probably not.

The Aspen Institute was not an unknown quantity for us. Long before the offer came about making me a full-fledged member of the staff, I moderated a number of seminars there. Seminars about what? Years earlier, shortly after the end of WWII, Walter Poepke, a successful businessman with ambitions and means transcending purely business goals, decided in his words "to bring classics to the American business community." At that time, Walter owned a good chunk of the underdeveloped village of Aspen. The Jerome Hotel, the only luxurious establishment, was his property, so was the railroad and the tiny airport. In short, he had enough assets to convert his dreams into reality. His wife, who outlived him by many years, shared his vision and helped implement it long after he was gone. The Institute was Walter's brainchild. He managed to convince the faculty and the administration of the University of Chicago to put solid intellectual input in the Institute's soul. In addition, he secured two intellectual giants: Robert Hutchins, at that time president of the University of Chicago, and Mortimer Adler, an Aristotelian philosopher, to initiate seminars for the business community.

But Walter's passions included another aspect of his interests: music. The Aspen Music Festival, still one of the major summer attractions, was inaugurated at the same time as the first seminar.

I jumped into the opportunity with zest. I loved the interplay of ideas. I felt at home inside the seminar room where participants, often taken out of their comfort zones, faced the difficult task of disrobing in public, of being forced to take the pragmatic approach when analyzing human nature, to look in the mirror, asking the key question about a potential conflict between the demands of the job on one side and a personal code of ethics on the other. The Aspen forum had an additional mission in mind: to educate the corporate sector and to make it aware of the historical continuity of the dilemma that leaders of humanity faced since the beginning of time.

The five years that I spent with the Institute, commuting between New York City, its headquarters, and Aspen, Colorado, was one of the highlights of my professional life. Aspen became the gathering of prominent and fascinating people from all over the world. Joe Slater had a generous vision of the Institute's role. He was determined, irrespective of the budgetary constraints, to make the place an intellectual Mecca. Thus, Aspen became a magnet for men and women from all over the world. Political leaders, prime ministers, heads of major financial institutions, experts in foreign and domestic policies, justices of the Supreme Court and military brass were almost daily visitors. Some came as speakers, but most of them were joining groups within the Executive Seminars program, my little domain. Stars from the literary, musical and arts worlds were equally attracted.

Each summer, our deliberations about Plato, Aristotle or Machiavelli were intertwined with music featuring Chopin, Mozart, Beethoven and others directed by some of the most prominent musicians of the world. No wonder Marysia and I considered ourselves to be exceptionally fortunate.

While our satisfaction with the institution was seldom interrupted by people for whom my style of conducting seminars was not fully acceptable, I knew that opposition was growing. Toward the end of my five years tenure, the administration changed.

Joe Slater left. His replacement, Colin Williams, a clergyman with a very different approach to the role of the Institute, took over.

It wasn't long before our philosophies clashed. It was not long before I was invited to face the "troika" of new members of the executive team and asked to resign. The irony of the moment was the fact that the program itself was booming, that my efforts to bring new companies, new participants and develop new readings, had just paid off.

I was crushed and tried unsuccessfully to reverse the decision. The executioner, Williams, looked at me with a cold, detached eye. I had a sense that he enjoyed his role in firing people, (I was one among many) that it gave him satisfaction. This, of course, was my perspective, a perspective of someone who was the victim.

So, after my discussion with the chairman of the Board, a discussion that I initiated hoping to reverse the decision, he made a date with me to deliver the final blow. While attending my last staff meeting, in the plush surrounding of the Wye Plantation, a Maryland property donated to the Institute by one of its trustees, I gave a message to my remaining colleagues. "Don't try to be successful, don't work too hard, don't attempt to exceed your own expectations. Look at me," I said to a hushed room, "I have been fired and I am departing from the top of my mountain. I just climbed it too eagerly."

The Institute, its people, its programs and its mission provided Marysia and me with a base to move forward, a base to expand and an opportunity to use what the two of us were especially well-equipped with, to be on our own. But at the moment of our divorce from Aspen, we were not aware that this was in the cards. Instead, we saw a grim possibility of drifting back to uncertainties and finding ourselves, once again, unattached and slightly lost.

During sleepless nights, a series of images crowded my mind, the image of a kitchen utensils salesman, the image of two of us packing food parcels to our native land and the image of working with people with whom we had nothing in common in order to earn our keep. What was wrong with me, I kept wondering? I did not fit into the Foreign Service. When I reached the official retirement age, I was not asked to continue at the Council on Foreign Relations. And now, after spreading my wings wide and sensing that my role at the Institute was almost a perfect fit, I was kicked out. What was wrong with that fellow called Zyg Nagorski?

A period of deep depression followed.

It did not last long.

It was Marysia, who always saw a silver lining in any situation and whose deep faith sustained her in moments of stress that picked me up and set me straight. "What are you complaining about?" she almost cried. "Five wonderful years gave you access to a multitude of fascinating individuals. It was a different access that you developed at the CFR. Here, it was much more personal, much more direct, making you feel like a full-fledged member of that Aspen community. The five years that gave you a renewed college education. Classical Greece, ancient Chinese philosophers, modern deliberations touching upon the nature of man and his place in society, all came alive thanks to the position that you held. What is America, Daddy? Remember that question? Come on, fellow!" she shouted at me. "Don't let yourself down because of a temporary defeat."

That night, I slept like a baby. Marysia, as always, gave me strength and faith in the future. That future arrived earlier than any one of us anticipated. An old friend, a man whom we met at one of the Aspen's gathering, called. He wanted to chat. "Is tomorrow evening free to chat?" he asked.

We did have a free evening. Jack Gottsman, the head of a small transportation company, settled himself on a sofa in our apartment at 91 Central Park West in New York, and with his traditional smile and readiness to banter, started a little sermon. "The Institute is a wonderful organization," he opened up his monologue. "It gave all of us a base, a perspective, a way to learn so much about each other. The way that you conducted executive seminars forced people to look inward, to examine and reflect. It also made a group of strangers develop close links, including personal friendships. Do you really want to abandon all that and go somewhere else?"

Marysia and I looked at each other with the air of bewilderment. "Do we have a choice?" I asked.

"Of course you do," Jack boomed in a way that walls started shaking slightly. "Of course you do. You can go on your own. You can shift your approach. You can build a new entity and no one, no one at all, will be in a position to kick you out. Your success or your failure will be in your own hands and in the hands of your future clients. Let's see what we can call it."

Thus our Center for International Leadership was born.

It combined the heritage of two organizations: the Aspen Institute and the Council on Foreign Relations. The former provided us with intellectual content, with an idea about a new direction that we decided to take. The latter, in addition to enriching further the intellectual content, gave us direct access to a multitude of men and women from political as well as from corporate worlds. Five years with Aspen deepened these contacts and expanded into additional world of academia. The two formed a solid base from which we could have started.

Jack was an Aspen alumnus. Other individuals who volunteered involvement were recruited from members of the Council. One of them was Dan Sharp, an executive of the Xerox Corporation, later President of the American Assembly. Dan learned about our bold decision. "There is a fellow," he mentioned in a casual way, "that might be of help. He is a corporate consultant. He is a very different personality from you. But who knows, you may click somehow. Try him," Dan mentioned. This was the way that Jim Bolt came into our lives.

I walked into Jim's office in Connecticut very unsure of myself. After all, I was brand new to the game. I knew next to nothing about the culture of corporate consultants. I was warned that this might very well lead me to a wrong address. Yet I had nothing to lose. I was ready to plunge into the unknown.

Jim, alerted by Dan of my interest, welcomed me warmly, as did his group of men and women that clustered around him. He was the mainspring of the operation. He was the one that provided corporate contacts and made connections between providers of services and corporate recipients, and developed his enterprise into a very profitable operation. Dan Sharp was correct. Our personalities did not jibe. But in spite of Jim's very pragmatic, very business-like approach, he sensed a value in what we were ready to offer. Our brand new Center was willing to undertake seminars and workshops dealing with ethics in business. This was a departure from the Aspen approach. The Institute was firmly rooted in humanities, in making corporate people better educated, better aware of history and more attuned to the challenges that humanity kept facing since time immemorial. What Jack Gottsman, Marysia and I concocted on that sofa in New York City, was a different approach. Using similar material that the Institute used, the approach would be to challenge ethical and value based corporate decision making and surface potential conflicts between the individual and collective values. Jim Bolt almost instantly perceived potential marketability of our program, in spite of the fact that most if not all his people dealt with very pragmatic, very down to earth topics.

At the very first meeting, Jim taught me a valuable lesson: don't sell your services too low. Companies are hesitant to contract with people whom they perceive as cheap. When I mentioned a figure of $1,500 per day Jim scoffed. "Much too low, much too modest."

"Would a higher fee limit acceptance?" I asked.

"To the contrary," responded my new teacher, "to the very contrary." I listened and I obeyed. It was a little later, when he helped to introduce the Center to two major corporations, that I fully understood his philosophy. His office expected a commission amounting to fifty percent of our earnings. The expectation caused our first slight disagreement, but it would not be fair to attribute his motives exclusively to his company's bottom line. I learned later that corporate clients view low tuition fees with suspicion.

"We are not looking for bargains," one of them explained to me. "We want top talent and we know that they do not come cheap." I listened and I followed.

During the first decade of the Center's existence, we earned enough money to rent a good office space in New York City, to hire a first class secretary and for me to earn more than I have ever earned before.

The very first seminar, however, was not the one that Jim Bolt was instrumental in generating. Jack Gottsman decided to expose his top people to our methodology and development approach. Appropriately enough, Jack chaired the session held in Vermont. Appropriately enough, since he was so instrumental in launching our Center, he was able to witness the birth of our very first major effort.

It worked just fine. I was able to use, to a much greater extent than at the Aspen Institute, the Socratic methodology. It suited me exceptionally well. I used to teach on occasion, I earned my living during the early stages of our American journey by lecturing, but I knew that, almost by osmosis, people learned much more, absorbed more easily and were able to tackle difficult topics by being active, rather than passive participants. In addition, I had my own selfish reasons. By asking questions, rather than providing answers, I was able to accomplish two objectives: hide my ignorance and to learn. It did not prevent me on some occasions to insert my own views framed as a question, more importantly, it created an atmosphere of interaction, of total involvement of everyone around the table.

The two companies that Jim Bolt introduced us to proved to be a tremendous boost. Weyerhaeuser and BellSouth put us on the road. Both, after a couple of initial sessions, decided to offer our seminars to a large number of employees, starting with the top brass. The Socratic methodology earned me a number of standing ovations. Weyerhaeuser lasted about three years during the time I commuted from New York to Eugene, Oregon about once a month. BellSouth lasted ten years. Hundreds of individuals were put through our seminars. As a rule, we did not take more than twenty at a time. At one point in our involvement with Weyerhaeuser, I was given a copy of a memorandum that the company sent around from its Tacoma Headquarters:

> This note should serve as a document the extraordinary value the Weyerhaeuser Forest Product Company has received as a result of the Humanities portion of the Leadership Institute. We currently have 600 managers enrolled in the Institute, the Humanities portion being a three-day integral part of the first week.

Then the note listed some of the objectives that the company hoped to achieve.

> To help participants to see how human values have a significant influence on how people think and the decision they make.
> To understand how decision-making can be influenced by the conflict between principles and expediency.
> To see how there can be many more alternative viewpoints than people had imagined.
> For managers to develop a broader sense of how their

personal leadership can be strengthened by a better understanding other people's point of view.

A steady flood of positive and, in some cases, enthusiastic evaluations testified to the effect that some of the objectives must have been reached. And yet, my mind kept wondering. Weyerhaeuser was a company devoted to development. Environmental groups had heavily criticized it for their policy of harvesting old trees. I remembered, vividly, one of the managers who openly voiced his amazement about people who admire standing trees, their foliage and their majestic crowns. "For me," he announced in a loud voice, "the beauty of a tree is when it is lying on a truck to be transported to its ultimate destination." And I stood there with my mouth wide open, unable to either contradict or comprehend.

Many of the men at the seminars - most of the groups were much more male than female - were born, lived in and were educated in small towns and villages. As a result, their horizons were rather limited and the community, often isolated from the regular flow of thoughts and ideas, influenced their views. Many of the participants had difficulty in dealing with such texts as Darwin, Dostoyevsky or Genesis. Some were even offended. Religion, faith, inner doubts - if any - were taboo as far as they were concerned. A case in point, a remark and a sense of discomfort came through when one of the men, a fellow slightly older than most of the others, proclaimed his own beliefs. "No one can be saved, no one can experience divine grace, unless that person recognizes Christ," he proclaimed in a rather timid, soft voice. His eyes listened with slight moisture, showing how strong his convictions were. The room felt silent. I was unable to resist a follow up question.

"How about people who were born before Christ?" I asked.

He looked at me with an air of bewilderment. It took him a minute or so to reply, with the entire room waiting in anticipation. "I guess they were just out of luck. Just out of luck."

Once again, I was reduced to silence.

There is, and probably remains forever, very little predictability in human life. In one of my father's letters to me, after receiving a rather discouraging report about our oldest daughter, he reminded me how difficult I was during my adolescence: lazy, a poor student and preoccupied more in playing bridge than in studies. "At that time," Father wrote (probably with a little smile), "no one would have foreseen you as a potential American diplomat." Then, with another wink, he recalled my first attempt to argue a civil case in a Polish court, a moment of total disaster. "So be patient before you judge your little girl. Be generous and be fully aware of natural human weaknesses."

As I've mentioned before, patience has never been one of my virtues. Neither was a willingness to abandon a plan or project, even when obstacles kept piling up, even when, in many people's judgment, I was following a wrong path. Father was always very cautious. I often wondered whether he would have been pleased or shocked by Marysia's and my decision to dive into the unknown, to listen to Jack and to embark on what in effect meant to create a mini-Aspen Institute, under a different name, with a different philosophy and methodology.

We did not have a financial base. We did not have any assurance of success. And yet the Center for International Leadership turned out to be the crowning accomplishment of our lives and a perfect platform of cooperation between the two of us.

Marysia has always been a critic, an analytical mind pointing to weaknesses and strengths and an editor who was also an idea person. I kept doing what the Aspen Institute helped me to perfect: leading and moderating groups.

In this capacity, I found something that I was able to do well. An army of individuals, representing all ages, various races and both genders kept telling me that I have touched their lives. How could this be predictable? Or possible? Or even imagined? How would I have known that an army of great thinkers, Mencius and Hsun Tsu, Plato and Aristotle, Kant and Darwin, Gardner and Freedman, were ready to be tapped, were ready to extend their helping hand by sharing with so many of us their wisdom and their talents? Without them, nothing would have been possible. Without them, minds of many of us, including my own, would have been dormant, idle, unchallenged and thus useless to others. All of them came to us via the Aspen Institute. It was there, either on the ski slopes of Colorado, or within the confines of the Wye Plantation in Maryland, that Marysia and I kept reading, refreshing our college years and digging deeper into the meanings of great philosophers.

All of a sudden, in our mature years, a wave of excitement engulfed our souls. The excitement grew with every encounter, with a group of men and women who came to Aspen to learn how to think. We kept sharing with them our questions, doubts and mysteries to which no human being as yet found a proper key. They began to share our excitement. They connected with each other much faster than anyone could have anticipated.

Another piece of the Center's puzzle, a puzzle that somehow we were able to decipher, has been the Advisory Board. Composed exclusively of men and women whom we have personally encountered, people who knew our goals and our potential, the Board provided us with respectability. Chairmen of the various corporate boards, heads of educational institutions and others of the same ilk, readily agreed to serve. We tried to take as little of their time as possible, holding Board meetings about two years apart. But on one important occasion, the tenth anniversary of the Center, the ballroom of the National Press Club in Washington was packed. The majority of the Board members came, as did a host of former participants. A series of skits, chaired by John Clandenin, Chairman of the Board of BellSouth Corporation, started by Jim Moore, one of the faithful believers and followed by former Senator Edward Brooke, brought the house down. We were grateful to Fyodor Dostoevsky, whose segment from "The Brothers Karamazov" served as a centerpiece of the entire performance.

Those have been some of the ingredients that made seminars a success, ingredients that allowed people to remember the encounters for years to come. No wonder that I grabbed the opportunity when it came to us. I welcomed every participant. I used and overused them. I kept wondering about the real nature of man and asked others and myself whether Mencius ("Man is basically good") or Hsun Tsu ("Man is basically evil") was correct. Together, we pondered the dilemma posed by Aristotle whether one can be a good man and a good citizen at the same time. "Difficult," wrote the Greek sage, "almost impossible," he would add as an afterthought. We spent hours dissecting Martin Luther King's call for creative tension, a tension that would lift all of us higher and would challenge our prejudices. And with equal passion, we would approach King's proposition that breaking an unjust law is the highest respect that anyone could pay to the legal system itself. Either at this point, or some other, we would start reading aloud Virginia Wolf's "Room of Your Own," inquiring about the position of women in contemporary society.

Is this what business people want to discuss? Are these issues in the minds of men and women working for corporate America, for multinational entities aimed at earning the maximum possible profits for their shareholders? Of course not, but because it is not what they are concerned with while working long hours every day to meet corporate goals, our approach worked. It not only worked, it touched people's lives.

"This seminar," wrote one of the people affected, "begins and forces an analysis of the process of individual thinking as it relates to business and life decisions. Although the Socratic method is very difficult for some, its value in making us explore ideas rather than conclusions is evident. Does it relate to business? Absolutely."

"This was not a seminar," commented another. "It was an experience that was enlightening, troubling, frustrating, moving and a great fun. Its value will be realized over time."

Self-disclosures and self-examinations, being forced to look within ourselves, avoiding easy ways out, stimulating new relationships with peers, bosses and subordinates, were some of the comments that emerged. Back in the office – now in our Washington, D.C. home - two women, the backbone of our entire operation, worked: Marysia and Ella Gifford.

We found Ella Gifford through an employment agency. She arrived on the first day, the agency having forgotten it was a holiday, and spent an hour or so on our doorsteps hoping that someone would open the door. When we finally connected, Marysia and I could not help wondering what kind of providence sent us this young person.

Her Japanese mother instilled in her an iron strong sense of commitment and duty. Through experience as a Peace Corps volunteer in Africa, she developed a sense of compassion toward people living in poverty. Thanks to her educational background, she was at home with the reading material that our Center used. In addition, over the years of her work with the Center, she developed not only an affinity, but also a strong intellectual commitment with our work. Listening to her descriptions of the Center's goals and purposes, I could not help feeling that she was often better, more convincing and more believable than either Marysia or me.

Our voices were heard as those of founders, but her voice was much more that of someone who came in cold and turned out to be a true believer. Ella was especially sensitive to the race problem. In Africa, she was a lonely, white female in a black society. Back home, she kept her involvement with various minorities. It was through her that we got to learn about Howard University and its strong position as a black oriented institution. During a rather spectacular celebration of the Center's tenth anniversary, Ella initiated a drive to create fellowships for a few needy black students. The outcome was excellent. Four of the students, selected from a large number of applicants, received the Center's modest supplementary funds. She was especially touched by some participants' comments related to the issue of racial inequalities. "The aspect of the program that was most valuable to me," wrote someone, "was the discussion of human nature and difference of races/gender. It was the first time I had read Martin Luther King's letter and it touched my feelings or rationale behind the belief of minorities. The fact that there are things we will never know or understand until we walk in the shoes of others."

Ella just beamed.

Nothing in human activities, no matter how nobly it is constructed or viewed, escaped criticism. Among a flood of supportive, positive voices there were also others. The Socratic methodology turned some people off. The probing and challenges often took people from their comfort zones. In some cases, I pushed too hard. In some situations, I turned out to be insensitive to different cultural backgrounds, to different ways of upbringing. In one specific case, I paid the ultimate price of being rejected.

Columbia University in New York had a long established program of executive education. Its content at one point included a segment dealing with corporate ethics. I was asked to participate. The limitations were severe. I was allotted half a day to deal with a large group, often exceeding fifty people from various parts of the world. Men (as there were only men) from Islamic countries were both unprepared and not too eager to accept the notion of strong inquiry of personal as well as corporate behavior. Their resentment to the Socratic methodology was shared with a number of European and American participants. There was little time to warm them up to the process. There was little time to bridge the other segments of the program with our Socratic methodology. The total time of the program usually lasted several weeks and used traditional academic and dialectic methods. At one point, I was accused of insensitivity to religious standings, particularly to Muslims. On occasion, the evaluations of the session resented the entire Socratic approach. The key principle, based on challenging one's prejudices, beliefs and convictions, was viewed as unacceptable.

After several sessions, the management of the Columbia program decided to drop the portion dealing with ethics. It must have been my fault for not being able to shift gears, not being in tune with the multicultural world or not being flexible enough to adapt to cultural differences. Or it could have been a small collision between a fairly aggressive leader (me) and an audience that preferred peaceful coexistence instead of confrontation. This was probably the same reason the new management of the Aspen Institute turned down my offer to get re-involved in my moderator's capacity.

Oh well. Evidently, I was not created to be an organizational man.

23

The Last Chapter

Glancing at the past, it was difficult to deny this particular truth. My entire life span, since our arrival at the American shores, was a continued story of rejections. The Chattanooga Times was different. I was simply not equipped, not smart enough to learn the day-to-day operations of a newspaper. Foreign News Service, run jointly with Marysia and being a part of a larger entity connected with the London based Federation of Free Journalists, was spent on a steady flow of disagreements. I attempted to create a unit totally independent from the London Headquarters. The London group was not too pleased with that approach, nor would I have been should our relationship have been reversed. The government service in Washington and overseas earned me high praise on accomplishments but mediocre or low praise on teamwork. Promotion was denied, and in at least one case a demotion resulted. A brief stay at the Hudson Institute was a marriage of convenience, with both sides fully aware of its temporary nature. The Council on Foreign Relations was a great period, but when the moment came for new management and the decision to ask me to stay (which I wanted badly) or to retire, they opted for the latter. Another attempt to fit into an organization (The Lehrman Institute) went the identical route.

It was the Center for International Leadership that provided Marysia and me with the challenge and opportunity of our lives. We started that tiny unit when we were reaching old age. It turned out to have been the crowning event of everything we had done since the days of our youths.

What is America, Daddy?

It is tempting now, after the full discovery of the new continent and a lifetime, to answer the little girl's question with a series of predictable banalities. It would be equally tempting to brush it off as something natural, typical of one immigrant's impressions. On the eve of our fiftieth anniversary of the American landing, I knew that the answer would never be adequate and that the very mosaic of our experiences, tribulations, joys, pains, satisfactions and disappointments would not permit a pat response.

America, my dear young lady, is a very complicated part of our world. Maybe I should try to find a nugget of truth in the quote that I used at the very beginning of this grand inquiry.

> He is an American, who leaving behind all his ancient prejudices and manners receives new ones from the new mode of life he has embraced, the new government he obeys. The new ranks he holds... Here, individuals of all nations are melted into a new race of men, whose labor and posterity will one day cause great changes of the world. Americans are the Western pilgrims, who are carrying with them the great mass of arms, sciences, vigor and industry, which began long since in the East... The American is a new man who acts upon new principles; he must therefore entertain new ideas and form new opinions. - *Hector St. John de Crevecoeur*

There was also another quote, in a letter written on October 11, 1952. My father, at the age of sixty-eight, reflected on the role that he - and we - were playing on the vast chessboard of population movements. It was at a moment when he faced a momentous decision to cross the Atlantic. He was doing it fully realizing that starting a new life, in a new country, on a new continent was bound to be dramatically difficult. He was joining his two sons, who were already there, and his younger brother and sister.

> The political exiles are hanging between our old country, which is departing from us every day further and further, and the new one, which is bound to remain alien to us. But we are neither new nor original. America is populated by people like us. We are consciously or unconsciously, creators of a new era that is always born out of a mass movement of people...

I strongly believe that the Polish seeds of creativity, often influenced and affected by forceful separations from the native soil, are bound to sprout everywhere, including foreign soil; and that the new wheat is bound to grow out of these seeds of creativity maybe on our native, Polish soil or somewhere else.

America, I keep answering my little inquiring mind, is that "somewhere else." It is here that Polish creativity, separated from its native roots, gave the rest of the world two Nobel Prize winners. It witnessed the election of the first Polish born head of the Roman Catholic Church. And it allowed the rest of us, the gray masses of exiles and immigrants, to fight the best way we knew how, for restoration of Polish independence, a goal that was achieved.

Was that enough? How about Crevecoeur's call for a "new man who acts upon new principles?" What about: "He is an American who is melted into a new race of men, whose labor and posterity will one day cause great changes in the world?" Have we gone that far in our transformation? Have we become true members of the society that by our act of defiance half a century ago we chose to live in?

We should probably leave the answer to these questions to the generations who come after Marysia and I depart to another unknown. They came to America not by free choice. Too young, too dependent on their parents' judgments, they found themselves without the baggage of "ancient prejudices and manners" that we carried along.

We look back and see them, a small crowd of the family members positioning themselves towards the possibility of causing the great changes in the world and somehow we sense the motion. Maria, the oldest, spends her waking hours attempting to improve the lives of young men and women whose circumstances deprived them of equal opportunities. Andrew, a gifted writer and a man whose earlier days led him to take a dangerous road to demonstrate against racial prejudices in the South and later oppose the Vietnam War, found a perfect outlet for his views and principles by being a foreign correspondent for an influential American publication. Terry, the youngest and the only one born on the American soil, combines her unique talents as a skilled craftsman, with her constant care of the underprivileged.

Tom Nagorski, my brother's only son, acquired a position within the most powerful medium, television, which allows him to travel worldwide and report on human miseries as well as human accomplishments.

Then comes the third generation: the four children of Andrew and Christina, a model mother whose zest of life permitted all of us to admire the way she combined tolerance with strict upbringing of her youngsters. Eva, the oldest, acquired an unbelievable treasury of creativity and writing talents. Sonia, an unexpected scientist, combines geology with deep concern for the preservation of the environment. Adam, a graduate student at the Columbia University Law School, is already on track to follow in his great-grandfather's footsteps. Alexander, a freshman at Muhlenberg College, has a passion for drama and the arts. Jonathan, Maria's son, found his niche in modern technology. Now, the entire family depends on his skills in explaining, patiently, the mysteries of computer science to rather inept and lost grandparents.

My father was so right. And the two of us, now late in our life, are so lucky to be able to watch seeds of "Polish creativity sprouting on foreign soil." The decision to cross the Atlantic, forced upon the family by circumstances beyond our control, opened the door to almost unlimited possibilities for our future generations.

Thus, Marysia and I, getting ready to meet St. Peter at the heavenly gates that he guards most carefully, are well prepared. He will probably ask a similar question that our little girl asked, not pertaining to America but about our contributions on a new continent and in our lives. And we will be so eager to answer that St. Peter may be forced to admonish us by asking us not to speak at the same time. We were simply rattling all the names that we were leaving behind. The old Saint Peter, accustomed to the usual bragging of the "new arrivals," is bound to listen, to check instantly on his specially constructed heavenly list, and after receiving an "all clear" signal, open the door.

Marysia and I would look at each other, and, remembering the day November 22, 1938, we would repeat our mutual promises to be together forever and ever after.

The ever after is on its way.

www.ingramcontent.com/pod-product-compliance
Lightning Source LLC
Chambersburg PA
CBHW070722160426
43192CB00009B/1277